# SPACE AUSTRALIA

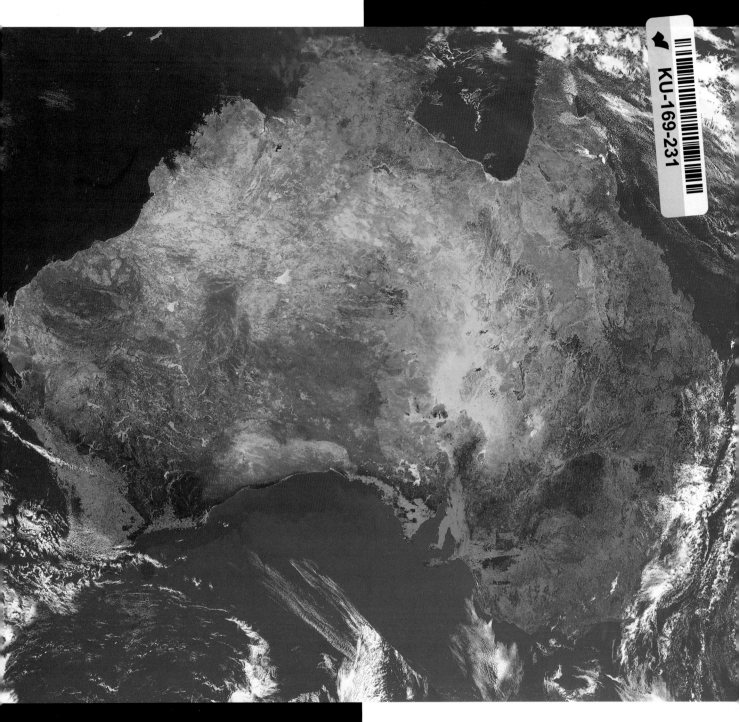

## THE STORY OF AUSTRALIA'S INVOLVEMENT IN SPACE

KERRIE DOUGHERTY + MATTHEW L JAMES

POWERHOUSE PUBLISHING

*Editor:* Jo Jarrah

*Designer:* Judy Hungerford Design Pty Ltd

*Production coordinator:* John O'Brien, Powerhouse Museum

Typeset in Baskerville 10½/14½ condensed and Techno bold by Post Typesetters, Brisbane

Printed by Griffin Press, Adelaide

CIP Dougherty, Kerrie. Space Australia. Bibliography. Includes index. ISBN 1 86317 034 0

1. Astronautics—Australia—History. 2. Astronautics—Australia—Communication systems—History.

I. James, Matthew L. (Matthew Leslie), 1957-  . II. Title. 629.40994

First published 1993 by Powerhouse Publishing, PO Box K346, Haymarket NSW 2000, Australia.

ACKNOWLEDGMENTS: The authors would like to acknowledge the invaluable assistance of the following people in the research for this book: Peter Anderson, Professor John Carver, Michael Crowe, Peter Davies, Mike Dinn, Dr Brett Gooden, Bruce Henderson, Mike Julian, Philippe Jung, Dr Ken McCracken, Dr Owen Mace, Professor Don Mathewson, Ted Mikosza, Philip Pearson, Dr Andrew Prentice, Graham Radcliffe, Robert Somervaille, Stanley Schaetzel, Dr Paul Scully-Power, Professor John Simmons, Professor Ray Stalker, Art Stolz, Steve Symons, Dr Andrew Thomas, Richard Tonkin, Dr Ian Tuohy, Mary Whitehead.

Our thanks as well to the reading committee (Dr Ken McCracken, Gina Grant, Terence Measham, Jennifer Sanders, Louise Douglas and Julie Donaldson), to our editor Jo Jarrah, to numerous Powerhouse Museum staff, in particular Samantha Cox (word processing) and Catherine Dunn (finished art), and to the many others who have assisted with pictorial material, information, advice and encouragement during production.

*A Note to the Reader:* Because of the many changes that have occurred in recent years to country, company and institutional names, in this book we will use the name that was correct in the particular period being mentioned.

**Cover:** The globe on our cover is a computer-enhanced image of the Earth, with Australia clearly visible, seen from space by Japan's Geostationary Meteorological Satellite in March 1991.

**Title page:** A mosaic image of Australia created from five scenes taken by a NOAA remote sensing satellite in September 1989.

# CONTENTS

## PREFACE

In 1988 the Powerhouse Museum opened Australia's first major permanent space exhibition, *Space—beyond this world*. This was the first exhibition in the world to bring together space hardware from the three superpowers, the US, USSR and China.

Our exhibition could also have told the story of Australia's own involvement with space were it not for the regrettable fact that little of our space heritage survives in forms suitable for museum display.

The answer for us was to tell the story through the medium of a book, one that has long been needed in any case. *Space Australia* provides this rich history for the first time and presents an overview of Australia's involvement in space technology which has far-reaching implications for the future.

For a small nation, Australia's history of space achievements is surprisingly varied: it has been home to one of the world's largest rocket ranges; was only the fourth country to launch its own satellite; has played a crucial role in US civilian and military space programs; and is today one of the world's major users of satellite systems for everything from communications and navigation to land management.

Australia is now poised to develop its space industry capabilities, expanding its role in international space activities and exploring the possibilities of spaceports at Cape York and the Woomera rocket range. The existence of a coherent history of Australia's involvement in space can only help to encourage understanding and promote this redevelopment.

This book will be of great value to the general reader as well as to those already interested in space activities. It will also be an indispensable resource and reference for students and teachers. There are so many positive stories still untold about Australian ingenuity and success in areas of science and technology. The Powerhouse Museum is committed to doing whatever is possible to help redress the balance, hence we are extremely pleased to publish *Space Australia*.

TERENCE MEASHAM
*Director of the Powerhouse Museum, Sydney*

# FOREWORD

DR PAUL SCULLY-POWER *was the first Australian-born person to travel in space. In 1984 he conducted valuable oceanographic research from space on board the CHALLENGER Space Shuttle. He comments on the value of space to Australia.*

In looking back over the history of involvement and notable achievements in space by Australia and Australians, *Space Australia* also points the way to the future. For whereas the history is ample proof of those three pillars of Australia's technological uniqueness—research ideas, innovation and that well-known 'have a go' attitude—they are the very same pillars that could propel Australia back into the forefront of the space industry. Yet in this last decade of the twentieth century there are several added prerequisites: an ability to exploit and commercialise new developments, flexibility, the identification of niche markets, and that elusive partnership between the public and private sectors.

In an age when technology is fast allowing a fusion of information science, telecommunications and computers, there are boundless opportunities for Australia to re-establish its status in space and space-related technologies, ranging all the way from 'high tech' service industries to electronic and fibre optic data compression techniques, 'designer' materials for specific applications, pollution control and environmental monitoring, through to global 'cellular' pocket telephones, faxes and computers and their unseen central nervous system—a galaxy of satellites in both low Earth orbit and at geosynchronous altitudes. Hence Australia can play a pivotal role, not only in the supporting technologies for these developments, but also in the new primary industry of specific application satellites and their launching, be they for communication, navigation, information exchange, broadcasting or national remote sensing for resource and environmental management and meteorology/oceanography. In all this it but takes a national commitment and the will to join in, be part of, and contribute to these new technologies on the horizon.

In the new global economy based on quick response in the marketplace, diversified products and efficient and ecological manufacturing, value-added products and services, and an increasing dependence on space-based information, Australia has a clear choice between being a net importer or net exporter of space hardware, technology and services, especially in the economic powerhouse now emerging in Asia. However, to be on the positive side of such a trade balance requires careful thought and planning, focusing of national resources, including scientific and technical talent, public understanding and support for a space economic strategy, and the firm backing and encouragement of the government. This vision is realisable and the time to act is now, for the consequences of delay and prevarication are to see Australia become increasingly dependent on importing such technology and services with the concomitant increase in the trade deficit.

Australia was one of the first nations in the world to launch a satellite, has been part of many multinational space projects, has made unique contributions to scientific progress in space, and has become one of the greatest per-capita users of space products. Yet it needs to build on this history, to encourage and support its indigenous space-related research-and-development organisations and industry, and to educate all Australians to be aware of Australia's role in space and its future economic vitality, which will be based to a large extent on space-related products and services. Indeed, education is the key to Australia's future, and this book is a great contribution to making all Australians aware of their space heritage and their inextricable dependence on future space products for their economic survival. The challenge now is to take the next step. Let it not be another lost opportunity.

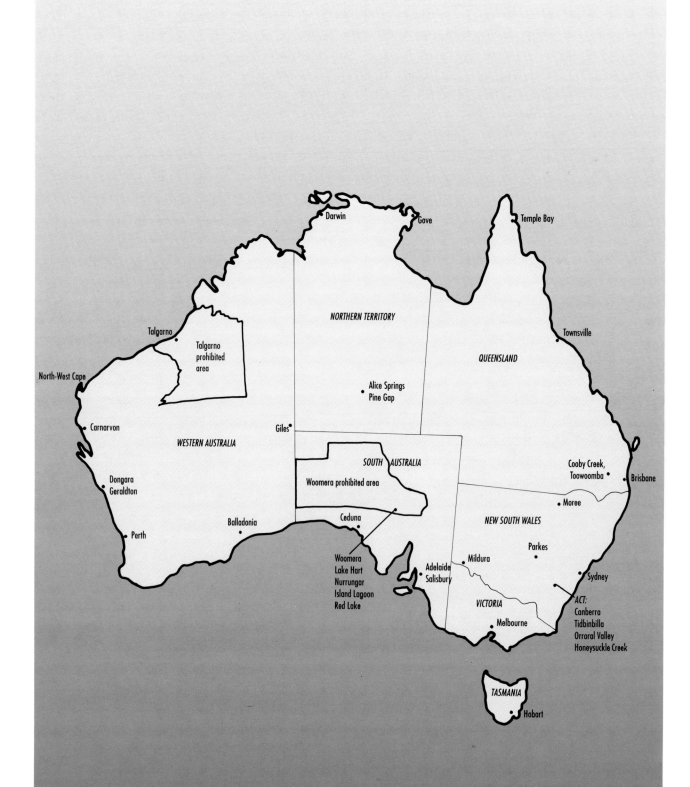

**Space places in Australia.** The locations of the main
Australian space facilities mentioned in this book are
shown on the map.

**INTRODUCTION**

# The Australian connection

The exploration and utilisation of space has been seen as the greatest adventure of the twentieth century and Australia has had its part to play in setting the world on the road to the stars, even though its contribution is not usually counted among this country's achievements.

Since the beginning of the Space Age, Australia has been involved with space activities. The Woomera rocket range, originally developed to test military missiles, enabled Australia to contribute to both British and European programs to develop rockets and launch satellites. Two satellites were successfully launched into orbit. At its height, Woomera was one of the largest spaceports in the world and, after a period of inactivity, it may soon be launching satellites again. Australia may also become home to the world's first fully commercial spaceport, at Cape York in far north Queensland, from which launch services would be provided to paying customers from anywhere in the world.

Australian scientists and engineers developed space expertise that enabled them to design and locally produce small research rockets and scientific instruments which made important contributions to astronomy and the physics of the upper atmosphere. It was this expertise and experience that gave Australia its place of honour as only the fourth country to launch its own satellite from its own territory, and the second to launch an amateur radio satellite. Today, Australian space scientists and engineers continue the tradition of excellence, participating in international space science programs, developing spacecraft instruments and experiments, and pursuing research in leading edge aerospace technologies that are set to revolutionise spaceflight.

Australia's geographical position has placed it in a unique position to participate in both the civilian and military space programs of the United States (US). The National Aeronautics and Space Administration (NASA) tracking stations located in Australia have assisted deep space missions exploring the Solar System, provided communications for crewed space missions from the Mercury program to the Space Shuttle and even received the first images from the APOLLO-11 Moon landing. The more controversial military space tracking stations have also brought this country into the realm of high technology space surveillance.

Whether or not Australians are aware of it, space technology touches some part of their lives every day. Australia was one of the first countries to participate in satellite programs for communications and weather monitoring, and today it is one of the world's largest users of satellite-based systems for communications, remote sensing, navigation and defence. With the vast area and comparatively small population of this continent, satellites are the only viable and cost effective means of obtaining accurate, nationwide information about our weather, natural resources and environmental health.

From breakfast table to bedtime, Australians are affected by space technology. Satellites monitor the crops we grow and aid the navigation of cargo ships bringing imports and exports to and from the country. At the office satellites aid domestic and international communications and at home they bring the news and weather report to the television screen. In times of natural disaster, satellites monitor floods and cyclones and help the emergency services to communicate. Town planners use satellites to help improve the built environment, while scientists and conservationists use them to monitor the effects of human activities on the natural environment.

Australia makes such extensive use of satellites that it has become a world leader in the development of software programs for manipulating satellite-supplied data, especially in the field of remote sensing. Australia is also producing world-class equipment for a variety of satellite applications. These skills form the basis for a small but growing local space industry, which has already flown instruments on some spacecraft and is beginning to export Australian expertise in the design and construction of satellite ground stations.

Every year, Australia spends many hundreds of millions of dollars overseas on the purchase of the space-based services it uses.

Soon, it may have to pay even more to acquire weather, natural resource and other data because the countries which currently provide the data free of charge are deciding to treat the information as a commercial commodity. The development of a strong Australian space program, with specialised areas of expertise and an indigenous launch capability, would aid this country's economic development and ensure our continued access to space-based services.

Australia's space history is a complex mixture of surprising achievements and disappointing lost opportunities. Through the conjunction of political and economic factors, this country has, at various times, both led and lagged among the world's spacefaring nations. *Space Australia* explores that fascinating and sometimes frustrating history and provides an overview of the country's current involvement with space. It will dispel some of the myths and misconceptions that surround Australia's space programs and consider some of the political, social and economic issues inherent in the country's use of space. Finally, this book will highlight the exciting potential for future Australian space activities, which will build upon the achievements of the past, achievements of which Australia, as a small nation, has every right to be proud.

**Keeping in touch with the world. Australia uses satellites for its international telecommunications, via Telstra's ground stations. This is Telstra's Oxford Falls facility, near Sydney.**

# CHAPTER 1

# SPACE IN TIME: Australian space activities in their world context

**Spaceship Earth. Images like this encouraged the concept of the Earth as the 'spaceship' of humankind. This photograph was taken by the crew of an Apollo mission returning from the Moon. Its unusual colour comes from the use of a filter which screened out all light except orange. The experiment for which this photograph was taken was related to the development of remote sensing satellites, which are now used to monitor the Earth's environmental health.**

Australia's space activities have not occurred in isolation. They have resulted from, been influenced by, and related to the space activities of other nations, in particular the United Kingdom (UK) and the US. This chapter provides a brief background of world space history and activities which will place the Australian space activities and programs outlined in the following chapters in their world context.

## ROCKETRY TAKES OFF

Although rockets have been known for about a thousand years, it is only in the last hundred or so that they have been recognised as the only practical vehicles for making the age-old dream of spaceflight come true. Rockets are the only means of transport so far developed that can both generate the necessary power to break free of the Earth's gravity and function in the vacuum of space.

In the early part of the twentieth century, two important space pioneers were active. Konstantin Tziolkovski was a Russian schoolteacher who published the first major work on astronautics in 1903, establishing all the basic principles of spaceflight. Robert Goddard, an American physicist, was the first person to successfully build and launch a liquid-fuel rocket in 1926. Inspired by their work, an international spaceflight movement developed in the 1920s and 1930s, with space travel and rocket societies being formed in many countries, including Australia. The German 'Society for Space Ship Travel' (*Verein für Raumschiffahrt* or VfR) was one of the most important amateur rocket groups at that time. After it broke up in 1933, many of its members worked for the German army on its rocket weapon projects. This work resulted in the A-4 rocket, which was known as the *Vergeltungswaffe-2* (or Vengeance Weapon-2), abbreviated to V-2. The world's first long-range missile, it was used in World War II.

The V-2 proved the military value of the rocket as a long-distance weapon and, immediately following the war, many countries began to establish rocket and missile programs. Larger, more powerful, more reliable rockets were developed, primarily for military use as long-range missiles. It was this interest in developing guided weapons (as missiles were also called) that led to the establishment of the Woomera rocket range in Australia and eventually brought this country into participation in space activities, as described in chapter 2. The national space policy which has guided these activities is discussed in chapter 8.

The success of the V-2 also demonstrated that it was possible to build rockets powerful enough to go into space. This inspired scientists to probe the atmosphere using small 'sounding rockets'. Tests were also carried out to ascertain how animals and people would react in space, in preparation for actual space exploration. Some of this scientific research was carried out in Australia and is outlined in chapter 6.

## SPACE AGE, SPACE RACE

The Space Age actually began when the world's first artificial satellite, SPUTNIK-1 ('travelling companion') was launched by the Union of Soviet Socialist Republics (USSR) on 4 October 1957. During its 1400 orbits of the Earth, it transmitted a continuous radio signal and was visible in many countries, including Australia, as a fast-moving 'star'. Australia's Overseas Telecommunications Commission (OTC) was one of the first agencies to record the bleeping of SPUTNIK's coded radio signal. SPUTNIK-2 rapidly followed SPUTNIK-1, carrying the first animal into space, a dog called Laika.

### SPUTNIK-MANIA

OTC monitored the SPUTNIK transmissions and was besieged by calls from the media and the public reporting the satellite or strange sightings. One amusing telephone call was received from someone declaring that he could distinctly hear the SPUTNIK sounds coming from his bedsprings! One country newspaper reporter telephoned to say he had heard that a flaming object had plummeted to the ground near a town in western New South Wales. OTC was able to establish that SPUTNIK was over Afghanistan at that time. It is also claimed that one Sydney resident was so alarmed by the prospect of SPUTNIK-1 crashing down upon his head that he took out what was probably the world's first insurance policy against damage caused by a satellite!

**Look! Up in the sky ... ! Crowds gather in Sydney's Hyde Park to watch SPUTNIK-1 pass overhead.**

**Astronaut Edwin Aldrin, second person on the Moon, with the US flag planted by the APOLLO-11 crew. The APOLLO-11 landing effectively won the 'space race' for the US, as the USSR abandoned its lunar landing program after the American success.**

After being plagued by a number of early rocket failures, the US launched its first satellite, EXPLORER-I, in January 1958. In the Cold War climate of the time, space achievements were seen as evidence of technological—and supposedly political and ideological—superiority, and a 'space race' developed between the US and the USSR, with both countries striving to achieve status-conferring space 'firsts'. Because of the political significance that was attached to the capability to launch satellites, Britain and other countries in western Europe banded together to form the European Launcher Development Organization (ELDO), with the intention of developing a European launch vehicle independent of the superpowers. Inviting Australia to become its only non-European member, ELDO tested its rockets at the Woomera range, a story that is told in chapter 2.

On 12 April 1961, Soviet cosmonaut Yuri Gagarin orbited the Earth in VOSTOK-1, becoming the first person in space. The first American, Alan Shepard, followed less than a month later aboard the FREEDOM 7 Mercury spacecraft. The Soviet Vostok ('east') and Voskhod ('sunrise') programs and the American Mercury and Gemini space missions were the first tentative steps in crewed spaceflight. These programs tested the spacecraft, equipment, and techniques for living and working in space.

In response to an apparent Soviet lead in the 'space race', President Kennedy set the US the goal of achieving a crewed landing on the Moon by 1970. This technologically demanding and ambitious aim was accomplished through the Apollo program, which succeeded when APOLLO-11 landed the first people on the Moon on 21 July 1969. Between 1969 and 1972 six Apollo missions landed on the Moon, effectively winning the 'space race' for the US.

Australia played an important role in the US crewed space program at this time through its many tracking stations, as will be outlined in chapter 3. The first pictures from the APOLLO-11 landing on the lunar surface were received by NASA tracking stations in the Australian Capital Territory (ACT) and the Commonwealth Scientific and Industrial Research Organization's (CSIRO) radio telescope at Parkes in New South Wales (NSW) and then transmitted to the world.

## SPACE AS A RESOURCE FOR THE EARTH

While the 'space race' was capturing the headlines in the 1960s, less spectacular but equally important programs were developing experimental satellites for a variety of uses. The success of early communications, weather and surveillance satellites led to the realisation that space could be utilised as a resource for the Earth by developing satellite networks. From the vantage point of space, they enabled large sections of the Earth to be observed at one time from high in orbit. Many nations sought to gain international prestige by launching their own satellites, and Australia achieved the distinction of becoming only the fourth country to launch its own satellite from its own territory, as described in chapter 6.

Throughout the 1970s and 1980s satellite networks for communications, weather observation, Earth resources studies, navigation, search and rescue, scientific research and military purposes were established, linking the world by invisible threads. In this way, space has become a resource for the Earth, allowing the special advantages of satellites to be applied in practical ways to assist a wide range of activities on Earth. The many ways in which Australia utilises satellites are outlined in chapters 4 and 5.

Australia is not only one of the world's largest users of satellite-based systems, it is also a world leader in many areas of space applications, utilising satellite systems and the data they provide to assist in the monitoring and management of this vast continent. Australia's space scientists and industry have contributed to the development of space applications technology and their achievements will be covered in chapters 5 and 7. Chapter 9 will look at some of the exciting scientific, technological and economic potential for Australia available through further utilising the resource of space.

| AUSTRALIAN EVENTS | | INTERNATIONAL EVENTS |
|---|---|---|
| Britain approaches Australia to develop a rocket testing range | — 1945 — | World War II ends |
| Overseas Telecommunications Commission created<br>Anglo-Australian Joint Project inaugurated | — 1946 — | US and USSR begin rocket tests with modified V-2s |
| Long Range Weapons Establishment created | — 1947 | |
| MINITRACK and SAO tracking stations established<br>Sounding rocket launches and hypersonic research begin at<br>Woomera | — 1957 — | International Geophysical Year commences<br>(concludes in 1958)<br>SPUTNIK-1, world's first satellite, launched |
| | 1958 | US launches first satellites, EXPLORER-1 and VANGUARD-1<br>NASA inaugurated |
| Australia assumes Chair of UNCOPUOS technical and scientific<br>sub-committee | — 1959 — | First USSR space probes to Moon |
| | 1960 — | TIROS-1, first weather satellite, launched<br>First experimental navigation and surveillance satellites<br>launched |
| | 1961 — | Yuri Gagarin (USSR) first person in space<br>Alan Shepard first American in space |
| ELDO established | — 1962 — | TELSTAR-1, first commercial communications satellite |
| North West Cape US military tracking station established | — 1963 — | Valentina Tereshkova (USSR) first woman in space |
| First ELDO launch<br>Australia becomes founding member of INTELSAT<br>Regular reception of satellite weather images begins | — 1964 — | INTELSAT established |
| | 1965 — | US and USSR achieve first spacewalks<br>INTELSAT-1, first commercial geostationary communications<br>satellite<br>France launches first satellite |
| First direct satellite link between Australia and UK | — 1966 — | First automated spacecraft land on Moon |
| Australia's first satellite, WRESAT, launched<br>Australia participates in global satellite television broadcast | — 1967 | |
| | 1968 — | APOLLO-8 first crewed spacecraft to orbit Moon |
| Australia receives first pictures from APOLLO-11 | — 1969 — | APOLLO-11 makes first crewed Moon landing |
| AUSTRALIS-OSCAR-5 satellite launched<br>Pine Gap US military tracking station established<br>Last ELDO Europa launch | — 1970 — | Japan launches first satellite<br>China launches first satellite<br>VENERA-7 probe makes first landing on Venus |
| ELDO withdraws from Australia<br>Nurrungar US military tracking station established<br>PROSPERO satellite launched from Woomera | — 1971 — | USSR launches world's first space station, SALYUT-1 |
| | 1972 | LANDSAT-1, first remote sensing satellite, launched<br>APOLLO-17 makes last crewed Moon landing |
| | 1973 — | US SKYLAB space station launched |
| Australia declines ESA membership | — 1974 | |

# PACE EVENTS

| AUSTRALIAN EVENTS | | INTERNATIONAL EVENTS |
|---|---|---|
| Australian sounding rocket program ends | 1975 | APOLLO-SOYUZ, first US/USSR joint spaceflight |
| | 1976 | VIKING-1 makes first landing on Mars |
| | 1977 | First GMS weather satellite |
| | 1978 | Czechoslovakian cosmonaut becomes first non-US/USSR citizen in space |
| British sounding rocket program at Woomera ends<br>Australia joins INMARSAT | 1979 | INMARSAT established |
| Anglo-Australian Joint Project officially ends<br>STARLAB project commences<br>Australia Landsat Station (ACRES) commences operation | 1980 | India launches first satellite<br>VOYAGER-1 spacecraft explores Saturn |
| Aussat established | 1981 | COLUMBIA, first US Space Shuttle, launched |
| Australia accepts NASA invitation to fly national payload specialist | 1982 | US NAVSTAR-GPS navigation system commences operation<br>COSPAS-SARSAT commences operation |
| | 1983 | US President Reagan proposes Strategic Defence Initiative ('Star Wars')<br>Sally Ride becomes first US woman in space |
| STARLAB cancelled<br>COSSA formed<br>Australian-born astronaut flies on Space Shuttle | 1984 | US President Reagan proposes Space Station FREEDOM |
| Madigan report on Australian space policy<br>AUSSAT-1 & 2 launched | 1985 | |
| Australian Space Board and National Space Program established<br>Cape York spaceport proposed | 1986 | VOYAGER-2, first space probe to Uranus<br>Space Shuttle CHALLENGER destroyed<br>MIR space station launched<br>First aerospace planes proposed |
| Australian Space Office established<br>AUSSAT-3 launched | 1987 | |
| First Ausroc amateur rocket launch | 1988 | US Space Shuttle flights recommence after CHALLENGER disaster<br>Cosmonauts spend full year in space<br>Israel launches first satellite |
| Australia joins COSPAS-SARSAT network<br>Cole report on Australian space science | 1989 | VOYAGER-2, first space probe to Neptune |
| | 1990 | HUBBLE SPACE TELESCOPE launched<br>MAGELLAN space probe begins radar exploration of Venus |
| ERS-1 launched | 1991 | |
| ENDEAVOUR payload flies on Space Shuttle<br>OPTUS B1 launched<br>Expert panel and BIE Australian space policy reviews<br>North West Cape military tracking station reverts to Australian control<br>OTC and Telecom merge to become AOTC (now Telstra)<br>Optus becomes second Australian telecommunications carrier | 1992 | International Space Year<br>NASA begins SETI search |
| Australian Space Council formed<br>First successful test of Australian SCRAMJET engine | 1993 | |

A NOAA satellite weather image of south-eastern
Australia, showing the Great Dividing Range, areas of
the New South Wales south coast and Gippsland in
Victoria. Snow can be seen on the mountains of the
Australian Alps.

## SPACE STATIONS AND SHUTTLES

In both the US and USSR, attention became focused, in the 1970s, on developing a permanent human presence in space. To do this it was considered necessary to develop space stations and a vehicle which would make access to space economical and routine—a reusable 'shuttle'.

Space stations act as laboratories in orbit, using the microgravity (weightless) environment of space to conduct a wide range of experiments of scientific and commercial interest. They may also serve as platforms for scientific, commercial and military observations of the Earth and could eventually form the basis of space manufacturing facilities.

The USSR launched the first space station, SALYUT-1 ('salute'), in 1971, and since that time has acquired considerable experience in long-term human space activities. In 1986, the USSR launched the first of a new generation of space stations, MIR ('peace'), which is capable of being expanded into a substantial space structure, permanently occupied by crews of cosmonauts. Despite the political and economic difficulties of recent years, the Commonwealth of Independent States (CIS) now plans to make MIR space station complexes the backbone of its space program into the twenty-first century.

America launched its first space station, SKYLAB, in 1973. This facility, which was occupied during 1973 and 1974, had a unique link with Australia. When it finally re-entered the Earth's atmosphere in July 1979, it crashed down in the vicinity of Balladonia in Western Australia, covering a wide but, fortunately, sparsely inhabited area with debris.

The US also plans to have a permanently crewed space station in orbit by the end of the decade, when the US-backed international space station FREEDOM will become operational. FREEDOM will be occupied by multinational astronaut crews and is expected to remain in orbit for up to 30 years. Its occupants will conduct microgravity research in a wide range of fields and also undertake remote sensing and other experiments. Recent discussions between Russia and the US have paved the way for a truly multinational space station, possibly combining elements of FREEDOM with MIR space station modules and the COLUMBUS and JEM modules being developed by the European Space Agency (ESA) and Japan.

Until the 1980s, all space missions were launched using expendable rockets that were used only once. This system, although it enabled the rapid development of spaceflight, was very wasteful of resources and made space launches very expensive. In the 1970s, the high cost of space travel encouraged the US to develop a 'shuttle' system, to make access to space economical and routine.

The US Space Shuttle made its first flight on 12 April 1981, exactly 20 years after the first crewed spaceflight. Launched like a rocket and landing like an aircraft, the Space Shuttle Orbiter is reusable, and its solid rocket boosters can be refurbished, although the huge external tank is only used once. Although the Shuttle was intended to replace conventional rockets, various design and operational deficiencies have meant that it is actually a very expensive system and, since the CHALLENGER disaster in 1986 (when a fault in the solid rocket booster design led to the destruction of the spacecraft), America has turned once again to expendable rockets to supplement the Shuttle.

In the future, shuttle vehicles may be replaced by aerospace planes which combine the reusable spacecraft characteristics of a shuttle with the easy launch and landing of an aircraft. They will be able to take off and land using existing airport runways, and so lower the cost of going into space. Future spaceplanes will use special combination rocket-jet engines known as Supersonic Combustion Ramjets (SCRAMJETS). Several designs are now under development, with leading-edge research being done in Australia, as will be described in chapters 6, 7 and 9.

## WHERE NO-ONE HAS GONE BEFORE

A major aspect of space activity has been the development of robot-controlled probes to explore the distant reaches of the Solar System. These automated explorers have revolutionised our knowledge of our nearest neighbours in space.

As early as 1958, space probes were launched to the Moon and nearby planets. These spacecraft discovered important information about the planets, information that could never have been discerned from Earth-based observations. They have revealed a Solar System profoundly different from what it was believed, just 30 years ago, to be.

Every planet in the Solar System, except Pluto, has been visited by robot explorers. They have discovered exotic worlds of extreme temperatures, strange gases, rocky and icy moons, volcanoes and ancient river beds. The Sun and comets have also been studied by a fleet of deep space probes of international origin. Four spacecraft—PIONEER-10 and 11, and VOYAGER-1 and 2—were sent to tour the outer regions of our Solar System. They will eventually become the first human artefacts to travel to distant stars.

Large radio antennas are used to track and keep in contact with space probes as they travel far from Earth. One such antenna is located in Australia near Canberra, and joins with others in Spain and the US to track space probes as they travel around the Solar System. See chapter 3 for more about Australia's role in tracking deep space probes.

Australia's space activities have been conducted against the background of the international space activities outlined here. These activities have influenced and even determined the path of much of Australia's involvement with space. Succeeding chapters will present the history, current activities and future plans of Australia's response to the challenge and potential of space.

The first Space Shuttle, **COLUMBIA**, makes its maiden
flight in 1981. Only the aircraft-like Shuttle Orbiter is
genuinely reusable; the solid rocket boosters are
sometimes too damaged to refurbish for reuse, while the
external tank is jettisoned as the Shuttle heads for orbit
and burns up in the atmosphere.

# CHAPTER 2

# LIFT-OFF! Australia's first space programs

The last Europa rocket launched from Woomera (F-9) makes a spectacular lift-off. The rocket motors functioned perfectly, but one heat shield did not separate and the test satellite failed to achieve orbit.

Australia's involvement with space activities goes right back to the beginnings of the Space Age, and its first space programs were an extension of the rocketry development programs initiated by Britain immediately after World War II. It was Australian participation in British missile programs that brought this country into the realm of international space activities and made it home to one of the world's major spaceports during the 1960s.

A captured V-2 rocket on display at an air show at the former Mallala Airport, near Adelaide, around 1954. This photograph was taken by space enthusiast Brett Gooden, who was about 11 years old at the time.

## ROCKETS IN THE DESERT

The use of the V-2 in World War II demonstrated that missiles could be effective weapons capable of striking at great distance. Recognising the strategic value of guided weapons, the major powers began to establish rocket and missile programs as the war in Europe came to an end. The UK was one of the many countries that decided to develop a missile capability and it began a major program of research and development in this field.

However, it was difficult to test long-range missiles in Britain, because the space was not available, in such a relatively small and densely populated country, to set aside the large, uninhabited area needed for a long-range missile test range. To accommodate the missiles that it was planning to build, Britain needed a test range up to 4800 kilometres long, with regular good visibility to allow visual tracking of the missiles during test flights. It was also preferable to have a land range, so that the missiles could be recovered in the event of malfunctions for assessment of developmental problems. The need for vast areas in which to test captured V-2s and newly developed missiles made Australia's immense size

an unexpected asset that carried this country into the forefront of early space activity.

Australia's vast size, its political loyalty to Britain and its economic stability made it highly suitable for the type of extensive weapons testing range required. From its southern reaches, Australia offered immense areas towards the west and north. Although both Aboriginal groups and white settlers lived in the proposed areas, the numbers were low enough for Britain to view them as suitably uninhabited. The harsh but fragile environment of central Australia was deemed to be less important than its remoteness, which was considered a critical security asset in the Cold War paranoia of the times. Few white Australians ventured inland from the coast; this meant an enormous slice of territory could be declared a restricted security zone, to reduce the presumed risk of espionage and sabotage, and most people would scarcely realise that it had gone. From a military point of view this made central Australia the ideal place to test V-2 rockets, which Britain had taken from Germany at the close of the war, and their technological descendants.

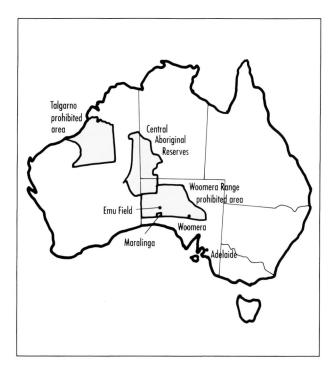

**This map shows the location of the Woomera range 'prohibited areas' in South and Western Australia. The locations of the Central Aboriginal Reserves and the Emu Field and Maralinga test sites are also indicated.**

In October 1945 the British government approached Australia with proposals to set up an experimental guided weapons testing range across the centre of the country. No detailed plans were presented, but the prime minister of the day, Ben Chifley, liked the idea. Although Chifley was eager to support the 'Mother Country', as Australians then viewed Britain, he had Australia's self-interest in mind in accepting the proposal. Australia's industrial plants and engineering skills had advanced during the war, but many of those plants were now idle, with skilled workers unemployed. The development of the weapons testing facility offered new opportunities to utilise and upgrade the manufacturing and technical sectors. Chifley envisaged potential benefits for the development of Australian technology and postwar employment, through the establishment of a British armaments industry here.

Chifley also saw the range as a means for Australia to ensure access to the latest weaponry in the event of another war: the Chifley cabinet had bitter memories of Australia being denied armaments from Britain, for use in the Pacific War, on the basis that they were needed in Europe. He agreed to the weapons facility proposal with the one firm proviso that Australia was to enter the project as an equal partner. Australia would share the development and maintenance costs of the rocket range in return for technology transfer, the employment of Australians within the facility and contracts to Australian industry. From this agreement the Anglo-Australian Joint Project was born, a cooperative agreement that was to last until 1980.

In 1946 an area near Lake Torrens, about 480 kilometres northwest of Adelaide, was chosen as the location of the new testing facility. Both the range town and the range itself were subsequently named 'Woomera', from an Aboriginal name for the throwing stick device used to give increased range to spears. From there, rockets could be launched and tracked, with any test failures presenting minimal danger to life and property because the desert areas of central Australia were so sparsely inhabited.

The effect that the Woomera project might have had on the desert-dwelling Aborigines living in the range area was of little interest to the British, but it was extensively debated in the Australian parliament in the late 1940s. Although the planned impact areas were located in the far north of Western Australia, the proposed centre-line of the rocket range would overfly the Central Aboriginal Reserves and both the safety and culture of the tribal people living there were deemed to be at risk, from crashing missiles as well as the intrusion of the observation posts which were to be located in the reserves.

## PLAYING THE ODDS

Initially, both Aboriginal rights campaigners and the white landholders whose properties were encompassed by the rocket range protested against the danger from crashing rockets. As a result the station communities were eventually provided with shelters into which they could retreat when rocket flights were being undertaken. Protection for the nomadic tribal Aboriginal groups of the reserves was not even considered.

However, the risk of injury was actually very low. The extremely low population density over the range area (one person per 400 square kilometres on average) and the relatively low rate of rocket firings meant that the likelihood of civilian casualties was very slight. In fact, no-one was ever killed or injured by rocket overflights from Woomera during the entire life of the range. No rockets flew over the reserves in the first decade of Woomera's operation. Of the few that did overfly the area during the ELDO period, only one ever impacted in the reserves, as the result of a malfunction.

Most Australians at the time had little interest in Aboriginal issues, but white Aboriginal rights campaigners did champion the Aboriginal cause in the early years. Although some of their arguments were based on wildly incorrect surmises about the type of work that would be carried out at the range, a government committee, which included state Aboriginal Affairs officers and a noted anthropologist, was convened in 1947 to examine the issues. No representatives of the affected Aboriginal groups were invited to participate, as the attitude of the day was that white experts knew what was best for the Aborigines.

The findings of this committee, perhaps not unpredictably, were that the measures the government intended to take for the physical and cultural safety of the Aboriginal people in the range area were adequate, particularly in view of the range's supreme importance to the defence of Australia and the West. This quieted public fears and Woomera ceased to be an important Aboriginal issue, as far as white Australians were concerned, for the duration of the Joint Project.

Australian government policy until the last years of the Joint Project was for the gradual, but eventual, assimilation of Aborigines into white culture and Aborigines living in the Woomera township area at the time of its construction had already had considerable contact with white pastoralists and miners. However, tribal Aborigines, with little previous contact with Europeans, ranged across the reserves over which Woomera's rockets would fly and culture shock, or cultural interference, during the construction and operation of the range, was considered a greater threat to them than the rockets themselves.

At the time Woomera was established, there were about 1200 Aborigines in the reserves and adjacent missions, with the population rising to around 2000 during the peak years of Woomera's operation. Despite early concerns over observation posts being established across the reserves, only one was ever established— the Giles Meteorological Station. However, several incidents occurred at Giles which vindicated the concerns of Aboriginal rights campaigners. A corps of white Native Patrol Officers was established to safeguard the welfare of the reserve Aborigines and, despite some complaints that they prevented Aborigines on

A downrange reconnaissance party encounters tribal Aborigines in 1950. The word 'woomera' (meaning 'a spear-throwing stick') is derived from an eastern Australian Aboriginal language, not the tongue of the local Kokatha people who lived in the vicinity of the rocket range.

walkabout from entering the test areas in 1958, they were generally deemed to have carried out their duties well.

The establishment of the range did restrict the local Kokatha people's access to their traditional lands and they were cut off from many of their cultural sites, which fell inside the prohibited areas of the range. In addition, the western branch of the Kokatha became separated from those living to the east of the range and this led to a physical dispersal of the Kokatha people away from their traditional lands.

By the late 1950s, the reserves were practically depopulated, with Aborigines drifting to townships or cattle stations. In the last years of the Joint Project, Aboriginal groups began to move back into the reserve areas, with the growth of the land-rights movement. The diminished scale of activities at Woomera meant that the range was not considered a hazard to the new communities, and the Kokatha people began to press for access to their sacred sites within the prohibited area. At the time of writing, they had not yet achieved that access, but their campaign is continuing.

## WOOMERA ROCKET RANGE AND THE WEAPONS RESEARCH ESTABLISHMENT

Once the site was chosen, a team was set up to plan the rocket range. An empty munitions factory at Salisbury, near Adelaide, became the backbone for Woomera and Australia's defence science establishment. As the headquarters of the Long-Range Weapons Establishment (LRWE), as it was first called, Salisbury became one of the principal centres of rocket-weapons research and development in the British Commonwealth.

In 1947 the LRWE began operations, intending to build a range starting from Woomera and extending across central Australia. However, because it was so remote, the cost of maintaining each person and each facility at Woomera was two and a half times what it would have been had the facility been established in the vicinity of a capital city. At the height of activity at the rocket range, the township boasted a population of around 6200 scientists, technicians, support staff and their families.

Two vast areas were declared as 'prohibited areas', to be developed for the rocket range: the Talgarno impact area in north-western Western Australia, some 1800 kilometres downrange from the launch area, and the short-range impact area in South Australia, extending about 400 kilometres from the launch sites. An impact area in the vicinity of Christmas Island, in the Indian Ocean, about 2400 kilometres from Australia's north-east coast, was also planned for the testing of the longest range missiles then under consideration for development.

A change in British defence policy almost led to the cancellation of the Joint Project in 1948, but Australia had already invested considerable financial resources in the establishment of the range and campaigned hard to keep the project alive. Britain

finally agreed to the construction of a small general purpose range, extending only 48 kilometres, to test guided weapons, radar, bombs and other armaments and aircraft.

Due to the advanced nature of much of the work being conducted at the time, the scientists and technicians of Salisbury and Woomera often could not obtain the equipment and instruments they required off the shelf. They had to build the technology they needed from their own designs and specifications. This gave them considerable expertise in many areas of advanced missile and rocket technology.

In January 1955 all the LRWE facilities established in South Australia were consolidated into one institution, the Weapons Research Establishment (WRE). Its main work related to the research, development and testing of British guided missiles, but it also conducted specific Australian defence projects. These involved additional research and development in the fields of high-speed aerodynamics, guided weapons development, rocket propulsion, chemistry and physics. As a result of this consolidation, the object of the Joint Project was redefined to focus on the testing and development of guided weapons, pilotless aircraft and air-launched equipment, including radio and radar control, and such agreed projects as could be carried out making use of facilities then in existence or planned. Australia was to provide range and support facilities, developmental facilities, and production

**A true 'company town', Woomera was developed from nothing to become a virtual oasis in the desert. In order to attract staff to work in such an isolated location, it provided every amenity possible. (Above) The Woomera township around 1960. (Below) Sailing on Lake Koolymilka: the Koolymilka Yacht Club only operated when there was water in the lake!**

capacity. Much of the equipment for the Joint Project at Woomera was supplied by the WRE itself, but there was also significant participation by Australian and overseas industry.

The Woomera rocket range actually consisted of a number of independent ranges, which were used for varying purposes, from

## NO NUKES AT WOOMERA

Despite popular misconception, no nuclear devices were ever tested at Woomera. Although there were unfounded early rumours that flying atomic bombs were going to be launched in the process, only inert ballistic dummies of nuclear bombs were ever dropped at Woomera, during bombing trials.

The infamous nuclear test sites of Emu Field and Maralinga were adjacent to the Woomera range but the atomic tests conducted at these sites between 1953 and 1963 came under a separate agreement with Britain that was not connected with the Joint Project. This agreement was drawn up under Prime Minister Menzies, whose attitude was that if it was good for Britain, it was good for Australia. Unlike the arrangement at Woomera, Australia had little control over the conduct of the nuclear tests, which have left large areas of radioactively contaminated land in central Australia.

The WRE's involvement with the atomic tests was confined to providing logistic support for the nuclear programs. Woomera also functioned as a recreation centre for personnel from the test sites, which were supplied by the RAAF from its base at Woomera. The Native Patrol Officers attached to the Woomera range did assist in policing the borders of the nuclear test areas as part of their duties and are known to have voiced their concern about the dangers of fallout to the population on the reserves.

bomb trials to rocket launches. The principal missile range was based at Koolymilka, about 40 kilometres north-west of the Woomera township. It provided a variety of separate launching aprons which allowed work to proceed on several projects simultaneously.

An elaborate network of instrumentation covered the trials areas. Adjacent to the main rangehead were airstrips and facilities for the operation of pilotless target-aircraft, such as the Australian-designed and built Jindivik. A MINITRACK space tracking facility and later a NASA tracking station were established at Island Lagoon, about 22 kilometres south-east of the town. By 1957 it was agreed that there was not a range in the Western world better equipped, better managed, or conducting a major program with fewer staff, than the WRE facility at Woomera. During its peak years in the 1960s, Woomera was the most heavily used space launching facility in the world, apart from Cape Canaveral.

## BLACK KNIGHT AND BLUE STREAK

In 1953 the British government reversed its policy on long-range missiles and decided, once again, that it needed such weapons. In 1955 the Blue Streak program was initiated, to develop a long-range ballistic missile capable of hitting a target in Europe if launched from either Britain or the Middle East (where Britain still had colonial territory). To investigate the problems associated with protecting the nose-cone of the Blue Streak, which housed the nuclear device, from being incinerated by the fierce

**Kinetheodolites were used as tracking cameras during rocket and weapons tests at Woomera. They formed part of the range instrumentation.**

## BALLISTIC MISSILES

A ballistic missile is one that is guided and propelled only during the initial phase of its flight. During the non-powered phase of its flight, its trajectory, like that of a bullet or artillery shell, is largely determined by gravity and atmospheric drag.

An intercontinental ballistic missile (ICBM) is a ballistic missile with a range of a few thousand kilometres. It normally travels out to the fringes of space before re-entering the atmosphere over enemy territory. ICBMs were developed as one of the main weapons of nuclear warfare deterrent during the Cold War. They were primarily intended to be launched from submarines, or underground launch sites known as 'silos'. Many of the world's civilian space launch vehicles were derived from modified ICBMs.

**One of the two launchpads originally established at Lake Hart for the Blue Streak program and later used for the ELDO launch vehicle development program.**

heat of re-entry, it was also proposed to develop a smaller research rocket, the Black Knight.

In April 1956 the Australian government formally accepted the twin proposals that the Black Knight and Blue Streak rockets be tested on its territory. The proposed time scale of the project was for the Black Knight to be launched in 1958 and the Blue Streak tested in 1960. Thus, ten years after the initial reconnaissance into the arid zone, a program to develop Woomera to the limits foreseen in 1946 was finally set in train. It was this program that would actually bring Australia into direct involvement in space-related activities.

The development and testing of Black Knight and Blue Streak would demand an effort far greater than anything that had gone before. The facilities at Woomera had become concentrated in a small area, but now a much larger area of the range would have to be put into use. This was a major engineering assignment requiring huge constructions at the planned Blue Streak launch sites at Lake Hart and the installation of tracking, measuring and recording instruments across the impact area in Western Australia. An enormous upgrading program was initiated: new roads were laid over hundreds of kilometres of untouched country and water pipelines, power supplies and telephone lines were extended to the new launch sites.

The main purpose of the Black Knight program was to test the aerodynamic behaviour of re-entry nose-cones, an important aspect of the development of ICBMs. Black Knight rockets were flown at Woomera from 1958 until 1965 and by 1960 they had won acceptance as the Western world's most reliable rocket. The Black Knight was so successful that, after the cancellation of Blue Streak as a missile in 1960, it continued to be used for various re-entry physics experimental programs, in conjunction with the US, Canada and Australia. The results obtained from these tests and

experiments were used in the development of American missiles, launch vehicles and spacecraft. The Black Knight was also used as a test vehicle for the ELDO launcher development program.

Unlike the successful Black Knight, the liquid-fuelled Blue Streak missile had become obsolete as a weapon while it was still under development and the Blue Streak project was cancelled, ironically while the first rocket was en route from Britain to Woomera for tests. The decision was sudden and taken without any real consultation with Australia. The WRE, despite a few earlier suspicions, had known nothing definite about the cancellation until the news turned up in the morning papers! The cancellation, after so many resources had been expended in developing the missile and its facilities at Woomera, caused a major outcry in both countries and severely embarrassed the British and Australian governments.

## WOOMERA SPACEPORT

Because of its association with missile development, it was a logical assumption in the 1950s that Woomera might one day be a launch site for true space missions. This concept appealed to British and Australian science fiction authors and futurists, and references to Woomera Spaceport abound in both the science fiction and speculative spaceflight literature of the 1950s and 1960s. It was even postulated, by supporters of British spaceflight, that the first crewed mission to the Moon might be launched from the Woomera range!

**Black Knight rockets ready for launch at Woomera in 1961. Note that the two rockets in this photograph have differently shaped nose-cones.**

## ELDO AND EUROPA

The Blue Streak was, however, not totally abandoned. Britain had previously investigated the feasibility of using the missile as the first stage of a satellite launch vehicle and now sought to recover from the cancellation debacle by offering it as the first stage of a satellite launching vehicle to be developed by a consortium of European nations. A British initiative, the European Launcher Development Organisation (ELDO) was established between 1961 and 1962, but did not formally come into being until 29 February 1964, because of the complexity of the international negotiations needed to ratify its charter.

A predecessor of the ESA, ELDO had as its objective the development of an independent, non-military European satellite launch vehicle. With the Blue Streak launch facilities already in place, Australia was the obvious site for ELDO launch operations and it consequently took another step forward in space activity by becoming the only non-European member of ELDO, joining Belgium, the Federal Republic of Germany, France, Great Britain, Italy and the Netherlands. At the insistence of the federal government, Australia became a full, but non-paying, member of ELDO, contributing its facilities in lieu of any financial contribution or commitment.

**The Europa launch vehicle's Blue Streak first stage ready for its first test flight. Note the diagonal pattern painted on the rocket's body. This was used to help the tracking cameras determine the rocket's movements in flight.**

| EUROPA 1 BASIC DATA | |
| --- | --- |
| *Total height of vehicle* | 104 ft 6 in (31.85 m) |
| *Total weight* | 110 ton (112 tonne) |
| **First stage:** *Blue Streak*, UK | |
| *Length* | 61 ft (18.59 m) |
| *Diameter* | 10 ft (3.05 m) |
| *Fuelled weight* | 93.5 ton (95 tonne) |
| *Fuel* | Kerosene and liquid oxygen |
| **Second stage:** *Coralie*, France | |
| *Length* | 18 ft (5.48 m) |
| *Diameter* | 6.6 ft (2.01 m) |
| *Fuelled weight* | 11.8 ton (12 tonne) |
| *Fuel* | Dinitrogen tetroxide and unsymmetrical dimethyl hydrazine |
| **Third stage:** *Astris*, West Germany | |
| *Length* | 13 ft (3.96 m) |
| *Diameter* | 6.6 ft (2.01 m) |
| *Fuelled weight* | 3.9 ton (4 tonne) |
| *Fuel* | Dinitrogen tetroxide and aerozine |

Sources: B Gooden, *Spaceport Australia*, Kangaroo Press, Sydney, 1990; Bruce Henderson, ARDU.

The satellite launch vehicle was known as Europa. The rocket used in the initial ELDO program, Europa 1, consisted of three stages: the first was a modified Blue Streak provided by Britain. France provided the second stage, called Coralie, and West Germany the third stage, known as Astris. The test satellite that the Europa vehicle was to launch was developed under the leadership of Italy, while the Netherlands and Belgium were responsible for the development of telemetry and guidance systems.

Launches were made from the Lake Hart site, using one of the two launchpads constructed for the Blue Streak program and a downrange guidance and tracking station was constructed at Gove in the Northern Territory. Between 1964 and 1970, ten launches of the ELDO Europa 1 were made from Woomera. However, despite three attempts to launch the test satellite (which was referred to as STV or Satellite Test Vehicle), the Europa rocket never successfully placed a satellite into orbit.

Because so many countries were involved, the program ran into difficulties over the years and many technical problems arose. The launcher underwent many modifications and costs began to escalate. Development and launch delays pushed the program schedule back and enthusiasm for the Europa vehicle began to wane when ELDO's sister organisation, the European Space Research Organization (ESRO), conducted successful satellite programs using American launch vehicles. In addition, as early as 1965, ELDO began to rethink its launch site requirements.

One of the purposes of ELDO was to launch telecommunications satellites. Although scientific satellites are often placed in polar or inclined orbits, which could be readily attained from Woomera, communications satellites are best placed in geostationary orbit (for more information on these orbits see chapters 4 and 5). To launch a satellite into geostationary orbit efficiently, a launch site near the equator is best, because the Earth's own rotation will add significant velocity to a rocket launched there toward the east. Unfortunately, at approximately 30°S, Woomera was too far south of the equator for a launch there to gain any useful velocity by firing to the east. In addition, an eastward launch was potentially dangerous to the more densely populated coastal regions of Australia. Although it would have been possible to achieve equatorial orbit from Woomera, 20 per cent more energy would have been required than for a launch from a site near the equator.

In 1968 Britain decided to withdraw from ELDO for economic and political reasons and, as ELDO became more interested in communications satellites, it decided to pursue further launches from France's equatorial launch site at Kourou in French Guiana,

## CORALIE RHYMES WITH *AUSTRALIE!*

The French second stage of the Europa launcher received its name in an unusual way. Earlier French rockets had been named after precious or semi-precious stones, and it had been decided to call the Europa rocket 'Coral', as the next development in the series. However, there was political opposition in France to this choice of name, so the scientists called the rocket Coralie, which contained its intended name and appropriately rhymed with *Australie*, the French word for Australia!

**EUROPA LAUNCHES IN AUSTRALIA**

| Flight | Launch date | Vehicle configuration | Remarks |
|--------|-------------|----------------------|---------|
| F-1 | 5 June 1964 | 1st stage only | Successful |
| F-2 | 20 October 1964 | 1st stage only | Successful |
| F-3 | 22 March 1965 | 1st stage only | Successful |
| F-4 | 24 May 1966 | Active 1st stage with dummy upper stages and dummy satellite | Flight terminated 136 secs after launch |
| F-5 | 13 November 1966 | Active 1st stage with dummy upper stages and dummy satellite | Successful |
| F-6/1 | 4 August 1967 | Active 1st and 2nd stages, dummy 3rd stage and satellite | 2nd stage failed to ignite |
| F-6/2 | 5 December 1967 | Active 1st and 2nd stages, dummy 3rd stage and satellite | 1st/2nd stage separation failed |
| F-7 | 30 November 1968 | All stages active, satellite fitted | 3rd stage exploded |
| F-8 | 3 July 1969 | All stages active, satellite fitted | 3rd stage exploded |
| F-9 | 12 June 1970 | All stages active, satellite fitted | All stages successful, satellite failed to orbit |

Source: Bruce Henderson, 'Satellite launch activities at Woomera 1964–1974', unpublished, November 1991.

now the site of the ESA's launch facilities. The last ELDO launch at Woomera occurred on 12 June 1970 and today little evidence of the ELDO project remains. The Lake Hart facilities were scrapped in the 1970s and the Gove tracking station was demolished, with the antennas now being used in research work at the support laboratories at Salisbury.

## LATER PROJECTS AT WOOMERA

In 1967 the earlier Black Knight re-entry studies were continued by Project Sparta, a joint American/British/Australian program which used American Redstone rockets as the first stage of the Sparta launch vehicle. The Redstone, derived from an early US ICBM, was the type of rocket used for the first two launches in NASA's crewed spaceflight program. Nine Sparta launches were carried out in 1967 as part of this program, which was especially significant for Australia: it was a spare rocket from the Sparta program that was used to launch Australia's first satellite, WRESAT, which will be discussed in chapter 6.

The Black Arrow project, commenced in 1968, was the last major rocket program to be undertaken at Woomera. It was

Britain's final attempt at developing its own, independent satellite launching capability. Developed from the reliable Black Knight, Black Arrow was used to drive specially designed nosecones back into the atmosphere at re-entry speeds. Four Black Arrow launches were conducted at Woomera. The last, on 28 October 1971, lofted into orbit PROSPERO, the second of only two satellites (the first was WRESAT) to be orbited successfully from the range to date. This made Britain the sixth nation in the world to achieve an independent satellite launch.

Following the withdrawal of ELDO and the demise of the Black Arrow program in 1971, the Woomera range was progressively wound down, as neither Britain nor Australia wished to expend the funds to maintain it at peak capacity. Its facilities were demolished or relocated, and its staff redeployed to other projects. Space-related work there came to a virtual standstill, apart from occasional sounding rocket campaigns for studies of the upper atmosphere and astronomy (see chapter 6). Gradually, Woomera became little more than a support facility for the Australian/US Air Force Joint Defence Space Communications Station at Nurrungar, about 10 kilometres from the Woomera township. This controversial space tracking facility is discussed in chapter 3.

Weapons testing programs continued, but at a reduced level, and the Joint Project was officially terminated in 1980. Today, Woomera has moved from the control of the Defence Science and Technology Organisation (DSTO, the successor to the WRE) to become the responsibility of the Royal Australian Air Force (RAAF). Some weapons testing continues and the Koolymilka rangehead facility remains, with two operational sounding rocket launchpads, and a new computer control system.

Effective as they were, Australia's early space manufacturing and launch capabilities were a response to other countries' space plans, and tied to the Anglo-Australian Joint Project and ELDO activities. At the time, the Australian government did not appreciate the opportunities provided by space programs, and so, apart from space tracking programs in conjunction with the US, did not initiate other forms of international cooperation or actively support a national space program. As a result, our early space effort went into hibernation following the transfer of European rocket-launching activities away from Australia in the early 1970s. Further discussion on Australia's space policies and their effect on space activities in Australia can be found in chapter 8.

Woomera may yet see a new lease of life, if proposals for developing a light satellite launching facility, using an Australian assembled launch vehicle, come to fruition. Chapter 9 has more information on these plans and their ramifications for Aboriginal land rights. Woomera is waiting for a revival—what it needs is government commitment, a responsible approach to Aboriginal land rights, financial input and a project worthy of its past achievements.

C O M M E N T A R Y

MISS MARY WHITEHEAD *was a mathematician working in the Trials Division of the WRE. She comments on her experiences as one of the few professional women employed on the scientific staff of the WRE in the early days.*

I completed an arts degree in mathematics in Melbourne in 1937, but could not get any work in the field until after the Second World War. Then there was a recruiting drive for mathematicians at the Long-Range Weapons Establishment and I got a job working in the Bomb Ballistics Section at Salisbury.

When I went to Salisbury, in January 1949, I was the only woman on the professional staff, and I found, somewhat to my horror, that I was to be in charge of a team of computing assistants [who were known as 'computers']. The work involved doing the computations and reading the film records and other timing records for the trials conducted by the Bomb Ballistics Group at Salisbury. Some of the formulae we were given, others we had to devise, so my work was a mixture of mathematical work, setting up computing schedules and looking after the computing team.

The team comprised half a dozen young women, most of them straight from school. We were the only women doing technical work at this time—there were not many women engineers or physicists at Salisbury until many years later. When the section began our only aid was mechanical calculators. They were so noisy, we had to have egg crates as sound dampers on the walls and carpets in the rooms.

The conditions of employment at that time were somewhat different from those of the present. Although I was a professional officer, I was always paid less than a man of the same classification. In fact, because Salisbury was a long way out of Adelaide, a special award category had to be created for the female 'computers', in order to attract good people. As a result we recruited women of a very high standard, some of whom went on to get their degrees. Anyone who left WRE was snapped up by the local contractors [aerospace companies with contracts for WRE work], because a woman who was trained in computing work was invaluable to their scientists and engineers.

**Mary Whitehead and some of her computing team at Woomera in the early days. On their early visits to the range (when there were very few women living in the area) the 'computers' were required to dress in army gear, to discourage amorous attention from the range staff!**

Working in what was primarily a male environment had its good points. It would often be a bit of an initial surprise to the men, but I think we were helped by the fact that in those early days there was quite a large proportion of British scientists, who had come to Australia to help set up the general missile ranges. They had been used to having women working in the computing field during wartime, and because of this they gave us a better run and the Australians did, too.

Generally I was treated with the same professional courtesy that one male would give another in the same field. The major problem was in the system of sending graduates in science and maths et cetera to Britain to get experience in defence science. The Chief Defence Scientist just made the rule 'No Women', so I was wiped completely. The men got tremendous help in their careers by getting that training, but opportunities for advancement were just not being offered to women.

Salisbury was our base, but the women went out to Woomera frequently, particularly in the earlier days. There was a shortage of people to crew the instruments at the range, and the chief of our group firmly believed that everyone should know as much as possible about the trials, so the girls went to operate the instruments. They would come back and analyse those records and the background knowledge would help their reading and interpretation and help them solve many problems. The trips to Woomera were also great morale builders. The girls operated the instruments often under very uncomfortable conditions. They were right out at a tiny little outpost—the wind could be very cold in winter and it could be scorching hot in summer. It wasn't easy going, but it was interesting and it really grabbed their attention.

Sending women to the range was quite controversial in the beginning. Woomera was run by the Services, and the Brigadier in charge didn't want women there. Because our chief had worked with the women in England, he knew these girls were all interested and because he believed that the experience would help their overall work, he won out.

Our quarters was a hut with a row of rooms and we had to use the showers and toilets before the men, as there were no separate facilities. We were living under pretty basic conditions, but we were all young and hardy and we were never at Woomera for more than a couple of weeks at a time. Later on they had permanent computing staff on the range and then they set up separate women's quarters.

We generally had to be out at the range at 8.00 am and would have our lunch at one of the more central posts out there. We would probably get back somewhere about 4 o'clock. Sometimes there were night trials, but we usually only went out at night because there were cameras that had to be calibrated by taking photographs of the stars.

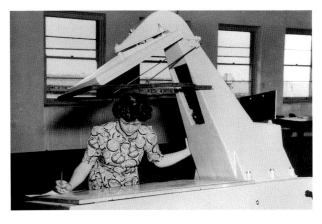

**A 'computer' reading a film record manually, using an overhead projector. Turning the information recorded on film into usable data was a labour intensive task.**

After working on the computerisation of our section, I was called back to work on the Black Knight trials. I would make a point of going up to the trial itself, but all the planning and computing work was done at Salisbury. I saw the launches, because being on the spot was important to get the feel of the information. It was also helpful because when the missiles broke up a bit as they came in, as they often did, you could relate that to the images that you saw on the camera plates.

I was fortunate to be involved in such interesting work—I was always learning. By the late 1950s we had the computer programs written. The girls still had to do all the reading and make measurements on the photographic plates but the programs had been set up and the results could be processed by the computer. We had a few trials before it was right, but it was a considerable advance on four weeks of hand calculating.

When, in 1960 I think, the Department installed its first IBM computer, we had a completely new ball game. It was very powerful, reliable and fast, and for a while all the required computing could be done in one day. However, the computer did not really supersede the ladies until the range was running down, because there was a tremendous build-up of knowledge that was required.

The Blue Streak trials were the end of my real work with data processing. My own modest contribution was the zigzag pattern on the rocket, which enabled us to make very accurate measurements of the missile as it rolled after leaving the launchpad. With the pattern there, the cameras that tracked the launch could easily measure if the rocket had rolled, depending on where that diagonal was relative to the top and bottom stripes.

I did work on WRESAT, overseeing another woman who did the detailed work to get the trajectory, but most of my later work was in the library, with information databases. I retired in November 1982.

# CHAPTER 3

# AN EYE ON THE SKY: Space tracking from Australia

A night-time view of the Island Lagoon tracking station at Woomera, with the 26- metre tracking dish illuminated.

When the US sought to establish space tracking networks for its spaceflight programs, Australia was strategically placed, both geographically and politically, to become the location for a number of tracking stations. Thus, while Australia participated in British and European space activities at Woomera, it also fulfilled a quite separate and vital role in the US space program. Spacecraft tracking has been Australia's longest continuous space activity, with stations operating in this country since 1957.

## KEEPING TRACK

An essential part of every spaceflight project is the communications system which transmits instructions from Earth to the spacecraft and returns data from the spacecraft to Earth. Tracking stations form the link between spacecraft and their mission controllers. Using antennas of various shapes and sizes, they transmit and receive signals from spacecraft as they orbit the Earth, or travel into deep space, and keep track of their position.

Because radio waves travel in straight lines, no single tracking station could communicate continuously with a spacecraft as it orbits the Earth. An individual tracking station can only keep in contact with a spacecraft as long as the craft is within its 'line of sight'. Consequently, a network of tracking stations is needed around the globe in order to maintain constant contact with an Earth-orbiting spacecraft.

Spacecraft travelling to the Moon and planets also need tracking networks in order to stay in touch with the Earth. Because the Earth is rotating, a minimum of three stations is needed, each located 120° apart so that, as the planet turns, at least one tracking station will always be facing in the direction from which the spacecraft's signals are coming.

Australia was particularly important to the US in the late 1950s as a tracking station location for a number of reasons. Because the first orbit of almost all spacecraft launched from Cape Canaveral would pass within sight of Western Australia, data obtained from tracking facilities in this area would aid in the confirmation and refinement of orbits, which are critical to the success of every space mission. Also, in order to maintain an unbroken network of contact with a spacecraft, tracking stations would be needed between Africa and Hawaii, and Australia

## ON TRACK

Complex antennas are used to communicate with spacecraft. As spacecraft move further away from the Earth, the signals they send back become very weak, so that receiving them is a bit like trying to watch a firefly in Perth from the distance of Sydney! Similarly, it is necessary to transmit very powerful signals in order to send commands to distant space probes. The size of an antenna depends upon the strength of the signals and the rates of information it is expected to receive. To receive images from space probes exploring the outer planets of the Solar System, huge antennas, up to 70 metres, are required.

Tracking station antennas are shaped to collect even very weak signals, which are usually reflected from the main dish into a sub-reflector, mounted on a support above the centre of the antenna dish. The sub-reflector focuses the signals into a MASER (Microwave Amplification by Stimulated Emission of Radiation—the microwave

analog of a laser), which amplifies them and feeds them into a receiver. When signals are being transmitted to a spacecraft, the process operates in reverse.

During space missions, each tracking station around the world communicates directly with the control centre in the US by teletype and voice circuits, to report on the position of a spacecraft and to pass on the latest engineering and scientific data received. The circuits in Australia have been provided and maintained by Telecom Australia and its predecessors, with special NASCOM (NASA Communications) switching centres established first in Adelaide and later at Deakin in Canberra. Communication between Australia and the US has been the responsibility of OTC/Telstra. Since 1979, ground-based communication links via telephone lines, undersea cables and radio have been supplemented and partly superseded by the NASA Tracking and Data Relay Satellite System (TDRSS).

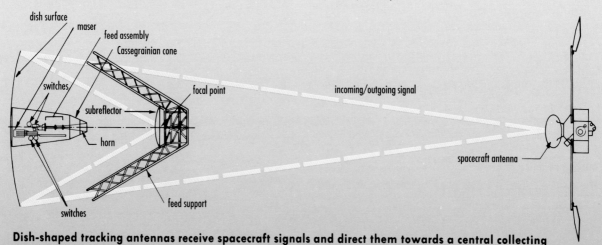

**Dish-shaped tracking antennas receive spacecraft signals and direct them towards a central collecting point, where they are focused and fed into a MASER for amplification. This type of antenna arrangement is called a Cassegrain feed system.**

**NASA's Muchea tracking station near Perth operated only for the Mercury series of space flights. It was closed down in 1963, and a commemorative cairn is all that remains to mark the site today.**

offered a good location for one or more stations, because the continent occupies such a broad swath of the Earth's surface.

In addition, Australia was a politically stable country and one friendly to the US. Had Australia not been prepared to host American tracking stations, the US would have been forced either to establish ground stations in South-East Asian countries that were considered politically unsuitable at that time, or to develop a large fleet of tracking ships, which would have been more expensive in the long term.

Because of its intention to launch a satellite during International Geophysical Year (1957-58), in 1956 the US government asked permission of Australia to install satellite tracking facilities at Woomera. This system was known as MINITRACK (*Mini*mum Weight *Track*ing). MINITRACK antennas were simple, but they could determine a spacecraft's position with great accuracy. They were used for measuring orbital data for American satellites such as EXPLORER and VANGUARD, and for recording the information they transmitted.

The MINITRACK station was established at Island Lagoon, about 27 kilometres from the Woomera township, but the agreement under which it operated was quite separate from the Joint Project. Australia insisted that it be managed by Australian staff and operated without direct interference from the US. However, as a goodwill gesture, the Australian government donated the land, buildings, and technical and scientific staff for the construction of the station. The MINITRACK system was later moved from Woomera to the Satellite Tracking and Data Acquisition Network (STADAN) facility at Orroral Valley near Canberra.

The establishment of MINITRACK was followed, in September 1957, by the installation of a Baker-Nunn optical tracking camera, also at Island Lagoon, which formed part of the Smith-sonian Astrophysical Observatory's (SAO) Optical Tracking Network. It had actually been developed as a rival to MINITRACK, so although operating at the same site as MINITRACK, it was deployed under a separate agreement with the SAO.

The Baker-Nunn camera at Island Lagoon was one of a network of 12 such cameras, which were used to take photographs of satellites orbiting the Earth. Baker-Nunn cameras were able to take remarkably clear photographs of satellites, even those in orbits of 37 000 kilometres! With the clear atmosphere at Woomera, some outstanding photographs were taken of small satellites at great heights.

## AUSTRALIA JOINS THE NASA NETWORK

In 1958 the US established the National Aeronautics and Space Administration (NASA) to manage its civilian space program and the MINITRACK facility was transferred to NASA control. At about the same time, US Department of Defense work on lunar probes was also transferred to NASA, along with control of the Jet Propulsion Laboratory (JPL) in California. As NASA assumed responsibility for lunar and other deep space probes, it began to plan the establishment of a tracking station network to monitor these spacecraft on their planetary exploration missions. Located in the Southern Hemisphere at approximately 120° around the globe from the tracking station being established in California, Australia was again ideally placed geographically to be a host location for such a station. It was important for NASA to have at least one tracking station south of the equator because there would be times when spacecraft would travel through areas not visible from the Northern Hemisphere.

**MAJOR NASA TRACKING FACILITIES IN AUSTRALIA**

| Station | Location | Years of operation |
|---|---|---|
| MINITRACK | Woomera, SA | 1957-66 |
| | Orroral Valley, ACT | 1966-85 |
| Baker-Nunn | Woomera, SA | 1957-73 |
| Muchea | Perth, WA | 1960-63 |
| Red Lake | Woomera, SA | 1960-63 |
| NASCOM Switching Centre | Adelaide, SA | 1960-67 |
| Island Lagoon | Woomera, SA | 1960-72 |
| Carnarvon | Carnarvon, WA | 1964-74 |
| Tidbinbilla | Tidbinbilla, ACT | 1965-present |
| Orroral Valley | Orroral Valley, ACT | 1966-85 |
| Honeysuckle Creek | Honeysuckle Creek, ACT | 1967-81 |
| NASCOM Switching Centre | Deakin, ACT | 1967-85 |
| Cooby Creek (mobile) | Toowoomba, Qld | 1966-70 |

Because NASA's plans for locating tracking stations in Australia were growing, a new agreement was needed to provide blanket coverage of all the facilities that it proposed to establish in the country. In 1960 the governments of Australia and the US formally agreed to cooperate in spacecraft tracking and communications. Australia undertook to establish and operate a number of tracking stations which would form part of worldwide networks under the control of NASA. The Australian Department of Supply, through the WRE, was responsible for fulfilling the local commitment under this agreement. Subsequently, this role has devolved onto the Department of Science and more recently the Australian Space Office. NASA's interests are overseen by a senior scientific representative, based in Canberra. Outside the US, Australia eventually had the largest number of NASA space tracking and communications antennas in the world.

Under the space cooperation agreement, NASA eventually established tracking stations in Australia for three networks: the Deep Space Network, for communications with interplanetary spacecraft; the Manned Space Flight Network, to support the US crewed spaceflight program; and the Space Tracking and Data Acquisition Network (STADAN), for tracking Earth-orbiting satellites. The different networks often assisted in each other's programs. In addition, NASA Communications (NASCOM) Switching Centres were established in Adelaide and later in Canberra as central communications facilities, responsible for coordinating the transmission of data received in Australia to the mission control centres in the US.

### The Manned Space Flight and STADAN stations

America's first piloted spaceflight program, Project Mercury, was initiated in 1958. Mercury spacecraft were small vehicles that carried only one astronaut but, like the Soviet Vostok program, they represented the first tentative steps in human exploration beyond the Earth.

In July 1960 a NASA tracking station was established at Muchea, near Perth in Western Australia, to support the planned Mercury orbital flights. The Woomera radar at Red Lake was also adapted for tracking use during this period. An Australian doctor served as Flight Surgeon at the Muchea station during the Mercury missions, monitoring the medical telemetry from the spacecraft, which reported on the astronauts' physical condition.

**Orroral Valley tracking station south of Canberra after a rare snowfall. Although most of the equipment was removed after NASA closed the station down, the site is still used today by Australian government departments for satellite monitoring and laser ranging programs.**

## THE SPACE COOPERATION AGREEMENT— AUSTRALIA BENEFITS

In the space cooperation agreement, NASA and Australia jointly established a management policy which has proved so successful that it has allowed the agreement to continue, virtually unchanged, until the present day. Construction and operation of the tracking facilities in Australia have always been financed by NASA, which has retained responsibility for system design and policy formulation. Australia has been responsible for the detailed facilities design and the installation, operation and maintenance of the stations.

Following the precedent established with the MINI-TRACK station, Australian staff are employed at the stations, which are operated by private industry under contract to the Australian cooperating agency (currently the Australian Space Office), with a civilian officer of that agency as director. At their peak, during the 1960s and 1970s, more than 700 Australians were employed at NASA tracking stations.

Because Australian industry undertakes all the tracking station construction, operations and maintenance work, this has enabled Australia to build and maintain considerable expertise in areas of electronic and mechanical engineering—for example, antenna design —relevant to the stations and the communications satellite ground sector. Australia also has the right to use the stations for its own scientific research, provided this research does not conflict with NASA's priority tasks.

After the conclusion of the Mercury program in 1963, NASA wanted to establish a larger network in Australia to support its more advanced spaceflight programs, so the relatively unsophisticated Muchea and Red Lake stations were closed down to make way for more advanced facilities.

The Mercury program was succeeded by the Gemini program which, during 1965 and 1966, used two-person spacecraft to test the equipment and techniques, such as space rendezvous and space-walking, necessary for accomplishing a mission to the Moon. To support the Gemini and subsequent Apollo flights, NASA established its Manned Space Flight Network (MSFN). The first MSFN station in Australia was at Carnarvon, Western Australia, which was opened in June 1964 in order to support the first crewed Gemini mission, GEMINI-3, in March 1965. Integral to the Carnarvon station was an international satellite communications ground station, operated by OTC, which allowed the tracking station to communicate with the US via an INTELSAT satellite.

To provide additional tracking and communications support for spacecraft around the Moon during the Apollo program (1968-72), Carnarvon was joined by a facility at Honeysuckle Creek near Canberra. Sited deliberately close to the Tidbinbilla tracking station, Honeysuckle worked in conjunction with it in tracking the Apollo spacecraft in lunar orbit. Typically, Honeysuckle would track the Apollo Lunar Module and Tidbinbilla the Command Module. In 1972 equipment from the closed Island Lagoon tracking station was shipped to Honeysuckle for use with the SKYLAB space station missions (1973-74) and to provide Deep Space Network support to the Tidbinbilla station. Honey-

---

CITY FORECAST: FINE AND HOT. MODERATE TO FRESH N.E. WINDS MODERATING IN THE AFTERNOON. MAX. 93DEG.

# The West Australian

78, No. 23,576. Registered at the G.P.O. Perth, for transmission by post as a newspaper. ••• PERTH, WEDNESDAY, FEBRUARY 21, 1962.     TEL. 21 0161     36 PAGES †  PRICE 4d.

# GLENN ORBITS EARTH, SAYS THANKS TO PERTH

American astronaut Col. John Glenn was rocketed into space from Cape Canaveral at 10.47 Perth time last night. Less than an hour later his spacecraft streaked across the sky above Rockingham on the first of three scheduled orbits.

The *West Australian* newspaper headlined Glenn's thanks from orbit. Australians were strongly interested in space activities in the early days of crewed spaceflight because of the US tracking stations here.

## UP GOES THE LIGHT BILL

The City of Perth and the adjacent town of Rockingham turned on their lights on a summer night in February 1962 to salute John Glenn, orbiting in his FRIENDSHIP 7 Mercury spacecraft. When Glenn asked Muchea about the source of the brilliant display that he could see and was told that citizens in both towns had turned on their lights for him, he thanked them publicly from orbit, thus bringing the two Australian towns to world attention. Soon after, on a wintry day in New York, the Mayor of Perth was present at ceremonies honouring the first US Earth-orbiting astronaut. Said Glenn to the Mayor, 'I hope I didn't run up your light bill!'

suckle Creek was later used to support communications with Space Shuttle flights, before being closed in late 1986.

Complementary to the MSFN was NASA's Satellite Tracking and Data Acquisition Network (STADAN), which was primarily intended for control and data reception of Earth-orbiting satellites. Australia's first STADAN station was at Orroral Valley, in the ACT. It was opened in May 1965 and used for scientific and applications satellites. The station also supported the APOLLO-SOYUZ Test Project (the first space link-up between the USSR and the US, in 1975) and Shuttle missions before closure in early 1985. The antenna was then moved to the University of Tasmania for use as a radio astronomy instrument. Tidbinbilla then took over the remaining tracking tasks for Earth-orbiting satellites, using the 26-metre antenna which had been transferred from the closed Honeysuckle Creek station.

Cooby Creek, near Toowoomba in Queensland, was a mobile STADAN station, used for tracking satellites in NASA's Applications Technology Satellite series from October 1966 until 1970. In 1967 it received some of the earliest live satellite television broadcasts into Australia, from Expo 67 in Canada and the America's Cup races. On 26 June that year Australia participated in the *Our World* program, the first live global television broadcast, via the Cooby Creek facility. NASA relinquished control of the station in 1970, and it was used by the Post Master General's Department (PMG) for a few years to conduct experiments with satellite communications for the outback, before it was finally removed and redeployed to Spain for another NASA program.

## NASA'S 'SUNSCREEN'

Associated with the Carnarvon tracking station was an observatory for NASA's Solar Particle Alert Network (SPAN), which was established in 1967 to monitor the Sun during Apollo Moon missions. Certain types of solar activity, such as solar flares, spew out streams of charged particles that would be harmful to astronauts outside the protective screen of the Earth's ionosphere. Astronauts on Apollo missions to the Moon were seriously at risk from radiation poisoning if a major solar event occurred during their spaceflight.

In order to ensure that spaceflights were not launched during dangerous periods of solar activity, NASA established the SPAN observatories to monitor the Sun continually. Three stations were established around the world to provide a 24-hour watch on the Sun.

Operating from sunrise to sunset every day, the Carnarvon observatory used two 6-inch (15 cm) telescopes to monitor solar activity. A small radio telescope was also used to 'listen' to the Sun in three different wavelengths, to detect signs of dangerous activity. In addition, the observatory operated a riometer, an instrument which could detect the disturbances created in the upper atmosphere by atmospheric nuclear testing. This device could be used to warn Earth-orbiting crewed spacecraft of areas of dangerous radiation created by nuclear testing.

The SPAN station was operated for NASA by the US Environmental Science Services Administration. Its two observers were employed by the Australian government.

## AUSTRALIA AND THE FIRST MOON LANDING

When APOLLO-11 made the first crewed landing on the Moon in 1969, Australian tracking stations played a critical role in providing live television coverage of the event. The signals from APOLLO-11 came through the Honeysuckle Creek and Tidbinbilla tracking stations, with assistance from the Parkes radio telescope. Honeysuckle and Parkes were tracking the Lunar Module, which was on the lunar surface, and Tidbinbilla was tracking the Command Module, in orbit around the Moon.

The initial broadcast of Neil Armstrong's famous words 'That's one small step for a man, one giant leap for Mankind' as he stepped onto the Moon was relayed via Honeysuckle Creek, with Parkes taking over the relay about ten minutes later. The NASA tracking station at Goldstone, in the US, was also receiving the signals from the Moon, but its reception was not good because of technical problems. NASA considered that Parkes was providing the best picture, and stayed with the radio telescope's signal for the rest of the broadcast. But

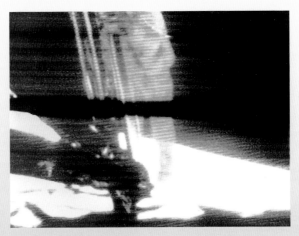

**Humanity's first step onto the Moon, as seen on television around the world, was broadcast via the Honeysuckle Creek tracking station.**

although Parkes provided the best and the majority of the APOLLO-11 television, the initial television came to the world via Honeysuckle Creek.

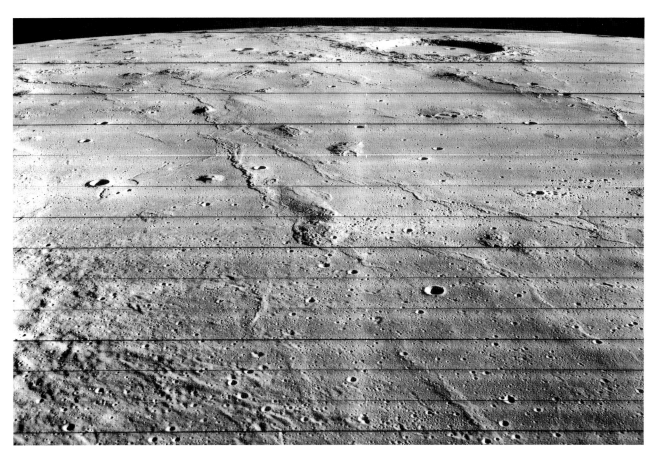

An image of the Moon's surface taken by LUNAR ORBITER-5. It was received at the Woomera DSN station as a series of strip images which were then combined together to create the overall photograph, hence the striped appearance of the picture.

With the slowdown in NASA space programs in the late 1970s and the development of its Tracking and Data Relay Satellite System (TDRSS) for communications, NASA no longer had need of its extensive MSFN and STADAN networks, which were gradually phased out by the mid 1980s.

### The Deep Space Network

The first Australian component of the Deep Space Network (DSN) was the Deep Space Instrumentation Facility built in 1960 at Island Lagoon, near the site of the existing MINITRACK and Baker-Nunn stations. The Island Lagoon tracking station supported many of NASA's early deep space exploration missions, including the Ranger, Mariner and Lunar Orbiter programs. The Ranger series of probes was the first step in America's lunar exploration program. Ranger spacecraft carried television cameras and returned close-up pictures of the lunar surface before crash-landing on the Moon. Lunar Orbiter spacecraft were placed in orbit around the Moon to take high resolution photographs of the lunar surface as an aid to the selection of suitable landing sites for the Apollo spacecraft.

NASA used the Mariner spacecraft to study the planets Mars and Venus. In 1962 Island Lagoon supported the MARINER-2 mission, which made history as the first spacecraft to fly past Venus and take measurements of the temperature and atmosphere of the planet. The Island Lagoon station operated until 1972, when it was closed down and its equipment shipped to the Honeysuckle Creek station.

In 1965 NASA established its second Australian DSN station, at Tidbinbilla near Canberra, just in time to support the MARINER-4 mission, which returned the first photographs of the surface of Mars. It went on to support the later Mariner missions to Mars and Venus, the Surveyor missions which landed on the surface of the Moon, and the Pioneer spacecraft, which were used to explore conditions in interplanetary space. Pioneers were also tracked by Island Lagoon. In the 1970s Tidbinbilla tracked the PIONEER-10 and 11 spacecraft as they sent back the first close-up images from Jupiter and Saturn, the giant planets of the outer Solar System, and helped receive the first striking images from the surface of Mars, taken by the Viking spacecraft.

Tidbinbilla has supported various crewed space missions, including the Apollo flights and the Space Shuttle, and has also assisted in tracking non-NASA space probes, such as the Soviet VEGA-1 and 2 and Japan's SUISEI and SAKIGAKE, which were sent to explore Comet Halley on its return to the inner Solar System in 1986. As the VOYAGER-1 and 2 spacecraft explored the

## A MESSAGE FROM MARS?

Because the signal from MARINER-4 around Mars was so weak when it arrived back on Earth, it was difficult to receive. When the spacecraft was due to make its closest approach to Mars, Tidbinbilla asked the civil aviation authorities to divert all aircraft in the area that might come between the station's antenna and the signal from Mars. This provoked jokes about little green men from Mars popping up to ask what was going on! Much to the surprise of the Tidbinbilla staff, just at the time when MARINER-4 passed behind Mars, they received a call on their special direct line from Canberra Airport (the first time ever), asking if they were experiencing interference from a UFO! Later the object was identified as an errant weather balloon.

outer Solar System in the 1980s, they were tracked by Tidbinbilla, which was able to receive signals so weak they were less than a billionth of a billionth of a watt in power, and translate them into the spectacular images of Jupiter, Saturn, Uranus and Neptune that have transformed our knowledge of the Solar System.

As the spacecraft it tracks have ventured further and further into the Solar System, Tidbinbilla has been expanded and its antennas enlarged in order to receive the ever fainter signals from deep space. It began operating with a 26-metre antenna, which was later extended to 34 metres. In 1973 a 64-metre DSN antenna was built, which was extended to 70 metres in 1987–88 in order to be able to receive the extremely faint signals from VOYAGER-2's encounter with Neptune. An additional 34-metre antenna was built in the mid 1980s.

Today, Tidbinbilla is the only major NASA tracking station in Australia and represents an American investment of approximately $400 million. It continues to track the Pioneer and Voyager spacecraft at and beyond the edges of the Solar System and supports more recent NASA deep space missions such as the MAGELLAN mission to Venus, the long-duration GALILEO flight to Jupiter and the MARS OBSERVER. With its 26-metre dish, the station is also used to track spacecraft in Earth orbit.

## OTHER CIVILIAN TRACKING PROGRAMS IN AUSTRALIA

Apart from its major spacecraft tracking stations, NASA has maintained a laser satellite tracking station on a property near Dongara in Western Australia since 1979 to support its Earth Dynamics program. This program uses lasers, reflected from the Moon and specially equipped laser-reflecting satellites, to make very accurate determinations of distance, which can assist in a wide range of studies such as polar motion and Earth rotation, the orbit and interior structure of the Moon, as well as studies of the tides and gravity.

The NASA mobile facility is complemented by a fixed station,

located at the old Orroral Valley tracking station site. This program is managed by the Department of Administrative Services' Australian Surveying and Land Information Group (AUSLIG). The old Orroral site is also used by the Department of Transport and Communications for international and domestic satellite transmissions monitoring with small antennas.

Australia has also assisted the European Space Agency (ESA) in tracking and controlling its Ariane rocket launches and spacecraft operations. In 1979 the ESA established a tracking station at Carnarvon, utilising and extending the facilities of the OTC satellite communications station already established in conjunction with the NASA station there. The Carnarvon station became a major site in the ESA network and was the prime command station for the GIOTTO space probe's encounter with Comet Halley in 1986.

After the OTC station at Carnarvon was shut down, the ESA re-established its tracking facility at the new OTC ground station at Gnangara, near Perth, Western Australia, from which it continues to provide coverage for its space missions. In 1989 this tracking station was instrumental in rescuing the HIPPARCHOS astronomy satellite after it failed to achieve its proper orbit.

Australia's radio telescopes have also assisted in space tracking programs. The CSIRO radio telescope near Parkes, New South Wales, has been involved in many space communications programs. It was used by NASA during the Apollo program and received some of the first images from the APOLLO-11 Moon landing. It also provided crucial tracking support during the APOLLO-13 mission in 1970, when the spacecraft's fuel cell exploded, causing severe damage to the spacecraft and a life-threatening situation for its crew.

The Parkes telescope participated in the Voyager encounters with the outer planets and has been used for other international programs such as the ESA's GIOTTO probe to Comet Halley. As a result of the Voyager missions, Parkes and Tidbinbilla are now joined by a microwave radio link, which allows the two facilities to work together on radio astronomy projects, as well as space tracking, forming the world's largest real-time interferometer radio telescope.

Since 1957 Australia's involvement in space tracking programs has enabled it to develop considerable expertise in space tracking technology and to participate not only in the space programs of the US, but those of other nations as well, in a manner which would not otherwise have been possible.

## BASES FOR DEBATE—MILITARY SPACE TRACKING IN AUSTRALIA

Apart from NASA stations, other US space tracking installations have been built in Australia for military purposes. Indeed, Australia's greatest current involvement in space activities is in military space tracking, although little is generally known about this because of the inevitable secrecy that surrounds it.

## WHERE ARE YOU, ET? THE SEARCH FOR EXTRATERRESTRIAL INTELLIGENCE

It is hard to imagine an event which would have a more profound effect on humanity than the discovery of intelligent life beyond the Earth. Astronomy has shown that there are enormous numbers of stars like the Sun and that the chemical elements characteristic of life are widespread. It seems virtually certain that suitable habitats for life are scattered about the universe, but if intelligent life has developed on them, how would we know it was there, or be able to make contact?

Just as tracking stations allow us to receive the signals from distant spacecraft, and radio telescopes the naturally produced radio signals of the stars, so they also provide a method of 'listening in' to possible communication from other intelligent beings. Artificial signals produced by technology have characteristics that distinguish them from natural radio emissions, and radio waves suffer least from interference by the natural background radiation of the universe as they travel through space.

The Search for Extraterrestrial Intelligence (SETI) has been conducted sporadically since the first SETI program, Project Ozma, in 1960. In 1983 the Tidbinbilla tracking station took part in a short-lived NASA SETI program. The CSIRO Parkes radio telescope has also been used for SETI experiments. In October 1992 NASA began a ten-year survey of the heavens for signals of extraterrestrial origin. The SETI High Resolution Microwave Survey (HRMS) comprises two parts: the Targeted Search is aiming radio telescopes at selected stars and scanning the electromagnetic spectrum in the microwave frequencies for signals originating from the stars' vicinities. Part of this search, the Parkes radio telescope is scheduled to scan the sky for 16 solid weeks beginning in August 1994.

The Sky Survey, the second part of the HRMS, is the responsibility of NASA's Jet Propulsion Laboratory. It is using NASA's existing DSN, including Tidbinbilla, to scan the entire sky in a frequency range between 1000 and 10000 MHz. An automatic pattern recognition system will be able to detect likely signals. The Sky Survey is 300 times more sensitive than any previous sky survey.

What would happen if a confirmed intelligent signal was ever detected? The implications for the world's governments, cultures and religions are profound. If the intercepted message was actually meant for us, would we reply? Or should we? Would the ETs laugh at us, or be prepared to share their knowledge with us? These are questions which deserve serious thought before the Search for Extraterrestrial Intelligence forces us to confront them by Contact with Extraterrestrial Intelligence!

The Tidbinbilla tracking station in 1992, showing its four tracking antennas. The largest dish (the 70-metre antenna) is capable of receiving very weak signals from spacecraft beyond the edge of the Solar System. Could it also pick up signals sent out by intelligent beings elsewhere in the galaxy?

Australia forms part of the US intelligence-gathering network through satellite ground stations established in Central and Western Australia following the signing of joint defence agreements by Australia and the US. These agreements were unrelated to the Joint Project or the NASA tracking stations. The three main bases are at North West Cape at Exmouth in Western Australia; Pine Gap, near Alice Springs in the Northern Territory; and Nurrungar, near Woomera.

These installations are vital elements of the US strategic command, control, communications and intelligence system which supports the US strategic nuclear posture, and their presence in Australia has been highly controversial. During the Cold War, their functions made them undoubted nuclear targets and one of the main aspects of the controversy surrounding them was whether the risks they represented were outweighed by their contribution to deterrence and arms control.

Other areas of controversy in relation to these bases have included Australian access to the intelligence data gathered, and the 'disinformation' campaign by successive Australian governments to obscure the bases' military roles. The use of euphemistic terms such as 'space research', 'upper atmosphere studies' and 'geological and geophysical research' in reference to the bases has had the additional unfortunate effect of tarring with the military brush genuine civilian programs in these fields.

The North West Cape Naval Communications Station in Western Australia was established in 1963, originally to provide communication with US nuclear ballistic missile submarines. It uses the US Defense Satellite Communications System (DSCS) for communication with the US surface fleet and attack submarines, a war-fighting role rather than a deterrent one. DSCS is also used by other military installations in Australia, principal among them the Australian Defence Signals Directorate in Melbourne.

Because the function of North West Cape, which does not need to be sited in Australia for geographical reasons, has not been related to arms control and because Australia has not had access to the communications passing through it, it has been well argued by opponents of the US bases in Australia that the station's risks outweigh its benefits. In 1991 the Minister for Defence announced that Australia would gradually assume total control of this base for its own military purposes as the US administration relinquished its participation, which it did by late 1992.

Regarded as the most important US installation in Australia, the Joint Defence Space Research Facility at Pine Gap, near Alice Springs, is one of the largest satellite ground stations in the world. This facility, which commenced operation in 1970, is controlled by Signals Intelligence (SIGINT) staff from the US Central Intelligence Agency (CIA), and there has been considerable controversy over the extent of Australian access to the data it gathers. The

A laser aimed at a satellite from the AUSLIG laser station at Orroral Valley contributes to NASA's Earth Dynamics program. Precise measurements of the orbits of satellites and the Moon are used to determine the structure, composition and motion of the Earth and Moon.

SIGINT satellites which Pine Gap monitors are the most secret of all US intelligence-gathering satellites and are designed to intercept a wide range of foreign signals. These signals include telecommunications, radar emissions and the telemetry signals associated with missile tests.

Although some of the intelligence gathered by Pine Gap enhances US nuclear war-fighting capabilities, much of the data are essential for the verification of some major arms control agreements and provide additional verification monitoring for others. Unlike North West Cape, Australia is a crucial geographical location for the Pine Gap facility and a very credible case can be raised for the need to maintain the base, even in the 1990s, because of the stabilising effect that arms verification has upon the global strategic balance.

The Joint Defence Space Communications Station at Nurrungar commenced operation in early 1971, under the control of the US Air Force and Australian Department of Defence. The station monitors US Defense Support Program early warning satellites, which detect the launch of ICBMs. Australia has had full access to the data obtained and staff from the station make up a sizeable proportion of the Woomera township's current population.

The Nurrungar facility has been particularly controversial. Although its early warning and nuclear detonation detection

## THE HIGH GROUND OF SPACE

Most satellites are for military use. They are intended for command, control, communications, navigation and surveillance or intelligence gathering. Surveillance or 'spy' satellites are used by many countries to gather military intelligence and include both photographic reconnaissance satellites and radar/infra-red satellites used to locate such things as concealed facilities and submarines and to provide early warning of missile launches. The resolving power of these satellites is much greater than that of civilian remote sensing satellites. Electronic intelligence satellites (ELINTs or Ferrets) listen in to radio, computer data and telemetry channels to discover political and military information and also to discern the capabilities of their opposition's weapons systems.

After the launch of SPUTNIK-1 in 1957, the principle was established that space is 'free territory'. This means that satellites are free to travel over whatever countries their orbits carry them without those countries claiming that their 'territorial airspace' has been infringed, despite the fact that the exact upper limit of 'territorial airspace' has never been defined. Because of this internationally recognised convention, spy satellites are tolerated and not removed by politically opposing countries (at least in peacetime).

Checking up on political opponents from above, surveillance satellites, euphemistically referred to as 'national technical means of verification', play an important role in verifying adherence to arms control treaties. Such verification is the only means by which disarmament is possible. Consequently, during the Cold War, the intelligence provided by surveillance satellites made an important contribution to the maintenance of the balance of power between the Superpowers. Space-based verification has contributed significantly to the prevention of nuclear warfare since 1945, and it continues to play an important role in maintaining world peace in the 'New World Order' of the 1990s.

The controversial North West Cape Naval Communication Station has been the site of many protests by environmental and anti-nuclear groups.

roles were important safeguards against surprise attack or accidental nuclear conflict during the Cold War, its capabilities could also make a critical contribution to US nuclear war-fighting capabilities. Nurrungar's activities are related to arms control, but its contribution is slight and the base could equally well be sited outside of Australia. This means that, of the three US bases, the arguments for and against it are the most equivocal.

With the end of the Cold War and the vast political changes that have occurred in Europe in the early 1990s, the role of the US bases in Australia and their place in the new global strategic balance must come into question. Until such time as they are finally removed they will undoubtedly remain a source of controversy within the community.

### Australian military space facilities

In addition to the US bases it accommodates, Australia operates its own secret, but regionally important, military space program. Since the downturn in activities at Woomera, this has actually been its most extensive space-related activity. Australia maintains its own SIGINT satellite interception facilities under the control of the Defence Signals Directorate, primarily concerned with obtaining intelligence relevant to Australia's regional security interests in South-East Asia and China. With over 1100 personnel, four communications monitoring stations and other facilities, the Directorate is the largest single Australian governmental agency involved in space-related activities.

Australia's ground stations are located at Stanley Fort in Hong Kong (in conjunction with a related British facility), Shoal Bay near Darwin, and the Kojarena facility near Geraldton, Western Australia. The Kojarena facility has been controversial on the grounds that its satellite monitoring capability exceeds Australia's legitimate regional intelligence requirements and is covertly acquiring additional intelligence information for the US. A satellite facility for intelligence communications via the US's DSCS system is also maintained at the Watsonia Barracks in Melbourne.

Space tracking, both civilian and military, has been one of Australia's major space activities since the beginning of the Space Age. Hosting NASA space tracking stations has enabled Australia to play a vital role in the US space program and, consequently, in the 'grand adventure' of space exploration. Although more controversial, Australia's role in military space tracking has also been significant and can be argued to have contributed to the maintenance of the global strategic balance during the Cold War.

**The Pine Gap intelligence satellite ground station near Alice Springs. This base gathers signals intelligence which assists in arms control verification. The domes in this photograph cover the actual tracking antennas.**

MR MIKE DINN *has had a long association with space tracking in Australia. Currently Director of the Canberra Deep Space Communications Complex, he comments on Australia's longest continuous civilian space activity.*

In 1965, while working for the Air Force, I saw an advertisement for Deputy Station Director at Honeysuckle Creek. I had an interview for that job, but was offered the job as Deputy Station Director at Tidbinbilla instead. I had no idea where it was! It was a very big transition from what I had been doing previously, but I had to learn quickly because the policy was that the Deputy Director ran the operations. So, literally within a month of arriving, I was sitting on the Operations Desk running things, which was initially quite frightening. It took me not too long to realise that, although I might make an error, there was no chance of me jeopardising the spacecraft or the station. Once I realised that, I moved on with confidence and in 1966 was closely involved with the Surveyor program.

I eventually moved to Honeysuckle Creek about September 1967. Honeysuckle had a poor reputation, and I realised quite quickly that one reason for this was that the station did not have confidence in itself. It tended to react too strongly to requests, suggestions and demands from NASA in the US. It took a few months to turn the place around, into having confidence in itself, and from then on it went from strength to strength.

I was at Honeysuckle until early 1971, during the Apollo program. That was the highlight of my career. Within three months of supporting our first Apollo mission, APOLLO-7, we were supporting the first lunar mission, APOLLO-8. Honeysuckle came into its own then and became a major player, for the first time. That really was memorable—our first Lunar mission, the first time we were a major part of the manned flight team.

Missions were happening at two-month intervals: December for 8; January-February for 9; March-April for 10; June-July for APOLLO-11. We were getting the documentation for the next mission before we had even flown the previous one, so it kept everybody on their toes. But it was very, very satisfying because everybody knew what they were doing, why they were doing it. There were no distractions—financial, organisational or contractual. We had about 110 staff, all there specifically to track the Apollo missions.

With APOLLO-11 we looked to the Parkes radio telescope for support for the mission. The signals from APOLLO-11 came through Parkes, Tidbinbilla and Honeysuckle. Honeysuckle and Parkes were tracking the Lunar Module and Tidbinbilla was tracking the Command Module, but the famous words from Neil Armstrong came from Honeysuckle. This has been a source of friendly argument between ourselves and Parkes for 20 odd years.

APOLLO-13 was very memorable. We were just coming up to receive the spacecraft signals when I heard the phrase 'We've got a problem. Houston, we've got a problem.' Very rapidly *we* ran into a problem, because the Lunar Module, which was being used as a 'life raft' after the Command Module explosion, transitted on the same frequency as the third stage of the Saturn 5 rocket. I had ten receivers, all trying to decide whether they had got the Lunar Module signal or Saturn signal. There were two separate transponders though, so eventually we pulled the frequencies apart. We turned the downlink from the Lunar Module off, the only mission where this happened. We were the last station to track APOLLO-13 before it re-entered.

After APOLLO-13, the opportunity came to return to Tidbinbilla and be Deputy Director. The new 64-metre antenna was starting to be built and it became clear that there was a need for someone to do system design to integrate that antenna into the station. One thing that the Jet Propulsion Laboratory [JPL, the control centre for the Deep Space Network, located in California] is not especially good at is system design. They are very good at the detail level, but when it comes to nailing it all in together in a system, they really don't do it very well. It was agreed that I [as Deputy Director] would go to JPL in 1972, to be responsible for system design for the 64-metre dish.

The Manned Space Flight Network was very satisfying to work with, being operationally orientated. They also struck a good balance between formality and informality in running the network. You felt you were really part of the team, treated as equals, whereas within the Deep Space Network, at times you get the impression that 'NASA knows best', despite having been proved wrong a few times.

When I got back from JPL I was ready for a change. I resigned and moved out of the system for 10 years. However, in 1983 I applied again for the Deputy job at Tidbinbilla and was more than happy to move back here. Since returning to Tidbinbilla, the

**The planets of the Solar System. Images taken by various space probes have been combined in this 'family photograph'.**

two Voyager encounters have been the highlights. I was responsible for the Parkes Uranus support. Because the VOYAGER-2 Uranus encounter was about a month before the GIOTTO Halley encounter, the ESA had got in before NASA to ask for Parkes' support with GIOTTO. There was a fair bit of politics between the ESA and NASA. The ESA could have had all the support they needed for GIOTTO from Tidbinbilla, but they had had some bad experiences with NASA pulling out of projects, so they negotiated downlink support with Parkes.

We had to put in a microwave link between Tidbinbilla and Parkes and that was a $2 million investment made by NASA. They agreed a full microwave link was worth the money. Of course, the big spin-off for the CSIRO and for Australia was that the microwave link which joined the two antennas gave us the world's longest real-time interferometer.

I became Director at Tidbinbilla in late 1988 and the VOYAGER-2 Neptune encounter was in August '89. The Neptune encounter was in some ways harder than the Uranus encounter, particularly the radio science, which relies on signals coming through the atmosphere of the planets and their moons to learn about those atmospheres and their composition.

I think Australia has gained a great deal from its involvement in the tracking network. In the network's heyday we had six stations in Australia, which added up to around 800 employees. The three ACT stations were a not insignificant contribution to its economy. I think our contribution to US–Australia relations, albeit in a very small area, is one very useful aspect of the arrangement. Because we have also tracked the odd Russian and Japanese spacecraft, I would like to think this country is recognised as a valuable contributor to international space cooperation.

Today, we are keeping a tradition going. The management arrangements have not fundamentally changed. There is a government to government agreement and an agency to agency agreement which has not needed to be rewritten these 30 years. I admire the people who set up this arrangement right at the outset. They made sure that Australia was going to be responsible for the operation and maintenance of these stations without undue interference. We bend over backwards to make sure we meet commitments at least as well as any other facility in the network.

I think Tidbinbilla has a long future ahead of it and the place will be here for 20 to 30 years. I think it is a very bright future.

# INVISIBLE LINKS: How satellites keep us in touch

**Keeping in touch via satellite: the Optus satellite system provides domestic communications across Australia.**

The NASA and military space tracking stations in Australia have specialised roles in space exploration and defence, but Australia also has other ground stations used for the everyday purpose of maintaining contact between countries around the world through the medium of communications satellites. International and domestic communications satellites help to link Australians to the world, and to each other across a vast continent—whether or not we realise it, they touch our lives every day.

## LINKED BY INVISIBLE THREADS—INTERNATIONAL COMMUNICATIONS VIA SATELLITE

'Live via satellite': once every television news program made this statement proudly when it carried a report from overseas. Today, when live satellite television broadcasts have become so frequent as to be commonplace, the phrase is rarely heard! Yet the first commercial communications satellite, TELSTAR, was only launched in 1962, demonstrating how quickly this space-based technology has been incorporated into our society.

### GEOSTATIONARY ORBIT

As early as 1945 it had been recognised that a satellite in geostationary orbit would offer stable links across oceans and be able to broadcast and receive signals across entire continents. In geostationary orbit, approximately 36 000 kilometres above the Earth, satellites travel at a speed which is equal to that of the planet's rotation. Consequently each satellite remains at a fixed point above the equator. In this orbit a satellite can cover about one-third of the Earth's surface, so only three satellites are needed, in any network, to provide worldwide coverage for international telecommunications purposes.

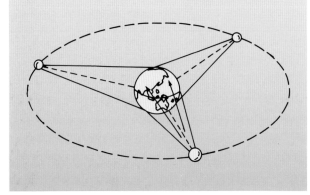

Once the first satellites proved the viability of orbital-based services, commercial satellite communications systems were quickly established. Today, communications satellites carry much of the world's television, radio, telephone and data (fax, computer, etc) transmissions. Worldwide international telecommunications are currently controlled by multinational agencies: INTELSAT serves most of the world's nations; Intersputnik, the states formerly aligned with the USSR; INMARSAT provides communications services to ships at sea, aircraft and other mobile vehicles. These agencies are funded by member countries, but their services are equally available to non-member states. Australia was a founding member of both INTELSAT and INMARSAT and is still INTELSAT's sixth-largest shareholder.

By 1964 the International Telecommunications Satellite Organisation (INTELSAT) had been established to provide spacecraft to link nations separated by the major oceans. The first INTELSAT satellite, INTELSAT-1, also known as EARLY BIRD, was launched in 1965. INTELSAT provides a global telecommunications satellite service, with its satellites located in geostationary orbit at various points around the Earth.

Australia uses INTELSAT satellites over the Indian and Pacific Oceans for its international telecommunications. The only alternatives to these satellite services are undersea cable networks or shortwave radio services reflected from the ionosphere, which are subject to variation in transmission quality. Australian INTELSAT facilities are operated by Telstra, the offshore arm of Telstra Corporation Ltd, formed in 1992 by the merger of Telecom Australia and the Overseas Telecommunications Corporation (OTC). The latter was created as a commission in 1946 to develop and manage all external communications to and from Australia. It became a corporation in 1989 and in 1993 was renamed Telstra. OTC/Telstra has been at the forefront of satellite communications use and has developed considerable expertise in telecommunications, playing a significant role in INTELSAT's advisory committees for satellite procurement and earth station development.

Although OTC had previously concentrated on undersea cable systems, in 1964 it was one of the original eleven signatories, on Australia's behalf, of the charter for INTELSAT. Other signatories included the US, UK, Canada and Japan. By the following year, the Australian government had approved construction of a satellite ground station near Carnarvon, Western Australia (which was to be used to provide a satellite communications link with America for the NASA tracking station). The Carnarvon ground station achieved Australia's first international satellite contact with the UK via an INTELSAT-2 satellite on 25 November 1966, when the television program *Down Under Comes Up Live* was broadcast from Australia.

In 1968 a second major ground tracking station began using Pacific INTELSAT satellites from Moree, New South Wales, providing a regular commercial television relay from the US. Satellites over the Indian Ocean were contacted from the Ceduna (South Australia) ground station established in 1969.

Improvements in satellite technology enabled OTC to close the Carnarvon and Moree ground stations in 1987 and relocate them closer to state capitals. The Australian ground stations for contacting INTELSAT satellites are now located at Ceduna in South Australia; Gnangara, near Perth in Western Australia; Healesville, near Melbourne in Victoria (established in 1984); and Oxford Falls, near Sydney in New South Wales, which was opened in 1987. In the late 1980s OTC also installed ground stations at Australia's Antarctic bases, to enable them to maintain direct contact with Australia and the rest of the world. Through these ground stations INTELSAT satellites provide 60–70 per cent of Australia's global telephone and television contact.

The huge 'feed horn' antenna at the OTC satellite ground station at Carnarvon, nicknamed the 'sugar scoop'. This station operated in conjunction with NASA's MSFN tracking station.

In addition to satellite communications, OTC/Telstra has been providing telemetry, tracking, command and monitoring (TTC&M) services for INTELSAT satellites since 1969. These services provide information about the satellite itself—for example, its position and the status of its equipment—and allow commands to be sent to it to correct problems or change its operations. OTC/Telstra's expertise in this area has been recognised by the ESA and INMARSAT, which have also commissioned it to undertake TTC&M support for their spacecraft.

In 1969 OTC began providing TTC&M services for INTELSAT from its Carnarvon ground station. In 1979 the ESA also located its regional tracking station at the Carnarvon site. These services were relocated to the new Gnangara ground station in 1987, where they were joined by a similar facility for INMARSAT satellites in 1990.

OTC also represented Australia in becoming a foundation member of INMARSAT, the International Maritime Satellite Organisation, a body similar to INTELSAT. Created in 1979, INMARSAT provides satellite communications services for ships and aircraft. This service has now expanded to provide communications for mobile vehicles such as trucks, and also has search and rescue capabilities.

Until 1992 OTC was responsible for all telecommunications carried by INTELSAT and INMARSAT satellites into and out of Australia. Following the reorganisation of Australian telecommunications which occurred in 1992, access to these satellite systems became available to both Telstra and the new telecommunications carrier Optus Communications Pty Ltd. After 1997, any newly licensed national telecommunications operator will also be permitted to use INMARSAT and INTELSAT satellites. Telstra has been actively marketing its various international services and recently has also moved to undertake provision of satellite communications services to Pacific nations. A regional network was provided in 1990 for members of the South Pacific Forum, an organisation representing the interests of Pacific islands.

Since the late 1980s INMARSAT and INTELSAT have been joined by private communications satellite systems, offering international services in competition with them. These new players make their profits in regions where INTELSAT does not have the capacity to meet with growing consumer demand for satellite communications services. One such area is the fast-growing Asia-Pacific region where, within the next few years, Australia will have access to communications satellites offered by companies like ASIASAT of Hong Kong. New direct broadcasting radio and television services will also reach Australia soon, beaming down a wide variety of new entertainment and informational programming, to compete with local domestic broadcasters.

While international satellites have some ability to provide domestic communications, they are generally not purposely designed to provide efficient local services, so some nations, like Australia, have established their own systems.

The CSIRO Parkes radio telescope, one of Australia's technological achievements seen in the *Our World* broadcast. The Parkes radio telescope has had a support role in space tracking in Australia as well as being responsible for major astronomical discoveries.

## AUSTRALIA BECOMES PART OF *OUR WORLD*

Between 5.00 am and 7.00 am on 26 June 1967, Australia participated in the *Our World* program, the first live global television broadcast which linked 30 countries via four communications satellites. A major achievement for both space technology and international relations (despite the Cold War, the USSR participated in the broadcast and allowed one of its satellites to be used for transmitting the program), the *Our World* broadcast was a potent demonstration of the potential reach of satellite television, with an estimated worldwide audience of over 700 million!

One of 18 countries to present material during the broadcast, Australia's contribution included an early morning visit to Melbourne, a tour of a CSIRO plant laboratory, and radio astronomy observations with the Parkes radio telescope. The broadcast was beamed into and out of Australia via NASA's Cooby Creek facility, and transmitted around the country with assistance from OTC, the PMG and the Department of Supply. It was the most complex television transmission ever attempted.

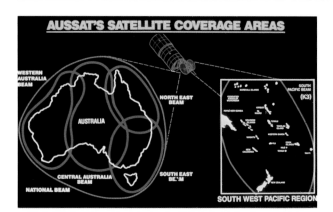

The satellite 'footprints' (areas covered by the satellite) of the first generation Aussat satellites. The second generation Optus satellites provide a similar area of coverage, but with enhanced capabilities.

## AUSSAT/OPTUS—AUSTRALIA'S NATIONAL SATELLITE SYSTEM

Apart from international telecommunications, individual countries also establish 'domestic' satellite services to improve their internal communications. Australia's domestic communications satellite system, originally established by the government as Aussat and now operated by Optus Communications Pty Ltd, was developed to improve telephone communications and radio and television reception in remote areas. Initially, Aussat used three satellites in geostationary orbit, with the first generation satellites being supplemented and gradually replaced by second generation Optus satellites from 1992. Since 1985, saucer-shaped antennas have sprouted all over the country to receive from, and sometimes send signals to, these satellites. Ground stations to control the system are located in every capital city. The system also serves New Zealand, Papua New Guinea and some western Pacific islands, but such places are at the limits of its range.

As early as 1977, a report commissioned by one of the nation's major broadcasters recommended that nationwide television network distribution services using satellites be developed. Although a report by Telecom Australia, conducted at the same time, concluded that a national satellite system was not economically feasible, the government established a task force to inquire into matters relating to a national satellite system for Australia.

This task force recommended in 1978 that planning for a government-owned system should commence immediately. In 1979 a successful test television transmission was beamed from Canada to remote areas in New South Wales and Queensland in special field trials using the facilities of a Canadian communications satellite. The experimental transmissions had been arranged to investigate the technological means to introduce satellite broadcasting direct to homes in the Australian outback. With the success of these tests, the decision was made to proceed.

Detailed plans and technical specifications for the system were developed by a team of engineers set up at the end of 1979. This group consisted largely of people drawn from the ranks of OTC, whose expertise in international telecommunications was invaluable in the development of the domestic satellite system. An OTC executive would eventually serve as managing director of Aussat Pty Ltd, the company set up to operate the new domestic satellite system in 1981. Potential users, including groups with an interest in outback communications, were also consulted.

Under the 1984 Satellite Communications Act, Aussat was initially 75 per cent owned by the Commonwealth of Australia, with the remainder owned by Telecom Australia. Complex funding arrangements were used to finance Aussat, with loan repayments derived from the revenues obtained by leasing the satellite's transponder capacity and other services. With a staff of about 300, Aussat had the highest concentration of satellite communications and space engineering expertise in Australia. The initial satellite system was designed to improve national business and remote area communications, providing a flexible and reliable service.

**The first Aussat satellite being launched from the cargo bay of the Space Shuttle ATLANTIS.**

## AUSSAT—PIGS MIGHT FLY?

To some people, the Aussat project seemed like a lot of expense to bring television shows to outback regions. As well, Telecom Australia opposed the project, suggesting that expansion of its own terrestrial communications system was a viable alternative. Some sections of the government bureaucracy also opposed the project on financial grounds, despite the decision to proceed.

However, Aussat was conceived in an era when national satellite systems were becoming a trend and an international status symbol. Aussat was initially proposed by powerful media interests which had strong persuasive powers to influence political support for the project. In the final analysis, it seems that their efforts won the day, even though the system could not become profitable.

In financial terms, Aussat was generally viewed as a marginal operation at best, especially as it later required direct support grants. However, Aussat's supporters claimed that telecommunications policy prevented the system from operating as it was designed to do, in competition with Telecom Australia's domestic services.

**Aussat was originally conceived with the intention of expanding television and communications services to isolated communities. The Queensland government uses the national satellites to provide interactive links between isolated students and teachers via the School of the Air.**

### Aussat takes off, Optus takes over

The establishment of the national communications satellite system has been one of Australia's largest expenditures on space-related activities through the purchase of satellites, launches and ground stations. Most of the $300 million spent on establishing the system went overseas for the purchase of three satellites from the US Hughes Aircraft Corporation and launches by NASA and the European Arianespace corporation. The Australian content of the first generation of Aussat satellites was largely limited to wiring harnesses produced by STC (Standard Telephones and Cables Pty Ltd) under an offset contractual arrangement. Two satellites were launched by the US Space Shuttle in 1985, and the third on an Ariane rocket in 1987.

Aussat operated eight major city earth stations providing for single point or multipoint contact across Australia, New Zealand and Papua New Guinea. The main control station was built at Belrose in Sydney, with a backup at Perth, to provide satellite control and system management. The other major city stations were automated and not normally staffed. A range of small, low-capacity, fixed and mobile ground stations for use by people living in remote areas was also developed, as well as several high performance transportable ground stations to provide television broadcasts from any desired location across the country. Major system uses include television and radio program interchange and distribution by major media networks, separate corporate and government communications networks, plus aeronautical services and Australian Defence Service communications usage.

In 1992 changes were made to the telecommunications scene in Australia. Aussat was privatised and sold to Optus Communications Pty Ltd for the reported sum of $800 million. Optus (the name means 'choice' in Latin) was initially 51 per cent owned by an Australian consortium which includes Mayne Nickless, AMP and National Mutual, with the other 49 per cent owned by two foreign telecommunications companies, Bell South from the US and Cable and Wireless from the UK. OTC, the nation's traditional international carrier, merged with Australia's domestic

### ANY DAY NOW

The launch of the first Aussat satellite was delayed for a few days, due to difficulties with the Space Shuttle. This inspired a clever piece of graffiti which appeared on a wall alongside a Sydney railway line:

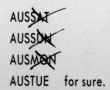

AUSTUE    for sure.

The main satellite control ground station at Belrose, on the outskirts of Sydney, established by Aussat and now managed by Optus. It provides command and control for the Optus satellites.

carrier, Telecom Australia, becoming the Australian and Overseas Telecommunications Corporation (AOTC) to compete with Optus in the provision of telecommunications services. In April 1993 AOTC was renamed Telstra Corporation Ltd.

In 1992 Optus began construction of two ground stations in Sydney and Perth to use the INTELSAT and INMARSAT system, while also taking over the existing Aussat installations and satellites. The Aussat satellite system became a backup for the national optic-fibre based telecommunications system established by Optus, while continuing to provide broadcasting, remote and mobile communications services. Following the sale to Optus, the Aussat satellites were renamed 'Optus'.

The first of the two satellites of the Optus second generation (or B series) was launched by a Chinese rocket in 1992. Also constructed by the American Hughes Aircraft Corporation, the first attempt to launch OPTUS B1 in March 1992 failed due to a fault in the engine's ignition control, but the second attempt in late August 1992 was a complete success. The second B series satellite, however, was destroyed as the result of an explosion about 48 seconds after it was launched on 22 December 1992. Although the Chinese rocket continued to function and placed the satellite's propulsion system into orbit, the B2 satellite itself fell back to the ground in pieces. At the time of writing, the cause of the accident was not known, although both an explosion on the satellite and the failure of the rocket's protective fairing have been suggested as possible causes. A replacement is being provided by

Hughes, under the terms of its contract with Optus. It is expected to be placed in orbit by June 1994.

The B series spacecraft were designed with much higher power and a range of new features to provide improved performance and flexibility compared to the first series. Like the first series, they were designed to provide television and radio, voice and data, and offshore services, but a special system enabled introduction of satellite services to mobile vehicles, to complement existing terrestrial cellular mobile telephone systems.

The second generation satellites cost around $360 million, including the launch fees. More than $20 million of this was used for Australian direct subcontract work for spacecraft systems and equipment. As well, there was a requirement that at least $100 million of the purchase be spent on offset contracts to Australian manufacturers to produce satellite and ground station parts. This represented a considerable rise in Australian manufacturing, compared to the first generation. (Chapter 7 provides more information on the space industry in Australia.) In addition to the components manufactured for the satellite in Australia, locally designed and manufactured high-precision optical laser reflectors ('cube corner' reflectors) were installed on each B series satellite as an aid to maintaining its precise position in orbit.

Satellite communications have become the world's first profitable space-related activity, as exemplified by the success of INTELSAT, INMARSAT and other systems. Australia has played a part in this success, through its long experience with ground stations for international and domestic telecommunications, and involvement with the Optus domestic satellites. Such activity provides the basis for a local industry capable of providing satellite systems and ground stations for other nations. A significant opportunity has also arisen for Australian industry to compete for production of mobile satellite terminals, which have an estimated global market value of $10-20 billion.

Satellite communications is a space application which has generated a profitable industry and provides a useful service to people worldwide. International satellite telecommunications have linked the globe by invisible threads, bringing people around the world closer together. The immediacy of contact which is now available has had a profound effect on the world's cultures and been responsible for unprecedented social change: indeed, some would claim that it has been instrumental in lowering global tensions and fostering the social consciousness of Western society.

## AUSTRALIS—AUSTRALIA'S HOME-GROWN COMMUNICATIONS SATELLITE

In the 1960s communications satellites were considered one of the great technological advances and amateurs, no less than professionals, were keen to utilise the new technology. As early as 1962, a group of American amateur radio enthusiasts had constructed the first Orbiting Satellite Carrying Amateur Radio (OSCAR). The successes of the Project OSCAR group encouraged a team of young Australians to build their own amateur radio satellite, the first to be constructed outside the US.

**Laser light reflected through an Australian-made cube corner reflector, like that installed on the Optus B series satellites to help maintain their position in orbit.**

AUSTRALIS-OSCAR-5, which became Australia's second satellite, was built by a group of undergraduate students at the University of Melbourne. In the mid 1960s these students had formed the Melbourne University Astronautical Society (MUAS). They set up equipment to track and receive signals from various US and Soviet satellites. One of their achievements was the first regular reception in Australia of meteorological images from early American TIROS and Nimbus weather satellites.

Several amateur groups in Australia were tracking satellites at this time, but the MUAS was the only one to receive images on a regular basis. Using their amateur equipment, they supplied visible and infra-red weather images daily to the Bureau of Meteorology before it established its own receiving facilities. On one occasion they were even able to assist NASA in identifying a fault that had occurred in a Nimbus satellite, because of a transmission that they received in Australia.

Among the satellites tracked by the group were the early OSCAR amateur radio satellites, developed by the Project OSCAR group (which, in 1969, became part of AMSAT, the Amateur Radio Satellite Corporation) and launched by the US Air Force. These satellites were developed to enable radio amateurs ('hams') to gain experience in satellite tracking and to conduct experiments in radio wave transmission through the atmosphere. After receiving signals from OSCAR-3 and 4, the MUAS was inspired to consider, in conjunction with the Melbourne University Radio Club, an Australian amateur radio satellite.

Although the students recognised that they did not have the technical skills to build an active communications satellite (one that would relay voice communications), they set themselves the goal of building a 'beacon' satellite which, like a radio beacon, would transmit telemetry data back to Earth on fixed frequencies. Such a limited technological goal proved to be a wise decision in view of the jungle of official approvals that was later found to be necessary, even for this simple satellite.

Work began on the satellite project, which the students called AUSTRALIS, in March 1966. Other university societies also assisted in getting AUSTRALIS off the ground, literally and figuratively. With virtually no funding, all the members of the group gave their time voluntarily and the necessary electronic and other components were acquired primarily by donation from suppliers, who were promised suitable acknowledgment as sponsors. Technical and financial assistance was also received from the Wireless Institute of Australia. The actual money outlaid to build the satellite was around $1300 (about $9000 at 1992 values), much of it paid for by the students working on the project.

In little more than a year the satellite went from drawing board to completion. University facilities were 'commandeered' to assist during the construction and testing of AUSTRALIS. The PMG and the Department of Supply also provided testing facilities. A

**Preparations for a balloon flight at Mildura to test some of the AUSTRALIS components.**

number of components, including the transmitters and command system, were tested on high altitude balloon flights to ensure that they were working correctly and were robust enough to withstand the rigours of spaceflight.

The completed satellite was delivered to the San Francisco headquarters of Project OSCAR in July 1967. There it remained while attempts were made to cut a way through the red tape surrounding the arrangement of a piggyback launch with another satellite. With the formation of AMSAT, the satellite was shipped to its headquarters in Washington DC during March 1969. It took another nine months for AMSAT to put the satellite into final shape so that it would be approved by NASA as suitable for launch, to arrange with NASA for the launch itself, and to wait out the many agonising delays caused by booster difficulties. NASA required that AUSTRALIS have some scientific or technological merit before a launch would be provided. AMSAT justified the launch on the basis that the amateur satellite would provide experience and training for radio amateurs and allow for the investigation of unusual radio signal transmission through the Earth's atmosphere and ionosphere.

## AUSTRALIS hits the heights!

After long delays at the US Air Force's Vandenberg Air Force Base, the satellite was launched at 9.31 pm (EAST) on 23 January 1970 by a Thor-Delta rocket carrying the TIROS-M (ITOS-1) weather satellite as its main payload. It was a textbook launch and the satellite was placed into an orbit which took 115.06 minutes, varying in altitude between 880 and 910 miles (1416–1464 kilometres). Once it was in orbit, the satellite was called AUSTRALIS-

OSCAR-5, AUSTRALIS, or simply AO-5. Its international designation was 1970-0008B.

Weighing only 39 pounds (17.7 kilograms) the satellite was constructed in the form of two cubic aluminium shells. It carried two small transmitters, each beaming the same telemetry signal on 29.450 MHz in the 10-metre band and 144.050 MHz in the 2-metre band. All antennas were made of flexible steel tape (cut from a carpenter's measuring tape!) and, as solar cells were too expensive for the group, power was supplied by two strings of chemical batteries.

The telemetry system was sophisticated, but designed for simple decoding without expensive equipment. The start of a telemetry sequence was indicated by transmitting the letters HI (the Morse abbreviation for 'hello') in Morse code. Seven parameters were then transmitted by the satellite. They provided data on battery voltage, current, and the temperature of the satellite at two points as well as information on the satellite's orientation in space from three horizon sensors. AMSAT applied an experimental paint pattern to the outer skin, to control the internal temperature of the satellite. However, this was not particularly successful and temperature data indicated that the satellite was operating with an internal temperature of around 50°C (122°F). Fortunately AUSTRALIS's instruments were robust and had been designed to function at high temperatures!

When AUSTRALIS was released from the second stage of the launch rocket, springs pushed it away into its own orbit. At the same time, the electronics were turned on, while the steel tape antennas unwound themselves. A passive magnetic attitude stabilisation system, which maintained the satellite's orientation by reference to the Earth's magnetic field, was used for the first time in an amateur satellite to stabilise AUSTRALIS and reduce its rate of spin. This system used a bar magnet and an eddy current damper (a device that reduced the pendulum-like oscillations of the satellite) to bring one axis of the satellite into alignment with the magnetic field lines of the Earth, just as a compass aligns itself with the Earth's poles.

A commercial cable circuit was leased to link the University of Melbourne with the OSCAR Control Centre at NASA's Goddard Space Flight Centre in Greenbelt, Maryland. The line was used for three hours beginning fifteen minutes before the launch. Every word and piece of information filtered through the control centre was fed live to a 'press room' at the University. Several AMSAT stations also transmitted the countdown and control centre commentaries live to radio amateurs around the world.

A special technique was devised to permit any station in the world, given several pages of computer-generated data and brief predictions at regular intervals, to track the satellite. The first radio amateur to report receiving the beacon transmission was on the island of Madagascar. He reported reception of the 2-metre signal at 66 minutes after launch. Another amateur in Darwin reported reception of the 10-metre signal a few minutes later. Other amateurs in Western Europe and North America also reported receiving both the 2- and 10-metre signals on the satellite's first orbit.

During its initial orbits AUSTRALIS-OSCAR-5 also passed within range of Melbourne and members of the Melbourne University Radio Club were able to tune in to the satellite. At the end of the first orbit, however, problems developed with the 10-metre transmission, which eventually became very difficult to decode.

With each successive orbit, telemetry calibrations, technical data, orbital information and predictions, and reception reports were collated by amateur radio operators. By the end of AUSTRALIS's first day of operation, AMSAT headquarters had already received more than 100 reports. Reports were received from several hundred stations in more than 27 countries. Several amateur clubs performed extensive tracking and telemetry data recording. Amateurs recorded their observations on standard reporting forms which were suitable for computer analysis.

The 2-metre signal was broadcast continually and operated until 14 February. The 10-metre transmission continued until the satellite's chemical batteries failed around 9 March. To conserve power until then, stations in Australia and the US had used a prearranged schedule to switch the transmitter on (mainly on weekends) and off (during the week) via the first successful command system installed in an amateur satellite. Although its batteries eventually failed, AUSTRALIS-OSCAR-5 remains in orbit and will continue to do so for several hundred years.

Following the success of OSCAR-5, the AUSTRALIS group did consider undertaking further satellite projects. Initially they proposed to build a multi-channel repeating satellite, which would both transmit and receive signals and be powered by solar cells rather than batteries. However, due to waning enthusiasm, the difficulty of finding sponsorship/funding and the need for the students to concentrate more on their studies and family life, this and similarly ambitious projects were to remain as ideas rather than realities.

Although the Project AUSTRALIS group did not undertake any further projects, Australian amateur radio enthusiasts have continued to use satellites and today AMSAT Australia operates as a division of the Wireless Institute of Australia. Operating independently of the American parent body, AMSAT Australia coordinates Australian amateur satellite activity and boasts several hundred members who utilise a fleet of satellites built by fellow amateurs in the UK, US, Germany, Russia, Korea, Japan and Argentina.

Australian amateurs use these satellites for relaying communications around the world, for remote sensing (via one satellite that transmits images of the Earth) and for computer data transmission, using a 'store and forward' satellite that acts as a digital

## OSCAR'S OSCARS

The success of AUSTRALIS-OSCAR-5 was a good example of 'amateurs' leading the way in a new field of technology. Apart from being Australia's second satellite, AUSTRALIS-OSCAR-5 chalked up a number of firsts:

★ It was the first OSCAR launched by NASA, the previous four having been launched by the US Air Force.

★ It was the first satellite to operate in the 10-metre band, which made it possible for a greater number of amateurs than before to receive satellite signals.

★ It was the first satellite, together with TIROS-M, to be launched by the then-new Delta-N booster rocket.

★ It was the first amateur satellite to be command-controlled from the ground, like a commercial communications satellite. Previous amateur satellites had not had the power-saving capability of being switched on and off like AUSTRALIS.

★ It was the first amateur satellite to contain a magnetic self-stabilising system to reduce spin, roll and signal fading, thus making its signals easier for amateurs to detect.

**The completed AUSTRALIS satellite, as it was when it left Australia. AMSAT later applied an experimental paint pattern to the outer surface.**

postbox. Satellites of this type receive computer text transmitted by radio amateurs, which is then stored in memory and transmitted to any other amateurs who ask for any messages addressed to them. As well as using satellites, Australian 'hams' also speak directly with the Space Shuttle and the MIR space station during their amateur radio experiments. After more than 20 years another Australian amateur group, ASERA, is also looking to build and launch its own satellites, following in the tradition of AUSTRALIS-OSCAR-5; their project is outlined in chapter 6.

DR OWEN MACE *was one of the student initiators of the AUSTRALIS-OSCAR-5 project, afterwards working for many years in the Australian aerospace industry. He comments on the student project that became Australia's second satellite.*

AUSTRALIS-OSCAR-5 had its origins in the Melbourne University Astronautical Society. We were a bunch of engineering and science students, except the driving force behind it, Richard Tonkin, who was a lawyer: he was more space-mad than the rest of us! Around 1964-65 we set up our own equipment to receive images from the early weather satellites and, indeed, you could say that Australia's satellite weather service actually started with the Melbourne University Astronautical Society.

I don't recall precisely how the AUSTRALIS project originated, but there were amateur radio people amongst the group and they knew of the Project OSCAR satellite experiments. We would meet at lunchtimes in a rooftop garret in the Physics Building at Melbourne University and one day somebody said, 'Oh hell, why don't we build an amateur satellite?'! It was one of those throwaway lines which, in other circumstances, you would laugh at and then get on to the next subject, but somebody else said, 'Yeah, why not? Let's do it.' Though I guess we thought in our hearts that it wasn't possible, we set off planning to do it.

I was what today would be called the program manager. I was the one that made sure everything happened. It was difficult but interesting, because I had a view of the entire project rather than just one corner of it. The thing that was new to me was the people management, the coordination of the team. Everybody was a volunteer, so to inspire them or to cajole somebody to deliver as promised was a very new experience for me.

It was an enormous step for us, because we had never flown anything before, so we decided on a number of test flights from balloons. We flew little packages, launching them from the university, quite illegally. We had no idea that we had to get permission for the transmitters to use certain frequencies. Every step of the way it was a learning experience: learning about bureaucracy, and I don't mean that in any negative way, but learning how society regulates itself and how we had to fit into that regulation.

We started work on this project about 1966. We had AUSTRALIS built before WRESAT was thought of, but it waited for a long time between building and delivery and flight—three years in fact! The satellite didn't take long to build, once we got stuck into it: from the time we said, 'Okay, we're building,' to the time it was actually finished and tested was under a year.

But there was a lot of preparatory work in several areas. We recognised that we had never met schedules before, so part of the reason for building the balloon payloads was so that we could set ourselves schedules and meet them. It was valuable training from many viewpoints. We had to convince suppliers that we were for real. We did an awful lot of media work, building up our presence. The companies were fantastic and we received almost no knock-backs. We gave acknowledgments of assistance and some companies advertised on the strength of it.

In terms of money, the project cost around $1300, but the vast bulk of it was donated in kind from sponsors. The electronics were all imported, although some components were made in Australia. There were some springs to kick the satellite away from the launch rocket: we went to a well-known mattress manufacturer and they made us a pair of matched springs, so that the force provided by the two springs would be as close as possible to equal, so that the satellite wouldn't spin when released.

In the overall OSCAR program, our project was a total maverick. The American OSCAR series was getting really sophisticated and here was somebody else starting from scratch again. AUSTRALIS was the first non-American OSCAR and we believe that the request for approval to fly went all the way to the Vice President: so it was highly significant, not just for us, but also within the NASA bureaucracy. The NASA representative in Australia at the time felt that he was encouraging a young country, so he helped us enormously and I think that sort of feeling went right through. It wasn't all one-way either. We came up with a scheme for helping the amateur network track the satellite that I understand was later picked up by NASA in its own tracking network.

In 1967 three of us took the completed satellite to the US. We delivered the satellite to San Francisco, where there was an AMSAT group, and the whole thing was on a scale that just amazed us. The AMSAT people delivered the satellite to Vandenberg Air Force Base, where it was to be launched, so we didn't have any involvement in the actual installation or launching.

The launch itself did not occur until 1970. We don't know what caused the delay, but I suspect that somebody decided that it

**Owen Mace (left), Richard Tonkin (centre) and Paul Dunn, at a press conference the day before taking the AUSTRALIS satellite to the US.**

had to be approved and therefore getting that through the bureaucracy would have taken a lot of time. Who knows what went on behind the scenes? We certainly never did!

After AUSTRALIS we did supply equipment for subsequent satellites, but it was such an intense activity that there was a degree of burnout. We just couldn't face another one and we dispersed and finished our degrees and went out and started learning what was *not* possible—what the real world was like!

AMSAT viewed the AUSTRALIS project as a success and we certainly felt that it was. It was a wonderful experience and there were some unique and world-first achievements that came out of it. Those were fun and very satisfying times. I guess in a way I

regret now that, if I had been older and wiser, I would have started a business out of it, because we had it all there. If we could have pulled it together as a space business, as Canada did for instance, then I think Australia would have already been one of the space-faring nations of the world today, rather than now aspiring once again to become one.

But I guess through it all, looking back on over 20 years ago, we were naive enough not to be burdened down with convention and what can be done and what can't. We thought, 'Hey, this sounds a good idea, let's give it a run,' and we did it. We had no idea that any sane person would say, 'No, you can't do that,' and would find all sorts of difficulties. We just went ahead and did it and I guess that's the wonderful thing about youth, that they are not burdened by what is supposed to be possible.

# OUR DAILY SPACE: How space assists life on Earth

The Nyngan floods, seen from space. Satellite imagery was used for surveillance of the situation around Nyngan in central New South Wales, during the disastrous floods of 1990. Compare this satellite overview with the ground view over the page.

Communications satellites are not the only way that Australia uses space on an everyday basis. Increasingly, the world is utilising space as a resource for the Earth through the development of satellite networks which enable us to monitor the environmental health of our planet, predict the weather, navigate ships and aircraft and locate people in distress. Satellites used for these purposes are broadly referred to as applications satellites, because they *apply* space technology to Earthly requirements. Australia utilises the services of a wide range of applications satellites and has developed considerable expertise in some areas of applications technology.

## WHAT SAT IS THAT?

Many abbreviated terms are used to describe different types of satellites. Some of these terms are used in this book and in many of those listed in the bibliography.

BIOSAT — Biological satellite: one carrying plants or animals into orbit to test their reactions to the radiation and microgravity conditions of space.

COMSAT — Any communications satellite.

LIGHTSAT — Any small, low-weight satellite that utilises modern high technologies and miniaturisation to save on launch costs. A lightsat generally weighs about 400–1000 kg.

METSAT — Any meteorological (weather) satellite.

MICROSAT — Any small satellite weighing less than 50 kg.

MINISAT — Any small satellite weighing 50–400 kg.

NAVSAT — Any satellite used to assist navigation for ships, aircraft and land vehicles.

SATELLITE — Any object that orbits around a larger body. The planets are satellites of the Sun, the Moon is the *natural* satellite of the Earth. Technically, spacecraft that orbit the Earth, whether crewed or automated, are *artificial* satellites of the Earth. In recent years, the term satellite has come to be used almost exclusively for automated Earth-orbiting spacecraft.

## THE EYE IN THE SKY—REMOTE SENSING SATELLITES

Many satellites study the Earth to help us learn more about our planet and its environment. The collection and use of this data is known as 'remote sensing' because the observations are made from many hundreds or even thousands of kilometres out in space. Satellites that view the Earth below are especially useful to Australia because the great size of the continent and its small population make the gathering of comprehensive data on the ground extremely difficult, if not impossible. Remote sensing satellites therefore play a key role in the management and mapping of this vast country.

Remote sensing satellites study our planet by detecting a wide range of electromagnetic wavelengths (such as infra-red, ultra-violet and radar), not just visible light, reflected from the Earth. Using computer-imaging techniques, this data can produce images which reveal details and information not discernible to the human eye. Remote sensing satellites provide huge quantities of valuable data for such diverse activities as agriculture, mining, environmental monitoring, land-use planning, water resource studies, ocean studies and atmospheric research.

## POLAR ORBITS

Remote sensing satellites generally travel in polar orbits at altitudes of 700–1500 kilometres. These orbits cross the north and south poles of the Earth, so that as the planet rotates the satellite passes over a slightly different ground track on each orbit. A picture of the entire area of Australia requires a number of successive passes over the country in order to build up a complete image. As each orbit takes the satellite over a slightly different ground path, it can be many days before a complete cycle of orbits brings the satellite into position to take an identical image of an area. Remote sensing satellites in polar orbit are able to resolve (see) objects as small as 10 metres across and future satellites will have even better resolution, down to about 6 metres.

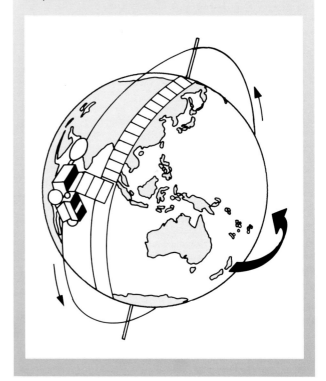

Many early weather satellites carried out Earth resources studies, but the first satellite specifically designed for remote sensing was ERTS-1 (Earth Resources Technology Satellite-1), also known as LANDSAT-1, launched by the US in 1972. It was the first of the Landsat series of satellites, which is soon to go into its seventh generation. Today Japan, France, India, China, Europe, the US and the CIS all have remote sensing satellites providing images for both commercial and scientific use.

Australia has been at the forefront of remote sensing research since the 1970s. As early as 1975, the CSIRO had obtained the first comprehensive digital archive of Landsat scenes of Australia, and in that same year the Department of Science recommended the establishment of an Australian Landsat receiving station at Alice

**The flooded town of Nyngan. Satellite images like the one on page 55 gave a broader picture of the flood situation than could be gained from the ground.**

Springs, with associated processing and archiving facilities at Belconnen, Canberra. These facilities were established in 1979 to receive and process imagery on a continuous basis, and became operational in November 1980. Equipped to receive, record and process data from all generations of Landsat satellites, these facilities have since been renamed the Australian Centre for Remote Sensing (ACRES). ACRES is part of the Australian Surveying and Land Information Group (AUSLIG).

ACRES now receives images at its Alice Springs station from many remote sensing satellites, including the US Landsat and NOAA (National Oceanographic and Atmospheric Administration) satellites, the French SPOT spacecraft and the ESA's ERS-1 satellite, to which Australia contributed. The imagery, which is available for any part of Australia, can reveal objects as small as 10 metres across. The satellite images are processed in Canberra for distribution to state mapping agencies in all capital cities. An Australian-designed computer, the Fast Delivery Processor (FDP) is used at ACRES to process the data from ERS-1. FDP technology is an area in which Australia leads the world and is further discussed in chapter 7. Imagery from CIS satellites and the MIR space station, some of which has a resolution of objects as small as 2 metres, is also available from ACRES.

Other remote sensing receiving stations located at Hobart, Townsville and Perth are operated in Australia by three local consortia of research groups. They receive data from the US's NOAA and other satellites for application in a variety of environmental and meteorological research programs.

The spectral signatures (electromagnetic radiation reflecting properties) of the Australian landscape are unique, so researchers have had to develop new hardware and software to make effective use of the data gathered by spacecraft designed to examine the greener, more temperate regions of Europe and North America. Australian and New Zealand researchers have made great contributions to the field of image enhancement. This involves the use of optical and computing techniques to highlight particular features of the Earth's surface such as crops or forests, or particular soil or rock types. Australia has in fact become a world leader in the development of remote sensing software.

Remote sensing is used in Australia for agriculture, geology, oceanography, surveying, meteorology, disaster monitoring and land management. Satellite surveillance has proved very valuable to farmers for crop management and has even been used to predict outbreaks of insect pests. Remote sensing techniques have also been applied to pasture management and used to identify eroded soils. The mining industry has made extensive use of satellite imagery in its search for new mineral deposits and likely oil-bearing strata, while other geologists and geographers have been able to obtain a greatly improved overall picture of the geological make-up of the continent and its geography. Bushfire control and flood and drought surveillance also use remotely sensed imagery, as do the authorities responsible for the management of Australia's water resources and fisheries. Oceanographers have used satellite data to assist with intensive studies of the Great Barrier Reef and the seas surrounding Australia, while ecologists and a

TION INDEX FOR SEPTEMBER 1989
MARINE LABS (HOBART) & WASTAC (PERTH)

**Vegetation patterns in Australia can be monitored from orbit, as illustrated in this composite NOAA satellite image, produced by the CSIRO. The green areas of major vegetation stand in obvious contrast to the arid parts of the country.**

wide range of government, university and private researchers apply satellite remote sensing data to their environmental studies. The vast territory of Antarctica, in which Australia has a special interest, has also been mapped and studied through the use of satellite imagery.

Australian scientists have utilised their expertise in remote sensing to participate in a number of international projects investigating global environmental change. Between May 1991 and December 1992 Australia took part in the International Land Cover Project, a global environmental monitoring activity for the International Space Year. COSSA participated in this project to study the extent and causes of global land cover degradation using satellite remote sensing data to monitor and record change over time. (See chapter 9 for more information on Australia's involvement in global change monitoring.)

Australian scientists and engineers have been involved in the development of remote sensing scanners since the mid 1980s. CSIRO and local industry designed a major component of the Along Track Scanning Radiometer (ATSR) instrument on board the ERS-1 remote sensing satellite and is developing further instruments for its successor, ERS-2 (see chapter 7 for more information on this program). Another Australian instrument that uses infra-red wavelengths to detect volcanic ash in the atmosphere has been installed in one of the US's NOAA satellites. Australian ideas and suggestions have also been incorporated into remote sensing programs such as the Shuttle Imaging Radar (SIR), which produces detailed images of the Earth's surface using radar, and the Japanese Advanced Earth Observation Satellite (ADEOS). Proposals are also underway for reception of radar satellite images in Australia and Antarctica.

## CYCLONES AND SATELLITES

Every year northern Australia is subject to the threat of cyclones, which can cause tremendous damage to people, property and the environment. Before the introduction of satellite weather monitoring, it was difficult to receive advance warning of where a cyclone would strike because they formed out over the Pacific or Indian Oceans, undetectable until they were close to land.

Weather satellites are able to observe the formation and growth of a cyclone over the ocean, providing timely warning of its development and path. They can also

**Tropical cyclone Fran prepares to strike the Queensland coast in 1992. Satellite early warning of the approach of a cyclone saves lives and reduces property damage.**

provide details of its wind speed and direction, which enable meteorologists to forecast the areas likely to be in the cyclone's path and to issue appropriate warnings. Once a cyclone moves to within about 300 kilometres of the coast, its progress can be tracked by weather radars, which provide a more detailed view than meteorological satellites.

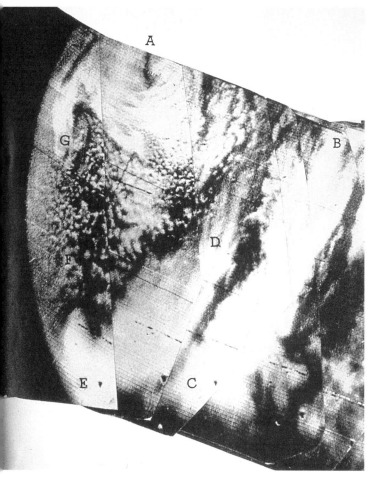

An early image from the first TIROS satellite, launched in 1960. Compare it with the modern meteorological satellite images in this chapter to see the improvement in weather imaging over the past 30 years.

## THE FORECAST FOR TODAY—METEOROLOGY SATELLITES

Allied with Earth resources and environmental monitoring, weather monitoring is a particular type of remote sensing. Today, the US, the CIS, the ESA and Japan operate networks of weather satellites that provide global coverage of the world's weather, night and day. Other countries, like China and India, have developed weather satellites that provide for their regional needs. From their vantage points far out in space, these satellites now enable data to be obtained on clouds, temperature, humidity, wind speed and direction, sea surface temperature and ocean currents, and atmospheric instability over areas that were previously inaccessible.

In addition to routine weather forecasting, this information is used in locating and tracking cyclones, in assessing the likelihood of floods, severe storms and bushfires, and in meteorological research. Weather satellites are also used for communications, relaying data from drifting ocean buoys, atmospheric balloons, and automatic weather stations in remote areas.

Experimental weather photographs were taken from high-flying rockets and balloons as early as 1950, and before the advent of weather satellites sounding rockets were used to undertake some meteorological studies of the upper atmosphere. Meteorological research formed part of the sounding rocket programs undertaken at Woomera from the late 1950s until the mid 1970s, which are outlined in chapter 6.

The first weather satellite was TIROS-1 (Television and Infra-Red Observation Satellite-1), launched by the US in 1960. Australian meteorologists were among the first in the world to receive live weather images broadcast directly from space from the TIROS-8 satellite. Test transmissions were received on Christmas Day 1963, with the first regular transmissions being received on 7 January 1964. This new capability had an immediate and profound impact on the quality of the weather forecasting and warning services provided by the Bureau of Meteorology. For the first time, many weather systems—such as tropical cyclones—were observed that previously went undetected because they were located over ocean areas devoid of conventional observational data.

By the late 1960s, real-time satellite imagery was being widely used for weather forecasting throughout Australia. Satellite reception stations were operated around the clock in Melbourne, Perth and Darwin, and other stations followed in Brisbane and at Australia's Antarctic bases. Early use of satellite images involved the identification, location, and extent of weather systems, and their development and movement.

Models of satellite-observed low pressure systems were developed to allow objective estimates of meteorological parameters, such as surface pressure, to be made directly from cloud images. Cloud imagery can also help to determine wind speeds and directions. Infra-red imagery of clouds can provide information on temperatures at different altitudes. These estimates are still used today as input to computer models (numerical weather prediction) for the analysis and prediction of weather over the Australian region and the Southern Hemisphere. Satellite data and computer modelling form a powerful combination in weather prediction. Australia makes extensive use of weather prediction analysis, utilising predictions derived from atmospheric modelling performed by supercomputers in Australia, Britain, Europe and the US.

During the 1970s, the first accurate quantitative measurements from satellites became available to Australian meteorologists. These data were processed to provide vertical profiles of atmospheric temperature and humidity, called soundings, and have contributed to a steady improvement in the accuracy of numerical weather prediction models in the Australian region. The Bureau of Meteorology opened its direct readout and processing system for sounding data from the US's NOAA weather satellites in 1980.

Compared with those of 30 years ago, weather satellites today provide much more data, more frequently, and at higher resolutions and a greater range of wavelengths. The Bureau of Meteorology now receives NOAA polar orbiting satellite data at acquisition stations in Melbourne and other parts of Australia. It also maintains a processing facility and provides orbit control functions for the Japanese Geostationary Meteorological Satellite (GMS), first launched in 1977. GMS, also called HIMAWARI, is now the major source of Australia's weather satellite imagery. In geostationary orbit directly north of Australia, GMS transmits low-resolution pictures every three hours, day and night, with high-resolution images available at hourly intervals in the event of severe weather such as a tropical cyclone. Two types of image are produced: 'visible', obtainable only in daylight; and 'infrared', obtainable day and night by sensing heat radiation from the Earth and its atmosphere. GMS provides a constant view of Australia and the South-East Asian region, and its images are seen every night on the television news in Australia.

## GUIDING STARS—NAVIGATION SATELLITES

In addition to observing our planet, satellites can be used as a means of determining location, because their orbits are precisely known and they can be seen from most parts of the Earth. With an appropriate radio signal receiver pointed at a navigation satellite, anyone can determine their position to within a few metres, or even centimetres, anywhere in the world.

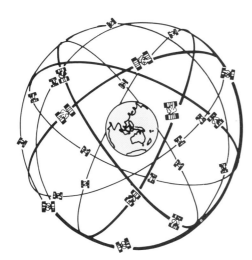

**The 24 satellites of the NAVSTAR-GPS navigation system travel in a series of orbits that form a network around the Earth. The overlapping orbital paths of the constellation of satellites means that four or more satellites will always be available to someone seeking to determine their location anywhere on the Earth.**

### HOMING IN

Military satellite navigation systems can instantly locate an object on the ground, in the air or at sea with a precision within five metres. This level of accuracy is required for targeting and intelligence purposes. Although military navigation satellites are available for civilian navigation use, civilian users generally only have instant access to a signal which provides a degraded level of accuracy of around 100 metres. This level is considered adequate for non-military use. The more accurate fixing system is denied to civilian users in order to prevent potential adversaries from gaining access to the system by simply obtaining civilian navigation equipment. The special receivers required to pick up the NAVSTAR military signal are restricted to the US and its allies.

Navigation satellites (navsats) allow ships, aircraft and land vehicles to determine their locations with much greater accuracy than do conventional navigation aids. They carry atomic clocks, accurate to one second in 33 000 years, and travel in orbits which are known with great precision. The ground receivers also carry very precise clocks, synchronised to keep the same time as those carried by the satellites. Consequently, when a ground station receives a signal from a navsat, it can use the difference between the transmit and receive time of the signal to determine its location in relation to the satellite. Signals from four satellites are needed to accurately locate a position on the ground.

Navigation satellites were first developed in the late 1950s for military use, but have become increasingly available for civilian use since 1967. The two main worldwide navigation satellite systems are the US Defense Department's Navigation System using Timing and Ranging-Global Positioning System (NAVSTAR-GPS) and the former Soviet Glonass system, now operated by the CIS. Both employ networks of satellites to provide global coverage for military and civilian use.

NAVSTAR-GPS is accessible to anyone carrying an appropriate receiver. NAVSTAR is the designation of the military system and GPS of its civilian counterpart, but both systems operate from the same satellites. These systems use a network of 24 satellites, travelling in six orbital planes with four satellites in each plane. During Operation Desert Storm in 1991, some US troops successfully utilised GPS for their tactical navigation requirements when there were insufficient NAVSTAR receivers for them to use the military system. Operation Desert Storm highlighted the ability that NAVSTAR-GPS provides for navigating in a featureless environment and accurate positioning to weapons systems.

The GPS system has a wide range of potential civilian uses, which are only beginning to be developed in the 1990s. Many commercial land, sea and air vehicles are now being fitted with

## VALUABLE DATA

Remote sensing and weather data are of major economic importance to governments, government agencies and businesses. At present, Earth resource, weather and environmental data can be received in any country that chooses to establish a ground station. The information can be used by anyone, to conserve or exploit the world's natural resources, to make money or for public good. Because of this economic value, remote sensing and weather data are increasingly being considered as economic products or commercial services and this raises many issues in regard to access rights and costs.

Because remote sensing and meterological systems are expensive to establish and maintain, and it is costly to archive the data, it has been suggested that only those countries which finance or contribute instruments to a satellite should have direct access to the information it gathers. Consequently, only those countries which supported a particular remote sensing or meteorological satellite system would be permitted to have ground stations to receive its data; other countries would then have to buy the data from the 'authorised' receivers.

A policy of this type would have particular ramifications for Australia, which is one of the world's largest users of applications satellite data and has invested heavily in ground receiving capabilities. If Australia was denied direct access to data, the cost of purchasing it from overseas would add considerably to the country's financial burdens. Australia has already contributed an instrument to the European Remote Sensing (ERS)-1 satellite and the remote sensing community in this country is encouraging the development of instruments for a wide range of proposed remote sensing and meteorological satellites in order to prevent future restriction of access to necessary data. (Australian involvement in the development of space hardware is discussed in chapter 7).

Treating remote sensing data as a commercial service has generated controversy over the pricing structure of the data and data products, such as processed images. Should data suppliers be charging scientists and other researchers the same fees as commercial companies, which plan to make profits from the information? Should poorer nations be allowed free or subsidised access to data, with the wealthier countries paying higher fees?

Access and cost in relation to remote sensing data have already become significant international issues, the importance of which will increase throughout the 1990s. Australia will have to confront these issues over the next decade and find solutions which allow the benefits of remote sensing and satellite meteorology to be retained for the country.

**Ozone depletion over the Antarctic has been observed since 1979 using the Total Ozone Monitoring System on board the NIMBUS-7 satellite. Important environmental data like this are currently freely available to Australia. The economic and environmental consequences could be very serious for Australia if direct access to such data was denied.**

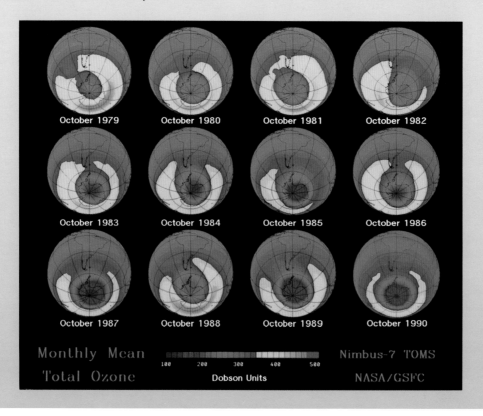

October 1979    October 1980    October 1981    October 1982

October 1983    October 1984    October 1985    October 1986

October 1987    October 1988    October 1989    October 1990

Monthly Mean Total Ozone    Dobson Units    100   200   300   400   500    Nimbus-7 TOMS    NASA/GSFC

computerised map display screens showing their GPS-determined position at any instant. In this way GPS can assist with air traffic control, as well as fleet management for transport companies. Already some companies with large truck fleets use GPS to enable their fleet managers to keep track of their vehicles. Wildlife researchers use GPS in a similar way to track the local movement and migration patterns of animals. Field workers and bush-walkers in remote areas are also using GPS to keep track of their location and avoid becoming lost.

Geologists, surveyors, oceanographers and environmental researchers use a special technique called High Precision Differential GPS to determine precise locations of geological formations, surveying points and scientific instruments established in remote locations. This technique is too complex for military or general navigation use, but it can provide locations accurate to within a few centimetres, or even millimetres! In this technique two or more receivers are used to fix one location relative to the position of a number of other receivers. This method significantly reduces the positioning errors that can occur as a result of atmospheric effects, imprecise orbital information or clock inaccuracies, but the navigation satellites must be tracked over a period of time in order to achieve such high levels of precision.

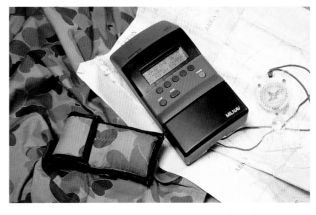

**An Australian-designed GPS receiver, produced by Auspace Ltd of Canberra. This device has the potential to capture a huge export market for Australia as GPS usage increases around the world.**

Australian scientists were pioneers in the development of the software for this technique and today they are undertaking a unique application of it in Papua New Guinea. There, the movements of the Earth's geological plates are being examined using High Precision Differential GPS. By this method, an accuracy of 1 centimetre or better is being obtained on measurements taken over a 1000-kilometre baseline.

## HELP IS AS CLOSE AS YOUR EPIRB

Marine and aviation authorities worldwide are encouraging companies and private citizens to equip their ships and aircraft with EPIRBs, which are needed to alert the search and rescue satellites. In some Australian states EPIRBs must, by law, be installed in seagoing vessels over a certain size. Compact and relatively light, EPIRBs can easily be fitted to any craft or vehicle, in much the same way as a portable fire extinguisher. There are even models small enough to be carried by bushwalkers, or fitted to a bicycle.

In an emergency, an EPIRB can quickly be operated, broadcasting its signal for help for about 48 hours. EPIRB signals can be detected by satellite, or by suitably equipped search and rescue aircraft and ships. Some EPIRB models even have the capacity to carry a coded message indicating the nature of the distress. The average time taken to detect and locate a distress signal in Australia and its coastal waters is around three hours. It has been estimated that by 1990 more than 1000 lives had already been saved around the world by this service.

**An Australian-designed and manufactured EPIRB. Designed for small boats, the beacon is compact enough to be carried in a backpack or canoe as well.**

## ALIVE VIA SATELLITE—SEARCH AND RESCUE SYSTEMS

Search and rescue systems use navigation satellite technology to allow rescuers to quickly locate people or craft in distress: ships, planes, even lost skiers can be located within as little as an hour, as long as they are carrying a small radio homing beacon. COSPAS-SARSAT is the major international search and rescue system, although INMARSAT and NOAA satellites also relay emergency messages and aid in search and rescue operations. The system name is derived from the Russian for 'space rescuer' and the English 'Search And Rescue Satellite'.

Operational since 1982, COSPAS-SARSAT uses four (CIS and US) polar orbiting satellites which detect distress signals transmitted by beacons that can be carried by planes, ships, land vehicles or even bushwalkers and skiers. These beacons are known as EPIRBs (Emergency Position Indicating Radio Beacon). When the distress beacon is activated in an emergency, one of the search and rescue satellites will receive the signal and relay it to a regional ground station, called a Local User Terminal (LUT). When the LUT receives signals from a satellite, it calculates the location of the distress beacon and then alerts the appropriate rescue services.

Supported by 18 countries so far, the system was extended from the Northern Hemisphere to global coverage in the late 1980s and Australia has been included in the network since October 1989.

Australia's LUT is located at Alice Springs. Through this station, the Department of Transport and Communications monitors the radio frequencies used by EPIRBs in the Australasian region. Prior to the availability of COSPAS-SARSAT, INMARSAT provided a distress beacon location service to Australia for some years.

In the 1990s, as space-based navigation and search and rescue services are coming to be more widely utilised, tremendous potential markets are opening up for GPS receivers and EPIRBs. It is estimated that the widespread use of EPIRBs could save many millions of dollars annually in Australia on futile searches for missing boats and aircraft. Australian-designed and manufactured EPIRBS are already marketed in this country and have had successful sales overseas. An Australian company, Auspace Ltd, has also developed a GPS receiver which, with versions tailored for different uses, is poised to capture a considerable share of the world market for navigation equipment. Thus Australia stands to benefit, not only from the use of satellite systems for navigation and search and rescue, but also from the international sales of products designed to utilise these systems.

Australia is one of the world's major users of space-based technologies. Every day, whether or not it is recognised, satellites play a part in people's lives: from the weather map on the nightly news to the cornflakes made from crops managed by satellite data; from the phone call to a loved one overseas to the imported car that arrived on a ship navigated by satellite, space technology impacts on Australia as the world utilises space as a resource for the Earth.

**Alive via satellite! Maritime rescue was the first use for search and rescue satellite systems, but they can be used to aid people in distress on land or in the air, as well as at sea.**

### C O M M E N T A R Y

DR KEN McCRACKEN *was a leading space physicist in the US in the 1960s. Returning to Australia, his work with the CSIRO resulted in a leading role in the practical applications of Landsat and other satellite data. He subsequently became the founding Director of COSSA, the CSIRO Office of Space Science and Applications. He comments on the early days of remote sensing and the value of space applications to Australia.*

While still an 'exchange student' in the US, NASA accepted my proposal to provide one of the instruments to be flown on the interplanetary spacecraft PIONEER-6 [see chapter 6]. Over the subsequent four years, my team and I built instruments flown on seven spacecraft. I even earned a nickname: 'Sir Launch-a-lot'!

Our instruments measured the properties of cosmic radiation, particularly those generated in solar flares. Our satellite data also allowed us to map the magnetic fields of the Solar System and see how closely they matched a theory I had proposed several years earlier [1960]. Our instruments had a very practical purpose: to decide whether astronauts, or passengers on high flying jets, would receive dangerous doses of radiation when a large flare occurs on the Sun. Some years later, when James Michener wrote his fictionalised account of the US space program, *Space*, I even had a 'walk-on' appearance in the book (not under my own name), as the young astronomer explaining my theory of 1960.

Returning to Australia, four colleagues and I were given the task, in 1970, of coordinating Australia's involvement in the US remote sensing satellite, Landsat. That involvement started Australia on a path that sees us, in 1993, being co-owners of instruments on three of Europe's remote sensing satellites. They make us a 'space provider' and keep us up with the latest technology.

Back in 1970, 'remote sensing' was very speculative: some called it 'remote non-sensing'! Luckily for Australia we had three excellent government laboratories that could 'see the vision': the Bureau of Mineral Resources, the Bureau of Meteorology and the CSIRO. They funded the research using Landsat and other satellite data. They could see the advantages that remote sensing could bring to Australia and they had the courage, and the stature, to ignore the jeremiahs.

Quietly at first, and then in a great rush, the Australian minerals industry adopted the Landsat technology. They almost besieged my laboratory in Sydney to gain access to our data tapes. Since that time, the mining industry has been the largest supporter by far, of both the research and applications of remote sensing. It was their strongly voiced need that convinced the Australian government to establish the ACRES data reception and processing facility in 1979.

By 1982 the US had developed a new form of Landsat scanner, the 'Thematic Mapper'. The data was transmitted on a new frequency and ACRES could not receive it. Australia was in recession at the time and the government could not provide the $15 million needed to upgrade the equipment. So we tried a new approach and proposed a low cost (about $1 million) alternative. The Chairman of the CSIRO called it 'McCracken's Dad's Army' proposal. The CSIRO agreed to provide 25 per cent of the funds if I could raise the rest of the money elsewhere. In the end we got the money and there were 24 'shareholders' in the thematic mapper project. This process developed a great team spirit between government and industry.

By now, no-one called it remote nonsense. We were not in space yet, but there were many people in industry and government who could 'see the vision' and our chance came in 1984. The British ran out of money to build a new remote sensing instrument to be flown on the first European remote sensing satellite. As an Australian scientist was one of the inventors of the instrument, the British approached me to see if we could 'find the money to help them'. Luckily for us (and them) it was only a small sum.

The government was sceptical, but on investigation they found extremely strong support for the concept and the previous nine years began to bear fruit! Australia agreed to join forces with the British. Australian industry and scientists became involved, culminating in the successful flight of ERS-1, and our remote sensing instrument, in 1991 [see chapter 7]. Almost 21 years to the day after my colleagues and I started Australia's involvement in Landsat, Australia became an instrument provider of remote sensing data. We had come of age.

The Australian Space Board (ASB) identified remote sensing as an activity of importance to Australia: we needed the results to manage our large continent; we were not too late to get a piece of the real action in space and commerce; our industry had the right level of skills to play a key role in the activity. As a consequence, the ASB accepted the opportunity to join the British in two more

**The geostationary viewpoint of the Japanese Geostationary Meteorological Satellite (GMS) allows weather patterns over the entire Asia-Pacific region, including Australia, to be discerned in one image. In this computer-enhanced infrared image, areas of high temperature are dark-coloured, while areas of low temperature show up in red and yellow.**

remote sensing satellites. Each time Australia sought, and was given, a larger part of the task. Each time our national space program, and our industry, has gained new skills. Our scientists, as the first people to see the new data, continue to be at the forefront of their field and new products are developed by them that lead to new commercial markets.

While we were developing the Landsat and ERS technologies, the Australian Bureau of Meteorology was taking great strides in the use of satellites in the prediction of the weather. Their interests, and those of the rest of the remote sensing community, converged in the late 1980s. As a result, Australia took the courageous step of pioneering the development of an entirely new concept—an instrument that will measure the atmospheric pressure from space. With that, Australia will make a unique and very important contribution to the worldwide applications of space [see chapter 9].

In short, Australia has come of age in one of the most important applications of space technology. The satellites we are participating in, and the instruments we are pioneering, will serve our nation well for decades to come.

Of course, remote sensing is only one of the many applications of space that we Australians use, day in, day out. Australia has a worldwide reputation as expert, and discerning, users of advanced technology. For example, navigation satellites are completely revolutionising our survey industry. Communications satellites occupy an important niche, which will undoubtedly increase as

new forms of communications are developed, for example, the 'cellular network in the sky' [see chapter 9].

I am convinced that our expertise on the ground, and our need to exert some control on the use of satellites, will lead us to become part-owners of satellites. Thus I believe that it is inevitable that, one day, we will need to become part-owners of a meteorological satellite. Other countries would prefer that we just pay money and let them build the satellites (and create jobs) in their countries. But that will not be our way. We now have proven ideas and a proven industry and we will build, perhaps, a scanner, or an atmosphere pressure sensor, or part of a spacecraft.

My crystal ball is too cloudy to predict the other applications satellites that Australia will participate in, but I have no doubt we will. The reason is simple: a small, dispersed population, in a large country, in the middle of a huge ocean, must have the most efficient means to communicate with, look at, and navigate to all parts of the country and its surrounding oceans. Satellites alone provide that capability. And if you don't have some ownership, you may not get the use of the satellite when you need it.

It took Australia a long time to recognise its needs and opportunities in space. It needed many things to happen simultaneously and, without the military catalyst that caused most countries to enter into space, it took Australia some 20 years for those strands to come together. Now they have and Australia is a real participant in space. There is no turning back!

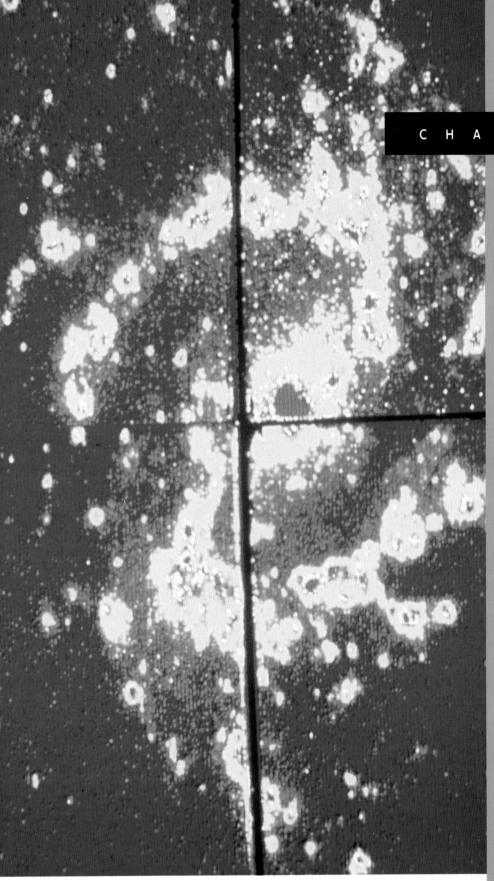

An image taken by the Australian-designed Large Format Photon Counting Detector. It shows the 30 Doradus nebula in the Large Magellanic Cloud taken in the light of hydrogen.

# CHAPTER 6

# REACHING FOR THE STARS: Australian space science and engineering

Australia has an international reputation in the science of astronomy and our expertise, especially in the field of radio astronomy, is well recognised. However, Australian space-science and engineering interests have extended far beyond ground-based astronomy (which is not covered in this book) and have included upper atmospheric studies, spacecraft payloads, space physics and space-borne astronomy, medical research and hypersonic aerodynamics. This research, in particular the development of spacecraft payloads, has provided the impetus for the establishment of a small but growing Australian space industry which will be further discussed in chapter 7.

Australian scientists and engineers, working both in Australia and overseas, have provided assistance to many NASA programs and those of other nations. Space science programs under the auspices of other countries have also been conducted in Australia, most notably at the Woomera rocket range.

## EXPLORING THE FRINGES OF SPACE—SOUNDING ROCKET PROGRAMS

Sounding (or geophysical) rockets are used to explore the upper reaches of the atmosphere and the fringes of space. They do not put satellites into orbit, but carry packages of scientific instruments that are recovered after the flight. Between 1957 and 1979, Australia was involved with sounding rocket programs at Woomera. These programs provided much valuable information on the physics of the upper atmosphere and infra-red, gamma and X-ray astronomy.

As part of their contributions to the International Geophysical Year from mid 1957 to the end of 1958, both Britain and Australia began programs of upper atmosphere studies, conducted at Woomera. Britain developed the Skylark rocket which, in its most advanced version, could carry around 200 kilograms of instruments up to an altitude of 270 kilometres. Between 1957 and 1979 more than 200 Skylark rockets were fired at Woomera, supporting research in upper atmosphere physics (such as the level of ozone, the structure and composition of the ionosphere and the measurement of high level winds), X-ray and ultraviolet astronomy, and investigations into remote sensing techniques.

Arguably the most important projects undertaken with Skylark rockets at Woomera were the X-ray and ultraviolet astronomy programs conducted by University College London and Leicester University, and by Australian researchers from the Universities of Adelaide and Tasmania. Major achievements of the X-ray astronomy research conducted by the Australian team included the discovery in 1967 of a powerful new X-ray source near the Southern Cross and their demonstration that X-ray stars varied in strength from day to day. Another major achievement was the British team's accurate determination, in 1971, of the location of deep space X-ray source GX3+1.

Side by side with the British program, Australia developed its own indigenous sounding rocket program, which also began in 1957, with initial experiments using 'rockoons', rockets carried and launched at high altitudes by balloon. This program was found to be unsatisfactory and quickly abandoned in favour of the development of Australia's first home-grown sounding rocket, the Long Tom. Originally designed as a small test vehicle to assist the Black Knight program, Long Tom was the first in a succession of more than ten Australian sounding rockets developed specifi-

**Australia's first locally designed and built sounding rocket, the Long Tom, ready for firing at Woomera.**

cally for research applications. Australian-designed and built, although often using British rocket motors, more than 400 of these scientific rockets were launched up to 1975, when the Australian program was cancelled as part of the winding down of Joint Project activities at Woomera.

Long Tom was succeeded in the early 1960s by the High Altitude Density (HAD) and High Altitude Temperature (HAT) sounding rockets, designed and built at the WRE to explore the atmosphere in regions around 75-120 kilometres. HAT rockets used dropsondes (instrument packages dropped from the rocket which fell to Earth on a parachute) to measure atmospheric pressure, temperature and ozone content as they descended. The University of Adelaide used HAD rockets in a joint program with the WRE to investigate the chemical composition of the upper atmosphere. This research was particularly significant because it led to the development of Australia's first satellite, WRESAT.

During the development of WRESAT virtually all Australian upper atmospheric work was suspended, as resources were allocated to the satellite project, and when the research was resumed, the HAD and HAT rockets were phased out in favour of a new generation of sounding rockets named after Australian birds, many of them using Australian-made rocket motors.

HAT rockets were superseded in 1970 by Kookaburra launchers, which were also used for dropsonde research up to an altitude of 75 kilometres. Later the interim Lorikeet and Kookaburra Mk 2 vehicles were introduced. More than 100 Kookaburra and 15 Lorikeet rockets were fired before the shutdown of Australian sounding rocket research in 1975.

HAD rockets were replaced by the Cockatoo rockets, which could reach altitudes of up to 130 kilometres. Upper atmospheric researchers used Cockatoo rockets to carry out lithium-trail experiments, in which clouds of glowing lithium vapour were released into the sky to provide optical measurement of winds and turbulence in the atmosphere at around 80 kilometres. Other Cockatoo research programs included measurements of ozone concentration, ultraviolet radiation and other conditions in the ionosphere. More than 60 Cockatoo firings were made between 1970 and 1975.

Another lithium-trail research program was carried out from 1968-1972 using the Aero High rocket, which could reach an altitude of 200 kilometres. Twelve Aero High flights, some conducted in conjunction with Kookaburra and Cockatoo experiments, carried 'grenades' which ejected lithium vapour and other chemicals into the atmosphere to create glowing clouds which enabled the detection of upper atmosphere winds and turbulence. Shortly before the conclusion of this research at the WRE, the Aero High rocket was superseded by the Corella, which saw only two flights before the end of the program.

Between 1970 and 1972, the WRE conducted a short program of meteorology-related atmospheric research using an American sounding rocket called HASP (High Altitude Sounding Projectile), which released clouds of metallised strips at an altitude of

## FALLING SPHERES

One of the main HAD rocket payloads was the series of 'falling sphere' experiments, which were later continued with Kookaburra rockets. Between 1962 and 1975, these payloads were used to provide measurements of air density, atmospheric temperature, and wind directions and velocities.

The 'falling sphere' experiments used a 2-metre balloon made of aluminised polyester film, which was packed with 'French chalk'. After the balloon was released from the rocket at 120 kilometres, it fell through the atmosphere until it collapsed at an altitude of around 30 kilometres. As it fell the balloon was tracked by radar and the 'French chalk' was released from it, appearing as an expanding cloud with the bright sphere at the centre.

In 1964 a series of 'falling sphere' HADs were launched simultaneously at Woomera and Carnarvon, in order to investigate variations in atmospheric density and winds over the western half of Australia. It was the first time that rockets had ever been launched outside the Woomera range and the firings were assisted by the NASA tracking station at Carnarvon.

By 1966, the HAD experiments had become monthly, providing routine measurements which are still considered one of the best consistent sets of seasonal atmospheric data available. These monthly measurements

One of the aluminised balloons used in the HAD 'falling sphere' experiments.

continued until 1975, when the program ceased. One important experiment in this series, in 1965, launched ten rockets over a period of 24 hours, in an ambitious program to examine the effects of atmospheric changes between day and night.

## UP, UP AND AWAY — BALLOON-BORNE RESEARCH

Like sounding rocket programs, balloon-borne experiments have been used for upper atmosphere studies, and many sounding rocket payloads were first tested on balloon flights. Australian balloon programs started at the University of Melbourne and the RAAF Academy in the early 1950s. Balloon-borne experiments have been flown from many sites around Australia and have led to significant advances in the fields of gamma-ray astronomy, cosmic rays, and infra-red astronomy.

In the mid 1970s the University of Tasmania constructed one of the largest detectors ever used for X-ray astronomy and had several flights with large balloons from Mildura in Victoria, Alice Springs, and Brazil. Ballooning became popular again during the advent of Supernova 1987A, with visits from the US National Scientific Balloon Facility team, and the French Centre National d'Etudes Spatiales (CNES) balloon team. In 1986 the University of Melbourne balloon team transferred to the Australian Defence Force Academy (ADFA) in Canberra. Since then it has been carrying out valuable research in X-ray astronomy using huge helium-filled balloons launched from Alice Springs.

60 kilometres. These strips could then be tracked by radar, indicating wind speeds and directions. Almost 100 HASP rockets were launched during this program.

After the Australian research program was discontinued in 1975, the Skylark program continued until 1979, with the University of Adelaide providing instrument packages for Skylark ultraviolet and X-ray studies in 1977. Since the final shutdown of the Skylark research, only spasmodic sounding rocket launches, carried out by other countries, have been conducted at Woomera. The most recent was in 1987, when NASA and West German teams utilised the Woomera range to launch sounding rockets to study Supernova 1987A, detected that year in the Magellanic Cloud.

## WRESAT—AUSTRALIAN SCIENCE GOES INTO ORBIT

The upper atmosphere research programs conducted at the Woomera range in the 1960s paved the way for Australia's first major indigenous step into space: the development and launch of its own scientific satellite. Until November 1967 only the USSR, the US and France had launched their own satellites from their own territory. On 29 November 1967 Australia joined this select club with the launch of its first satellite, WRESAT (Weapons Research Establishment Satellite).

The WRESAT project was actually something of an international affair. The satellite was built by the WRE and carried a scientific payload designed and constructed by members of the Physics Department of the University of Adelaide. The launch vehicle and its preparation team were provided by the US Department of Defense from its Project Sparta program at Woomera. Joint Project facilities were used for launch operations, which were funded by the UK in return for access to the experimental data. In addition, NASA's global Satellite Tracking and Data Acquisition Network (STADAN) provided tracking support for the mission and donated the tracking data tapes to Australia.

The impetus for WRESAT came towards the conclusion of the US Department of Defense's Project Sparta. This was a tripartite program conducted at Woomera by the US with British and Australian involvement. The project examined the physical phenomena associated with the re-entry of objects at high velocity into the Earth's atmosphere. Ten Redstone rockets were brought to Australia for the tests, but only nine were eventually needed to complete the program.

When it was realised, towards the end of 1966, that the tenth rocket would be spare, two senior WRE officers approached the American team with an informal suggestion: rather than waste money shipping the spare rocket back to the US, where it would probably be scrapped, it could easily be modified to launch a small Australian satellite payload from Woomera. The Department of Defense officials liked the idea and responded positively, considering the project an important encouragement to international cooperation in space. They may also have viewed the Redstone as a 'thank you' to Australia for its extensive involvement in the NASA space tracking network. In any case, both the Department of Defense and NASA gave freely of their assistance in what eventually amounted to a $1 million gift to Australia (approximately $6.7 million in 1992 values).

The WRE had to move quickly to make the offer official and secure the necessary funding to build the satellite payload, as the Sparta project was due to conclude towards the end of 1967. Cabinet debated the funding at some length, but was eventually convinced by the Minister of Supply's arguments: that the project would provide valuable scientific data (building on existing WRE sounding rocket programs); that the launch would be good practice for the range personnel prior to the planned ELDO and Black Arrow launches; and, most importantly, that Australia would be able to gain the prestige of joining the 'space club' very cheaply, as the launch vehicle and most of the associated launch and spaceflight services were being provided or paid for by the US and the UK. In fact the final cost to Australia of the satellite project was around $250 000 (approximately $1.7 million in 1992 values).

Design work on WRESAT began at the WRE and the University of Adelaide early in 1967, with the intention of developing a satellite that would extend their current upper atmosphere research programs. The data would, in addition, be relevant to US, ELDO and British launch trials being conducted at the Woomera range.

**Australia joins the space club as its first satellite, WRESAT, lifts off. The WRESAT logo painted on the rocket shows a kangaroo (symbolising Australia) and a woomera launching a spear (acknowledging its Woomera launch site).**

## THIRD OR FOURTH?

Confusingly, Australia has sometimes been credited with being the third country to launch its own satellite from its own territory, rather than the fourth. This discrepancy has arisen because in the 1960s every country was eager to claim space achievements for itself, yet there were no clearly established 'rules' for establishing many claims to space fame.

The USSR and the US were indisputably the first and second nations to launch their own satellites. Britain and Canada flew their first satellites in 1962, but these were developed with US assistance and launched on American rockets by NASA. In 1965 France launched its first satellite, A-1 (also called ASTERIX), from its rocket range at Hammaguir, in the French colonial territory of French Sahara (now part of Algeria) in north Africa. This satellite was entirely French-designed and built and it was launched by a French-designed and built rocket, the Diamant. However, for various political reasons its place in the succession of first national launches has been disputed.

Those who did not regard colonial territory as 'national territory' discredited France's claim to being the third country to launch its own satellite from its own territory and gave the honour to Australia. However, given that Australia did not provide the launch vehicle for its first satellite launch, the authors of this book follow the now more generally accepted order and give France the credit of third place.

The scientific instrument packages developed for WRESAT were continuations of experiments that had been conducted for some time by the WRE and the Physics Department of the University of Adelaide, using HAD and other high altitude sounding rockets to study the physics of the upper atmosphere. The WRESAT project gave them the opportunity to extend this research by using the satellite to study the heat balance between radiation from the Sun and the Earth.

The payload developed by the scientists consisted of sensors designed to measure radiation from the Sun at the three wavelengths which have the most effect on the temperature and composition of the upper atmosphere. Ion chambers were used to detect ultraviolet radiation, as well as, in another experiment, to measure the density of molecular oxygen. X-ray counters were used to detect X-rays, while another sensor detected ozone densities by using a filter which admitted only light of a wavelength that is strongly absorbed by ozone. The satellite also carried a special telescope to measure radiation scattered by hydrogen atoms around the Earth.

Some of the electromagnetic wavelengths studied by WRESAT had not previously been used in satellite research. Its data were later correlated with ionospheric soundings taken by balloon and rocket at Woomera and other world centres, coinciding with each satellite overflight, in order to provide information on how the upper atmosphere responded to radiation conditions in space.

In addition to its scientific instruments, WRESAT carried a radio telemetry transmitter, a magnetometer (a form of magnetic compass) and two instruments for accurately determining its position in space, a tracking system, a temperature control system and a power supply. The satellite's temperature was regulated in space by its paint finish. The outside was painted black, with some silver striping to balance out the heat absorbed by the sunlight areas of the satellite and radiated by the shadowed side. The inside of the satellite was painted white to ensure even heat distribution. Power for the satellite was supplied by chemical batteries, as it was not possible to design a solar panel array in the time available for the satellite's development.

Both the WRE and the university carried out tests to ensure that the satellite structure, with its measuring instruments and components, would operate satisfactorily in orbit for at least two weeks. Acceleration and vibration tests were devised to prove the design under simulated conditions of ground handling and launch. Special vacuum chambers simulated the conditions that the satellite would experience during orbital flight. The standards required to meet the test specifications called for advanced engineering and scientific skills, and much was achieved in the limited time available for the development and testing phases of the complex project.

WRESAT was designed, built, tested and launched in less than a year. Basically an instrumented nose-cone made of aluminium alloy, the satellite was 5 feet (1.52 m) high, with a base diameter of 30 inches (0.76 m). Its weight, 107 pounds (48.5 kg), was less than that of the world's first satellite, SPUTNIK-1. WRESAT's Red-

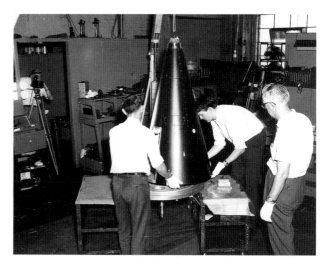

**WRESAT under construction in the workshops of the WRE at Salisbury. A section of the outer skin is about to be fitted to the satellite's structural framework.**

## THE WHITE PAINT INCIDENT

The white paint to be used on WRESAT's interior, selected on advice from the Americans and ordered from the US, was supposed to have special heat-distributing properties. Fifteen quick-drying coats had to be applied to the interior surface of the satellite and the work was done by two WRE officers in a straight 48-hour stint, during which they were sustained by visits to the pub.

Only after the satellite was ready for launch was it discovered that the wrong paint had been supplied from America and that WRESAT's interior had been coated with a matt internal wall paint! By the time the error was revealed it was too late to repaint the satellite, but, despite this problem, the temperature regulation system worked perfectly and the satellite's interior remained close to predicted temperatures.

stone launch rocket was 65 feet (19.81 m) high and 6 feet (1.83 m) in diameter. It had three stages: the first was liquid-fuelled, and the second and third stages used solid fuel. The third stage was actually an integral part of the satellite and went into orbit with it.

The satellite's launch was originally planned for 28 November 1967, but the launch attempt failed when the release mechanism of a heater–cooler unit on the side of the Redstone failed to release just before lift-off. Many of the dignitaries who had come to Woomera for the launch were greatly disappointed as they could only stay for the day, and the media made much of the anticlimactic launch abort. However, the following day, the launch proceeded smoothly and WRESAT lifted off at 2.19 pm local time. Australia's first satellite was on its way!

The first stage of the launch rocket impacted in the Simpson Desert, with the second stage falling into the Gulf of Carpentaria. The first stage was located in the desert in 1989 by aviator and explorer Dick Smith, and recovered the following year. It has since been set up for display at the Woomera township.

WRESAT, whose international designation was 1967-118A, was placed into an elliptical polar orbit of 106.5 x 776 miles (169 x 1245 km), with each orbit taking 98.98 minutes. Reports from the ELDO tracking station at Gove and the NASA station at Carnarvon confirmed that it had achieved orbit. WRESAT transmitted scientific data from its onboard instrument packages for 73 orbits (about five days), after which time its batteries were too weak to sustain the experiments. Although the ozone sensor malfunctioned, the other instruments supplied useful data, including a good determination for the minimum temperature of the Sun's atmosphere. After data transmission ceased, enough power remained for WRESAT to continue to transmit a signal for a further five days, at which point the satellite finally fell silent. WRESAT re-entered the Earth's atmosphere over the Atlantic

Ocean somewhere between Iceland and Ireland on 10 January 1968, after 642 orbits.

Despite the initial media bagging of the aborted launch, the successful launch received extensive media coverage, including a live radio broadcast of the launch by the ABC. Prime Minister Harold Holt described the launch as 'a notable scientific achievement, demonstrating a remarkable advance by Australia', and the Secretary General of ELDO sent his congratulations. Over the following days, congratulations were also received from the US, Britain and many other countries. Even the Soviet Union acclaimed the launch, despite Cold War tensions.

The satellite's success was a notable achievement for Australian scientists and engineers, who hoped that its success would be the key to convincing the federal government to invest in a modest ongoing Australian space program. At a ceremony in February 1968, when the WRESAT team was awarded the Fairchild Australia company's Planar Award for outstanding achievement in the Australian electronics industry, the sentiment was strongly expressed that WRESAT was the beginning of a growth in Australian space activities. Unfortunately, although the satellite succeeded in its scientific mission, it failed to provide the hoped-for impetus for a commitment to space from the government or the development of a national space policy.

## AUSTRALIAN SPACE PAYLOADS

WRESAT was not an isolated example of an Australian payload for space science. Many Australian space projects have centred around locally developed scientific payloads for both sounding rockets and a variety of satellites. Some instruments have been designed by Australian scientists working for NASA and other space agencies, while other payloads have been designed and manufactured in Australia, to be launched by other nations. These projects have involved local industry input into the manufacture of equipment and actually helped to provide the stimulus for the revival of Australia's space industry in the 1980s.

Australian scientists have flown locally designed instrument packages as part of sounding rocket programs overseas. As early as 1963, the CSIRO flew equipment on US geophysical rockets, as part of an upper atmosphere research program that ran until 1966. The CSIRO undertook another American sounding rocket program in 1970 to measure Very Low Frequency (VLF) radio noise in the ionosphere. In 1978–79, the University of Adelaide, continuing its long-term research program, provided ozone sensors for NASA's international ozone-sonde sounding rocket campaign.

In addition to its sounding rocket programs, the University of Adelaide was associated with a series of cosmic ray experiments on NASA Pioneer satellite flights between 1965 and 1968. These satellites were used to investigate the physical conditions in interplanetary space. The University also provided instruments to measure electrical conditions in space on the two NASA/West German HELIOS spacecraft, which studied the physical conditions in the vicinity of the Sun in 1974 and 1976.

With the demise of the sounding rocket programs at Woomera, Australian space science activity was considerably curtailed for some years, as government science and technology policy made funding difficult to obtain. However, a significant revival in Australian space science and engineering began in 1980 with government support of the joint Australian, Canadian and US STARLAB ultraviolet astronomy satellite project.

### STARLAB and ENDEAVOUR—the revival of Australian space science and industry

The STARLAB project was instrumental in promoting a revival of Australian space science. Its success in lobbying the Australian government for funding engendered a new interest in Australian space activities, which eventually led to the revitalisation, at least at a low level, of local space science and industry and the impetus for a national space program.

Australia's involvement with STARLAB was proposed by the Australian National University (ANU), which was already involved with ground-based ultraviolet astronomy. The ANU had

**One of two cosmic ray detectors designed by Australian space scientist Dr Ken McCracken. Flown on the PIONEER-6 and 7 spacecraft, they were used to detect the presence of high energy cosmic radiation in interplanetary space.**

considerable expertise in the development of photon-counting detectors, the type of instrument needed for the satellite telescope, and had already developed an instrument, called a Large Format Photon Counting Detector, which was more advanced than any other detector of its type in the world.

The project was funded by the government because of the potential of STARLAB to provide space qualification experience to local industry, which Australia had lost due to its downturn in space activities in the 1970s. This experience would be invaluable to the development of the proposed Aussat satellite communications system. In 1980 the ANU called the Australian Space Industry Symposium, to assess the level of Australian industry space capability in meeting the requirements of the STARLAB program. More than 100 companies expressed interest in the project and fifteen supported it with financial backing for the research and development that was needed.

The STARLAB design was for a 1-metre diameter space telescope which would provide high resolution ultraviolet imagery of large regions of space, in order to pinpoint areas which would be recommended for closer examination by more powerful space telescopes like HUBBLE. In fact, the STARLAB spectrograph design concept was later used in an instrument aboard the HUBBLE SPACE TELESCOPE. The Australian design studies for the project were well underway when the Canadian government, in a switch in their space policy, decided to support Canadian involvement with SPACE STATION FREEDOM instead of STARLAB and withdrew their support, causing the cancellation of the program.

However, the developmental work done for STARLAB was not lost. Australia could provide a near-identical instrument to that developed for STARLAB for the ESA's proposed FUSE/LYMAN ultraviolet telescope, which was intended to investigate the origins of the universe by studying gaseous regions and radiation in galaxies. A one-year feasibility study of the mission commenced in May 1987, in preparation for the ESA's selection of spacecraft payloads in late 1988. The studies involved Auspace Ltd (an Australian space company that was itself an outgrowth of the STARLAB project) and the ANU. Australia eventually withdrew from the FUSE/LYMAN program on financial grounds, after the government declined to fund any further involvement, although the US did utilise many of Australia's design ideas in the final LYMAN spacecraft.

Despite the fact that STARLAB and FUSE/LYMAN did not proceed, they lived on as the basis of the ENDEAVOUR space telescope. This instrument was originally intended to be the space-qualifying version of the proposed ultraviolet detector hardware for the FUSE/LYMAN project, prior to its acceptance by the ESA. After Australia's withdrawal from FUSE/LYMAN, it

**An artist's conception of the proposed STARLAB space telescope as it would have appeared in orbit.**

became an Australian space industry space qualification project in its own right. When it flew on the Space Shuttle, it became Australia's first major spacecraft payload since WRESAT.

The ENDEAVOUR space telescope is the most sophisticated space payload yet built in Australia. It consists of a compact 100 mm binocular ultraviolet telescope housing a Large Format Photon Counting Array Detector, with associated controls and data recorders. Developed entirely by Australian science and industry, principally Auspace Ltd and the ANU, ENDEAVOUR was designed to be housed in two 'Get Away Special' canisters (GASCANs). These containers, about the size of a household garbage bin, are used to carry small, self-contained experiments in the cargo bay of the US Space Shuttle. They are used as a way of obtaining cheap access to space for scientific experiments. The first canister contained the telescope and its control electronics, while the second contained the data video recorders and power supply.

**The ENDEAVOUR ultraviolet space telescope under construction. The technician is dressed in a special 'clean suit' to prevent dust from contaminating the telescope's delicate instruments.**

Originally ENDEAVOUR was proposed for launch by the Space Shuttle in 1988, as an event for the Australian Bicentenary. However, after the CHALLENGER accident and the subsequent delays in the US space program, the flight did not occur until 22 January 1992, when ENDEAVOUR was included on Space Shuttle Mission STS 42, aboard the Shuttle DISCOVERY. The ENDEAVOUR flight had three main aims: to obtain ultraviolet images of violent events in nearby galaxies, as a contribution to Australian astronomical research; to allow Australian engineers and industry to develop the skills necessary to design and manufacture space systems and hardware; and to space qualify the ultraviolet instrument for use in larger space telescopes.

However, the ENDEAVOUR mission proved to be controversial. Australia had accepted that the ENDEAVOUR telescope could not be pointed at individual stars on the flight, due to requirements of the Space Shuttle mission which had a higher priority than ENDEAVOUR. This meant that no astronomical images could be obtained and thus the flight could not fulfil one of its main aims, which led to criticism from certain sections of the space community. In addition, the detector only operated for two of the four scheduled observations, as its safety systems detected temperatures in the cargo bay higher than the operational limits of the telescope and so would not permit it to operate. Although critics panned the mission because of these apparent 'failures', the fact that the safety systems operated as they should have done proved that ENDEAVOUR was capable of functioning correctly while in space and probably saved it from self-destructing. Consequently, ENDEAVOUR was able to be space-qualified, even though it could not achieve its scientific objectives. A second flight, possibly in 1994, has been proposed to undertake the scientific observations.

### THE SATELLITES THAT NEVER WERE

In September 1985, the Australian government invited proposals for experiments for a national spacecraft to be known as MIRRABOOKA, which is an Aboriginal name for the Southern Cross. Four proposals were received. The two selected involved X-ray astronomy using an unusual wavelength, and a remote sensing experiment to investigate the effects of water vapour on imagery. However, like ENDEAVOUR, this project was affected by the CHALLENGER disaster and, instead, the proposals became candidate payloads for the development of an AUSTRALIAN SCIENCE AND APPLICATIONS SPACECRAFT (ASAS). Although a survey of Australian research institutions identified a number of potential astronomical, physics, ionospheric, remote sensing and solar experiments suitable for the proposed spacecraft, no further funds were forthcoming for the project and these experimental payloads did not proceed.

In the 1990s a wide range of sensors designed to be used with aircraft but with the potential for space science application are in development. They range across the electromagnetic spectrum from ultraviolet to visible light, through infra-red to radar wavelengths. The CSIRO has been involved with the construction and flight of prototype instruments such as the Atmospheric Pressure Sensor (APS), the Ocean Colour Scanner (OCS), the Global Atmospheric Methane Sensor (GAMS) and a detector of atmospheric volcanic ash, all of which have the potential for spacecraft deployment and could contribute to the growth of Australia's space industry.

## SPACE PHYSICS AND ASTRONOMY

Australian scientists and engineers have worked on a large variety of space experiments. They participate in ground and space-based studies in solar-terrestrial physics, which is the study of the electromagnetic waves and particles emitted by the Sun and their interrelationship with the Earth and its environs, both in Australia and overseas. This fundamental research has many practical applications in Australia and has even led to the suggestion that a small Australian equatorial orbiting satellite be built, to study the electromagnetic conditions of the upper atmosphere over the equator as well as tropical meteorology.

Currently, Australian space scientists are collaborating internationally on a number of space experiments. Scientists at La Trobe University have been involved in ionospheric and space physics for many years, leading to participation in the US/Canada/Australia Waves in Space Plasma (WISP) experiments, due to fly on the Space Shuttle in 1995. La Trobe University is also involved with an ultraviolet imaging system, in conjunction with NASA's Marshall Space Flight Centre, and, in addition, is working with the Goddard Space Flight Centre on studies of the Venusian ionosphere and magnetic field and on the data from the DYNAMICS EXPLORER-2 satellite.

Apart from their activities in ground-based astronomy, Australian physicists and astronomers have long been involved in aspects of space astronomy. As earlier sections of this chapter have outlined, Australia has been involved in many ultraviolet, X-ray and infra-red astronomy programs using sounding rockets, balloon-borne instruments and space telescopes.

In the 1980s Australian radio astronomers became interested in participating in Very Long Baseline Interferometry (VLBI) space missions. The technique of VLBI involves linking radio telescopes many kilometres apart, so that they effectively act as a giant single radio telescope, with a diameter equal to the distance across the array of telescopes. This greater diameter means that higher resolution can be achieved in astronomical observations. Australian radio astronomers are able to combine the Australia Telescope and Parkes radio telescope with the facilities at Tidbinbilla, the

## GUEST WHO?

NASA provides many opportunities for foreign scientists to participate in its projects. This 'guest investigator' status provides an important means for Australians to gain some access to space research and data. Australian scientists and engineers have been selected under this scheme to participate in projects connected with a variety of spacecraft such as ERTS-1 (LANDSAT-1), HEAO-1, SMM, VIKING, ISEE, PAGEOS, LAGEOS, GEOS-C, HCMM, SAS-3, MAGSAT, SKYLAB, NIMBUS, ATS-1, TIROS, LDEF, SEASAT and EXOSAT. For astronomers, guest investigator status has been particularly valuable on the IUE and EINSTEIN observatories and, more recently, on the HUBBLE SPACE TELESCOPE.

ACRES receiving station and the ESA satellite control centre at Gnangara in order to create a vast VLBI array.

In the 1980s proposals originated in Europe, the US, the USSR and Japan to develop orbiting radio telescopes, which could link with radio telescopes on the ground to form VLBI arrays many tens of thousands of kilometres across. The first of these, QUASAT, was to be a 15-metre space antenna, with a launch scheduled for the early 1990s. Australian radio astronomers were represented on the study team for the development of this ESA/NASA satellite due to this country's position as one of the leading nations in radio astronomy. Although QUASAT was eventually cancelled by the ESA, Australia remained involved in VLBI, and in 1986 and 1988 the Tidbinbilla tracking station and a Japanese radio telescope were used in conjunction with NASA's Tracking and Data Relay Satellites (TDRS) to create an interferometer with a base-

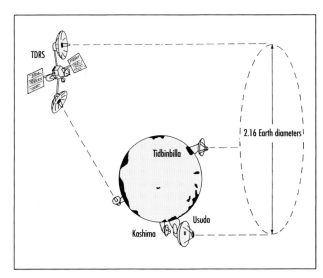

**The Tidbinbilla tracking station and a Japanese radio telescope combined with a NASA TDRS satellite to create a VLBI telescope with an effective diameter of 2.16 times the diameter of the Earth.**

line 2.16 times the diameter of the Earth to study remote radio sources in deep space.

Australia's involvement with space-based VLBI has also resulted in a direct link with two other international space astronomy missions, to determine very accurate radio source positions in the sky, which can then be compared to precise optical measurements of the same region of space. In these experiments measurements from the ESA HIPPARCHOS satellite and the HUBBLE SPACE TELESCOPE are being combined to assist in the precise location and identification of celestial radio sources.

In the next few years Australian radio astronomers will have the opportunity to participate in further space-based VLBI missions, contributing to the CIS RADIOASTRON space radio telescope and the Japanese VLBI Space Observatory Program (VSOP), further details of which will be outlined in chapter 9.

In addition to space-based astronomy, other Australian scientists have made notable contributions to planetary studies. Geophysicists and geochemists at the ANU and the University of Melbourne played a major role in the analysis of Moon rocks obtained by the Apollo missions. The participation of Australian investigators in this work occurred because of their special scientific skills, international reputation and this country's unique laboratory facilities for geochemical analysis.

Martian geomorphology and planetary formation are some other areas in which research has been undertaken by Australian scientists. Dr Andrew Prentice, an Australian physicist and mathematician at Monash University, has developed a controversial theory of planetary formation to describe the origin of the Solar System. He predicted the location of moons around the planets Uranus and Neptune, which were subsequently confirmed by the findings of the Voyager space probes.

## BIOMEDICAL SPACE RESEARCH

Australians have also been active in the biomedical space sciences. Australian doctors have specialised in aspects of space medicine and some have served with NASA in the US. An Australian ophthalmologist with the RAAF assisted NASA by designing wrap-around, anti-glare spectacles to shield the Apollo astronauts' eyes from the harsh glare of the Sun in interplanetary space. He also designed instrument hood glasses, which limited vision to forward gaze only and reduced interference from reflected light within the spacecraft. These glasses were used during spacecraft rendezvous and docking manoeuvres, where clear forward vision is essential.

Australian medical researchers have flown scientific experiments on board NASA and Soviet spacecraft, in order to study the medical effects of microgravity. Two groups at the University of Sydney have developed space medicine payloads. One group conducted joint experiments with NASA to study the flow and aggregation of blood cells in space, using a locally designed and manufactured space-rated experimental apparatus. This equipment, the Aggregation of Red Cells (ARC) experiment, has been Australia's most successful space medical experiment to date. It was the brainchild of Dr Leopold Dintenfass, a medical researcher at the University of Sydney. From the late 1970s he fought for funding for this project, which would examine the effect of microgravity on the aggregation of normal and diseased human red blood cells.

Dr Dintenfass designed the experimental apparatus, which was built by local industry with the support of a variety of sponsors, including real estate company Jones Lang Wootton. Dr Dintenfass contacted them on the basis of an advertising campaign that they were undertaking, which used the slogan 'We put more people into space than the Americans and Russians combined'. He convinced them to put their money where their slogan was!

The ARC experiment operated by passing blood samples through slit-capillary photoviscometers (devices for measuring

Prototype instrument hood glasses for use during spacecraft docking operations. Designed for the Apollo program by Dr John Colvin, then an RAAF ophthalmologist.

## BATTLER OF THE PLANETS

The term 'Aussie battler' may well be applied to Monash University mathematician Dr Andrew Prentice, who has been fighting a long battle with overseas theoreticians about the nature of the formation of our Solar System. Although he successfully predicted, in advance of discovery by the two NASA Voyager probes, some of the characteristics of the outer planets and their moons, he is still fighting for recognition of his theories, gaining considerable media exposure but not much status in the world of science.

Dr Prentice's 'Modern Laplacian Theory' seeks to explain why the planets all travel on the same plane in almost circular orbits. The late eighteenth century French astronomer and mathematician Pierre Simon de Laplace conceived of the Solar System as emerging from the contraction of a hot, rotating gas cloud. This contrasts with the traditional theory that presupposes formation of the planets within a disc of gas that surrounded the young Sun. This theory had been used to provide a reasonable model of the inner Solar System, but did not successfully explain the outer planets.

While Laplacian theory had long been discredited, Prentice proposed a new version, with supersonic turbulence that produces hot convection gas eddies shot out in the gas clouds to produce planets, which in turn create their moons. Thus the planets would form within gas rings around the proto-Sun. Supersonic turbulence remains unproven, but new studies in the US suggest that the

phenomenon may be possible. However, opponents claim that the energy loss from turbulence would serve to undermine the phenomenon, and Prentice has been unable to demonstrate it mathematically.

Prentice's theory does explain the formation of the outer planets, in line with observations. 'Predictions' of his which have been confirmed by subsequent spaceflights include: some characteristics of Jupiter and that a rocky ring would be found around the planet; Saturn's rocky inner moons, and their icy outer companions; Uranus's satellite ring; Neptune's new moons and their composition—they were found at orbital locations within 7 per cent of their predicted locations; the existence of dry ice on Neptune's largest moon, Triton; the mass of Saturn's moon Tethys; the orbits of two Uranian moons, plus the existence and orbits of a set of inner Neptunian moons.

Prentice's theory has other more far-reaching ramifications. He suggests that the infant Sun formed from a cloud with a dense core of dust and cometary matter. If this were so, the resulting Sun would have had a different evolution to that currently believed to have taken place, with a doubling in brightness at the beginning of the Cambrian era, 600 million years ago. Such a doubling may have caused the end of the pre-Cambrian ice age, and the explosion of life forms noted in fossil records from the era. The theory also generally suggests that most stars will have planets, boding well for the Search for Extraterrestrial Intelligence.

**Dr Dintenfass readying the ARC equipment for flight at Kennedy Space Centre. The experimental apparatus is now in the collection of the Powerhouse Museum.**

the viscosity, or fluidity, of blood) developed especially for the experiment. The blood samples in space were to be photographed simultaneously with control samples on the ground. Because the blood samples used in the experiment had to be fresh, volunteer donors paid their own way to the US in order to be available when required prior to the experiment's launch.

In January 1985 Space Shuttle flight STS-51C carried the ARC experiment aloft. Post-flight analysis showed that aggregation of red cells does occur in microgravity conditions, with apparently different results in healthy and diseased bloods.

Given the importance of such a discovery, which could aid in the treatment and cure of certain diseases, the experiment flew again to clarify the results on STS-26 in 1988, the first Shuttle flight after the CHALLENGER accident. NASA was so pleased with the results of this flight that the experiment was scheduled to make a third trip into space when the untimely death of Dr Dintenfass brought the project to a halt. Since then, no-one has undertaken to follow on with the ARC experiment and the research remains uncompleted.

The University of Sydney also has in train a proposal for an experiment designed to study changes in muscle tissue structure

under the influence of low gravity. The experiment was designed to fly rat subjects on board the ESA/NASA SPACELAB-4 Shuttle flight. Originally proposed a decade ago, this project has faced delays in the Spacelab program and a lack of local funding.

Another project that did make it into space was undertaken by medical researchers at the ANU. Their apparatus to investigate the three-dimensional structure of influenza molecules was flown on the Soviet MIR space station in 1991, providing interesting data on the molecular structure of the virus.

## HYPERSONIC RESEARCH

Hypersonic research, the study of flight at more than five times the speed of sound, began in Australia during the late 1950s, when both Joint Project partners were interested in the possibility of hypersonic aircraft. Hypersonic research is also relevant to missiles and spacecraft, since both reach hypersonic speeds when re-entering the Earth's atmosphere. The WRE began to undertake hypersonic aerodynamics studies in Australia in 1957. Because wind tunnel and computing technology were not advanced enough at that time to permit simulation research in hypersonic wind tunnels, a sounding rocket capable of reaching hypersonic speeds was developed to conduct the research. In conjunction with the British Royal Aircraft Establishment, the Hypersonic Research Vehicle (HRV) was designed and tested at Woomera. This rocket became known as the Jabiru.

The first fully operational Jabiru was flown at the end of 1960. A second generation Jabiru came into service in 1964 and was used until 1971. A third generation of Jabiru was produced in Australia between 1971 and 1974.

Jabiru rockets carried experiments which were mounted in the head of the rocket and were projected into free flight on their own when the rocket's propulsion ceased. The later experiments were recovered by parachute. The experiments were usually specially instrumented models, sometimes in the shape of nose-cones, sometimes reproducing aircraft-type wing forms. These models examined the effect on aircraft and missile designs of aerodynamic heating caused by the friction of high-speed flight through the atmosphere.

Hypersonic research emerged in Australia in the 1950s in a push to extend the boundary of aerodynamic flight. Although wind tunnels to aid this research were initially unavailable, Australia led the world in developing such facilities in the 1960s and has remained at the forefront of this technology ever since. Hypersonic wind tunnels, capable of generating very high-speed airflows in the Mach 10 to 25 range, enable real gas simulations on the ground of the high altitude conditions encountered by aircraft travelling at hypersonic speeds and spacecraft re-entering the Earth's atmosphere. Currently, the only technology capable of producing the necessary high-speed airflows is the free-piston shock tunnel, which was invented in Australia in the early 1960s by a small group at the ANU.

A shock tunnel consists of two long tubes end to end, with one of a larger diameter than the other. The larger diameter compression tube contains a free piston and is separated by a metal diaphragm from the second, smaller diameter shock tunnel. At the end of the smaller tube a nozzle and test chamber are attached. In tests of aerodynamic models, the piston is driven along the compression tube at speeds up to 300 metres per second. The head of the piston compresses the helium gas, with which the tube is filled, so much that the diaphragm separating the compression tube from the shock tunnel bursts. Helium then flows into the shock tube displacing the test gas (usually air) with which it was filled. A shock wave travels down the tube, creating a pocket of test gas which expands through the nozzle at the end of the tube at hypersonic velocities and flows into the test chamber containing an airframe or engine model.

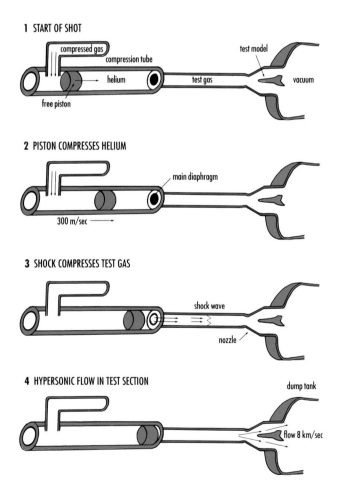

**Basic outline of a free piston hypersonic shock tunnel. Four versions of this unique Australian research tool have been constructed already.**

The special capabilities of such a shock tunnel have been recognised for many years and four tunnels have been built in Australia. Three were constructed at the ANU in the 1960s, ranging from 3 metres to 12 metres. The fourth, at the University of Queensland, is 35 metres long and commenced operation in 1987. The worldwide resurgence of interest in hypersonics for the development of aerospace planes has involved Australia in various international aerospace plane projects, providing hypersonic test facilities for research models of the HERMES, NASP, HOTOL and SANGER vehicles. The ANU facility undertook testing for the British Aerospace HOTOL vehicle, and the European Space Agency's HERMES Spaceplane. It has also tested a design for an Aero-Assisted Space Transfer Vehicle for return from planetary missions and high orbits.

The University of Queensland facility has been specifically designed to test full-scale SCRAMJET modules, SCRAMJET technology being necessary to provide the engines for future aerospace planes. Developmental research for the Re-Entry Air Data System (READS) for the Space Shuttle has also been conducted there.

Now there is a new proposal to develop a more advanced hypersonic wind tunnel at Woomera, which would provide the ability to test SCRAMJET powered flight vehicles for research into engine and materials technology and aerodynamic design. This new facility will allow the flight vehicles under test to accelerate to speeds of 6 kilometres per second for up to 60 seconds. No other existing facility can provide this type of hypersonic environment for more than a few milliseconds.

## AUSTRALIA'S SPACE ROLE AT THE UN

Since 1959 Australia has played a very special role in world space science through its participation in the United Nations Committee on the Peaceful Uses of Outer Space (UNCOPUOS). This committee was initially formed in 1959 as a response to the many Cold War concerns that arose over the potential military use of space. It became a permanent United Nations (UN) advisory body in 1961. UNCOPUOS consists of three subcommittees—general, legal, and science and technology—and an Australian has always been the chairperson of the science and technology subcommittee since its inception.

Just two Australians have occupied the chairperson position in more than 30 years. The first was a CSIRO scientist, Dr David Forbes-Martin, who held the position from 1959 until his death in 1970. Since then the post has been held by Professor John Carver, one of Australia's premier space scientists.

Australia's chair position in UNCOPUOS puts the country in a very influential position with regard to UN decisions on space activities. It provides opportunities for Australian scientists and space bureaucrats to meet with space policy officials from other

Shock waves surrounding a test model of the Space Shuttle Orbiter in the shock tunnel at the University of Queensland. This test was part of the developmental research for the READS system for the Space Shuttle.

## AN AUSTRALIAN IN THE HOT SEAT

How did Australia come to play such a major role in the monitoring of international space science activities? The answer goes back to the Cold War tensions in the UN in the 1950s and 1960s. In that period, Soviet Premier Kruschev was insistent that in each UN body there should be a trio of committees or participants—one from the Eastern bloc, one from the West and a representative from a neutral country.

This arrangement was followed with UNCOPUOS: the general subcommittee was chaired by an Austrian (a neutral), the legal subcommittee by a representative from Eastern Europe, while Australia was the Western nation chosen to chair the science and technology subcommittee. In the late 1950s Australia was considered a suitable choice for involvement in this subcommittee because of its space-related activities at Woomera.

countries at a very senior level, and enables Australia to have a voice in many space issues of international importance. Such issues have included the development of principles regarding the use of nuclear power sources in outer space and the promotion of education and training programs in remote sensing for developing nations.

## STUDENT PROJECTS

Professional scientists and engineers are not the only Australians to be involved in space science and engineering. Many students and amateurs have participated in, and even initiated, space projects. It should not be forgotten that Australia's second satellite, AUSTRALIS-OSCAR-5, was a student project, undertaken by 'amateurs' with no previous space experience.

In 1983 the Australian Space Education Association initiated an Australia-wide contest for schools, encouraging students to design experiments which could be flown in the Getaway Special

**Student winners of the Space Shuttle Science Contest with astronaut Joe Kerwin (left) and contest organiser Mark Rigby in Brisbane.**

canisters onboard the Space Shuttle. The competition aimed to find the most original and practical experiments for GASCAN payloads. Three winning experiments were chosen from more than 360 entries across Australia. They were:

★ **Perfect spheres.** An attempt to produce a perfect glass sphere in microgravity conditions by melting and resolidifying glass within a radio frequency field that would prevent the melted glass touching the walls of its container. This experiment was proposed by a student from Melbourne, but was eventually judged not to be practical and did not proceed to final development.

★ **Paper chromatography in zero gravity.** An examination of the efficiency of the separation of chemical components by a solvent. Proposed by a student from Berri, South Australia, the space results from this experiment were intended to be compared with ground-based control experiments.

★ **Cells in space.** This experiment, proposed by a student from Perth, was planned to examine the effects of microgravity on the biological processes of streptomyces spores.

Originally it was intended that the experiments would fly on a Shuttle mission in 1986, but the CHALLENGER accident delayed them and by 1993 they still had not flown. The possibility that the successful students will now see their experiments in space is, unfortunately, doubtful, although they did receive the contest's main prize of a VIP tour of NASA's Kennedy Space Centre.

In 1984 NASA launched the Long Duration Exposure Facility (LDEF) which carried numerous experiments to test the effects of long-term exposure to the space environment. One of the experiments onboard the satellite consisted of packets of tomato seeds, which were intended to be distributed to schools around the world, after their return to Earth, to allow students to participate in a space experiment.

In 1991, 100 Australian schools received packets of the 'space tomato' seeds that were carried onboard the LDEF spacecraft, and attempted to grow them as part of their science projects, to determine if cosmic radiation had any effects upon the seeds. One such school, Red Hill Primary School in Canberra, received its space seeds through the CSIRO Double Helix Club and raised two generations of 'space tomatoes' without detecting any mutations caused by cosmic radiation. The Red Hill school also provided second generation space tomato seeds to Thornlands State School in Brisbane, which succeeded in raising another generation of plants showing no evidence of radiation mutation.

## AUSROC AND ASERA — AUSTRALIA'S 'AMATEUR' SPACE PROGRAM

The Australian program of local rocket development, carried out with sounding rockets at Woomera, has today been revived by the dedicated Ausroc amateur rocket program. The objectives of this volunteer program include the design, manufacture and launch of small rockets as a publicly visible space education program. Ausroc plans to progressively construct and launch larger sounding rockets, bringing together the resources of many individuals and organisations across Australia to eventually develop the world's first amateur satellite launch vehicle.

Initially conceived as a student project by final year mechanical engineering students at Monash University in Melbourne, AUSROC-1 was developed by them with the assistance of the university, interested professional engineers and corporate sponsorship. Based on a simple liquid-fuelled design developed by the US Pacific Rocket Society, the first AUSROC-1 was launched from the Pucka-punyal army camp in Victoria in February 1988. It reached a height of almost four kilometres on its successful eight-second flight, thus accomplishing many of the goals the student group had set itself.

AUSROC-2 was a much more ambitious project involving the development of a larger, more complex rocket, powered by liquid

**AUSROC-1 under construction in the Department of Mechanical Engineering at Monash University.**

oxygen and kerosene, designed to carry a recoverable instrument package to an altitude of 12 kilometres. It was planned to be launched from Woomera in 1992, making use of the remnants of the WRE facilities there. Unfortunately, when ignited AUSROC-2 failed to leave the launchpad due to an oxygen valve failure, which prevented the liquid oxygen from entering the rocket's combustion chamber. The kerosene fuel burned away and the heat of the fire caused the liquid oxygen to explode, damaging the rocket's casing and instruments. Although the AUSROC-2 launch received considerable media coverage, much of it jeeringly focused on the rocket's failure, overlooking the considerable achievement inherent in bringing such a major amateur project to the point of launch. Undaunted by this setback, the Ausroc team planned a second AUSROC-2 launch for March 1994.

To follow on from the AUSROC-2 program, the team is also developing AUSROC-3, which will be the largest amateur rocket ever built. This sounding rocket will have a payload capacity for a 100-kilogram scientific instrument. With assistance from the Defence Science and Technology Organisation (originally the WRE), the Australian Association of Aerospace Industries, space societies and universities, AUSROC-3 will be capable of reaching an altitude of 500 kilometres, which is higher than the average Space Shuttle orbit. AUSROC-3 is currently planned for launch in 1994 or '95.

The ultimate goal of the Ausroc program is to carry a micro-satellite of 20–50 kilograms into a polar low Earth orbit, using the AUSROC-4 vehicle. AUSROC-4 will be a three-stage launcher using four AUSROC-3 modules as its first stage, a central core module as the second stage and a solid-fuel rocket motor mounted atop the core as a third stage. Whether or not AUSROC-4 comes to fruition will depend upon the success of AUSROC-3 and the amount of commercial support the team can attract. In the meantime, several spin-off rocket programs have occurred under the auspices of Australian Space Engineering Research Association Ltd (ASERA).

ASERA is an amateur organisation formed in 1990 to co-ordinate a non-commercial space technology research and development program. A non-profit group, ASERA is developing a low-cost complete rocket and satellite system using existing resources wherever possible. Volunteer participants come from universities, research organisations and industry across Australia. The ASERA program includes a sounding rocket program, the development of a space-qualified near-infra-red imaging system and the design, construction and launch of a microsat or lightsat.

The sounding rocket program includes the Ausroc project and is also proposing some Ausroc derivatives such as the CARATEL, a small sounding rocket based on AUSROC-1. Upper atmosphere research using high-altitude balloons is also proposed, in conjunction with the Australian Defence Force Academy. One

ASERA balloon research proposal involves the use of AUSROC-3 nose-cones as 'drop capsules', which would be released from high-altitude balloons to encounter about 60 seconds of microgravity. The drop capsule would carry recoverable scientific experiments for microgravity research. In addition, ASERA plans to build a microsatellite, to be called VKSAT-1 ('VK' being the Australian amateur radio callsign) or AUSTRALIS-2, which would operate within the amateur radio network. This tiny satellite, with a cubic body about 36 centimetres along each side, will be a remote sensing craft with a weight of less than 50 kilograms. It will have greatly improved control and data relay capabilities compared with current amateur satellites built overseas.

In May 1993 the Ausroc and ASERA groups merged to form the Australian Space Research Institute Ltd (ASRI). Combining the programs of its predecessor groups, ASRI proposes many ambitious activities, which could assist in developing the base of space expertise in Australia and may contribute to the further development of Australian space industry capability.

## AUSTRALIAN ASTRONAUTS

Since Yuri Gagarin's flight in 1961, astronauts and cosmonauts have been considered national status symbols, and many countries have participated in the American and Soviet/CIS space

**A launch accident caused the AUSROC-2 rocket to catch fire and explode on its first attempted launch.**

**Paul Scully-Power's flight provoked a number of cartoons about the attributes of an Australian astronaut.**

programs in order to achieve this distinction. Although no Australian citizen has yet flown in space, there have been three Australian-born astronauts who had become US citizens prior to their selection by NASA.

Australia's first astronaut trainee was Dr Phillip K Chapman. Born in Melbourne in 1935, he was chosen as a scientist-astronaut by NASA in August 1967. He was one of the first two naturalised US citizens to be chosen as an astronaut. A physicist and a specialist in instrumentation, Chapman had studied at the University of Sydney and the Massachusetts Institute of Technology (MIT), from which he obtained a degree in aeronautics and astronautics. He had studied auroras in Antarctica, as part of the Australian expedition there during the International Geophysical Year, and worked on aviation electronics in Canada. He was a physicist at MIT's Experimental Astronomy Laboratory at the time of his selection as an astronaut.

Chapman was chosen as one of a special group of 11 scientist-astronauts whom NASA intended to use in the Apollo Applications Program, the planned follow-on from the initial Apollo Moon-landing program. This program was to have included additional lunar landings and three orbiting research laboratories. However, cutbacks in the NASA budget over the next few years reduced the Apollo follow-on program to the single SKYLAB space station, and Chapman resigned from NASA in 1972 when it became clear that, despite serving on the support crew for APOLLO-14 in 1971, he would have no opportunity to fly in space until the Space Shuttle came into service, at the end of the decade at the earliest.

The first Australian-born person to actually make a spaceflight was oceanographer Dr Paul Scully-Power, who served as a payload specialist aboard the STS 41-G Space Shuttle mission in 1984. A payload specialist is not a permanent member of the astronaut corps and receives a spaceflight assignment on the basis of being an expert necessary to conduct specific experiments or research aboard the Shuttle. Few payload specialists make more than one spaceflight.

Born in Sydney in 1944, Scully-Power graduated from the University of Sydney with a degree in education and applied mathematics and established the Royal Australian Navy's first oceanographic group in 1967. He headed this unit until 1972, when he went to the US as an exchange scientist connected with the US Navy at its Underwater Systems Centre in Connecticut. While working with the US Navy, Scully-Power became involved with briefing and training the SKYLAB astronauts for oceanographic observations. In 1974 he planned and executed project ANZUS Eddy, which was a year-long joint Australian, New Zealand and American oceanographic study, and in 1975 he was again involved in the briefing of astronauts for the APOLLO-SOYUZ Test Project.

After acting as principal investigator on an experiment onboard the 1976 Heat Capacity Mapping Mission satellite, Scully-Power became a US citizen in 1977 and took up a permanent post as senior scientist and deputy to the Associate Technical Director for Research and Technology with the Underwater Systems Centre. In this position he coordinated large technology programs, was a major contributor to the Navy's technical strategies and managed the Navy Summer Faculty Research Program for five years. He was also a flight crew instructor in the NASA Astronaut Office at Houston between 1980 and 1986.

In June 1984 Scully-Power was selected to fly on the Space Shuttle STS-41G mission when the reassignment of that mission from the Shuttle COLUMBIA to the Shuttle CHALLENGER (which had one additional crew seat) allowed NASA and the US Navy Space Oceanography Committee to add another payload specialist to the crew.

During his flight, Scully-Power conducted visual oceanographic observations of three-quarters of the world's oceans. Because of the Shuttle's orbital height (200–400 km), Scully-Power was able to observe ocean current features that could not be detected from the much higher orbiting remote sensing satellites. He made the important discovery that spiral eddies (circular ocean currents about 8–48 km across) were not the rare ocean features they had previously been thought to be. Scully-Power found that, in fact, spiral eddies are common throughout the world's oceans, in the Mediterranean Sea and the Persian Gulf, occurring in complex fields of interconnected systems extending for hundreds of kilometres.

Since atmospheric and oceanic systems are directly interrelated, further research on ocean eddies will eventually lead to a better understanding of large-scale ocean movements and their effects upon the world's weather systems, which will ultimately

**Spiral eddies (numbered 1–3) in the Mediterranean Sea, photographed by Paul Scully-Power during his 1984 mission on the CHALLENGER. The other numbers on this image mark the wakes of ships (4), and current shears (5), which are indicated by displacements visible in some ship wakes.**

improve the accuracy of long-term global weather forecasting. Consequently, the discoveries made by Scully-Power during his space mission are of major importance to oceanography, meteorology and a number of other earth sciences.

In 1992 a third Australian-born scientist, Dr Andrew Thomas, was chosen to become an astronaut. A specialist in microgravity research, he was selected as a mission specialist and will be eligible for his first spaceflight in 1995. Mission specialists are permanent members of the astronaut corps, responsible for the various experimental and research programs carried out on Shuttle missions.

Born in Adelaide in 1951, Thomas obtained degrees in mechanical engineering from the University of Adelaide. In 1977 he joined Lockheed Aeronautical Systems Company-Georgia in

**Andrew Thomas conducting microgravity research onboard NASA's KC-135 research aircraft, nicknamed the 'Vomit Comet' because of the effect on many of the researchers of its aerial manoeuvres to create microgravity conditions.**

the US, where he worked on a variety of aerodynamics research projects. In 1983 he became manager of the company's Advanced Flight Science Department and became a US citizen in 1986.

In 1987 Thomas was appointed manager of the Lockheed Flight Sciences Division, which was responsible for performing design and wind tunnel evaluation of advanced aerospace systems. In 1989 Thomas joined the technical staff of NASA's Jet Propulsion Laboratory (JPL) in California as task manager for Non-Contact Temperature Measurement Advanced Technology Development. In this role he was responsible for the development of temperature measurement techniques to support microgravity studies. He was also involved in the design and conduct of some low-gravity flight experiments on board NASA's KC-135 research aircraft and began to clock up valuable experience working in a microgravity environment.

In 1990 Dr Thomas became group supervisor of microgravity research at JPL, responsible for the management of scientists engaged in experimental and analytical investigations targeted at the NASA US Microgravity Laboratory series of Space Shuttle flights. Through this work he acquired considerable experience

and expertise in microgravity studies. This was an important factor in his astronaut selection as microgravity research will be a major focus of NASA space science programs in the latter half of the 1990s.

Thomas was selected as an astronaut in March 1992 and will be in training until 1995. He will then be eligible for a flight assignment and may join the crew of the US Microgravity Laboratory flight currently scheduled for the second half of 1995, or be assigned to a later microgravity research flight.

Although Australian-born American citizens have become astronauts, no Australian citizen has yet flown in space. Although Australia was one of the first countries to express interest in NASA's 1982 offer to allied nations to train and fly a national payload specialist, the offer has never been taken up. There were proposals to fly a national payload specialist in conjunction with both the first Aussat launch and the planned ENDEAVOUR Bicentennial spaceflight in 1988, but neither came to fruition. Although there has been considerable interest from the military, the scientific community and the general public, none of the national payload specialist proposals have proceeded, due to lack of funding.

## COMMENTARY

PROFESSOR JOHN CARVER *is former Director of the Research School of Physical Sciences and Engineering at the Australian National University. Chair of the UNCOPUOS subcommittee on space science and technology, he has been involved with activities in Australia since the early 1960s, including the development of Australia's first satellite, WRESAT. He comments on early space science activities in Australia.*

In 1961 I was appointed Professor of Physics at the University of Adelaide, which had the advantage of being very close to the laboratories of the WRE. I decided that I would involve myself, and as much of the department as I could, in work associated in some way or other with rockets at Woomera. I received a lot of encouragement from the people directing the rocket research program at the WRE and set up some experiments that we could do in small rockets fired from Woomera.

We had an arrangement with the WRE that we would get something like six rocket flights a year, through the defence program already in operation. I didn't realise at that time how generous that was, until much later when I had to start paying for the rocket flights. We set up a program of looking at the absorption of ultraviolet radiation in the atmosphere, measuring oxygen and ozone densities. At the same time I also established some laboratory work in support of the rocket work. This was very important because if the students had a rocket failure (and they were not infrequent at that time), at least they had their laboratory experiments related to the absorption of ultraviolet radiation in atmospheric gases to go on with.

I spent a lot of time at Woomera watching rockets going off, and not going off. It was a very interesting place, even though the scientific group would really have very little to do when they got there, apart from making sure that the experiments were operating. Then you waited till all the firing conditions were right and off went the rocket. I read a lot of novels at that time! We had a very good camaraderie at Woomera. It was a curious place because there was a sort of military hierarchy, but it was quite sociable and happy. It was unusual because it was so isolated, and at that time it seemed to be unnecessarily 'classified'. There was a lot of security there: you couldn't go into Woomera without a pass, although there was certainly nothing that we university people were involved in that deserved a security classification.

We got very generous treatment from the WRE. At that time there was a courier from London to Adelaide once a week, that carried staff involved with the Joint Project. It was a free service and I sent research students several times to the UK, and went there once myself, that way. We collaborated with the British researchers working on the Skylark rockets, although we ourselves mainly used a whole range of rockets which were locally built and entirely produced by Australians. At that time there was a great capability in rocket production available in this country, but unfortunately that has since disappeared, many of those skills being lost as the work stopped in the 1970s.

WRESAT was a great opportunity. There was only one snag in the whole arrangement—we were told that the whole thing had to be done within twelve months, because then the American crew went home and took their Sparta-Redstones and everything else out of the country! Nevertheless we were enthusiastic and we got the satellite and the experiments built, using many of the experiments we had been putting on our small rockets up to that time. We had the most wonderful cooperation from the WRE throughout this project: priority in the workshops and people working overtime with great enthusiasm.

In November 1967 we had completed all the work. We had a countdown on the 28th and got down to within a minute or two of lift-off and the whole thing was canned. The press were there and said the usual things about launches from Woomera and we went home with our tails between our legs, feeling very despondent. The next day the launch crew went and did something about as sophisticated as giving the rocket a good kick in a particular place—I think they actually did kick it, bashing a bit of rust here and there! After that we had a very smooth countdown and launch.

The rocket went of with a great rush and was a very spectacular sight. Again the cooperation we had was remarkable: tracking stations all around the world received the data and we got good reports back to Woomera as WRESAT was picked up. Within half an hour or so we were very confident that it was in orbit and we watched the first couple of orbits with great pleasure. We were able to check the received data ourselves, so we could see the experiments were all working. We had good press the next day, with bright banner headlines on all the morning newspapers.

My great regret over WRESAT was that there was never a WRESAT-2. The Americans offered us a significant number of Redstones at a very modest price, but the Australian government decided that there was not an interest in developing a space program. Consequently, although at that stage we were the fourth country to have launched a satellite from its own territory, we didn't take up the opportunity.

After WRESAT, an attempt was made to 'civilianise' the rocket program at Woomera through research grants. In fact, I got what was at that time a very large grant, some $250 000, to fire rockets from there. By that stage, as the Joint Project was folding down, the WRE was starting to want us to pay for our rockets ($40 000 for a small rocket) and this grant bought them for us. That did not last for very long as it became clear that we were not going to be able to maintain the rate of rocket firings on research grants. I kept the rocket program going for a bit, but it gradually became less important, and in the mid seventies it essentially folded up.

After I became Director of the School of Physics at ANU in 1978, the STARLAB program got going with great enthusiasm and energy and encouraged a lot of interest around the country. It looked as if it was going to be a great stimulus to the rebirth of space science in Australia, but all that was eventually left of STARLAB itself was ENDEAVOUR. This was a small telescope to be flown on the Space Shuttle, designed to test out the photon counting equipment detectors which were going to go in STAR-LAB. ENDEAVOUR was designed not to do science itself, but merely to provide a test of the accuracy of its detecting system.

ENDEAVOUR and WRESAT were as different as chalk and cheese. With WRESAT, we built the payloads entirely ourselves in the university, and the satellite was constructed in the workshops of the WRE. But ENDEAVOUR is a beautiful, professionally built piece of equipment, which provided a space qualification for the Auspace company by forcing them to work at very high standards. There are more than two or three generations between WRESAT and ENDEAVOUR.

Australia is one of the beneficiaries of space technology—in fact, it has more to gain from space than any other country, through the use of satellites. But those benefits are dependent on Australia being involved with the international community. I would like to see us more involved in international space science, because often a space payload is the ticket into other activities that provide skills for this country. It is in the national interest for Australia to be heavily involved in major international programs, and we have to make sure that we maximise those benefits and develop a local space industry. We need to have a vision, to take the dramatic steps needed to get things done. WRESAT was a sort of half-dream which might have come to fruition and given us the vision to build on. STARLAB was a wonderful dream from which, unfortunately, we were woken before we were able to realise its benefits.

**Professor John Carver at an UNCOPUOS meeting at the United Nations.**

# GROUND-WORK: Space industry in Australia

**The Fast Delivery Processor is an Australian-designed supercomputer that's set to revolutionise image processing for remote sensing.**

Australia's space activities—at Woomera, in communications, remote sensing and other space applications, as well as in space science—have led to the development of a local Australian space industry. Although small by world standards, it has utilised Australia's specific high technology strengths to contribute to local and international space programs and begin the development of niche-market space products and services that may assist Australia's general economic development through the generation of export markets and the enhancement of local technological capabilities.

## ROCKETS AND WRESAT—EARLY AUSTRALIAN SPACE INDUSTRY

Space industry in Australia began during the Woomera years, when the WRE manufactured much of its own equipment in conjunction with local industry and international companies who established subsidiaries in Australia to participate in the work at Woomera. The production of missiles and sounding rockets formed the basis of this early space industry, giving Australia a high technology manufacturing capability held by very few nations at that time. Local defence contractors had the capability not just to 'build to print' from foreign designs, but also to design, develop and manufacture rocket casings and components, motors, instruments, telemetry and tracking systems and ground station equipment.

In the 1960s Australia had the potential to develop a significant space industry capability. The pool of expertise that was created during the development of Australia's first two satellites, WRESAT and AUSTRALIS, could have been combined with local rocket manufacturing capability to form the nucleus of a strong Australian space industry. The lack of the necessary seed funding required from government to initiate a significant Australian space industry, building on local expertise, meant that,

### OPPORTUNITIES LOST

As a result of the need to develop tracking and guidance equipment for the weapons and rocket programs at Woomera, Australia led the world in the 1960s in rocket guidance and optical tracking technologies. However, as activities at Woomera wound down, so did Australian research in this field. The technology was sold to Sweden, to be utilised in European space programs.

WRESAT was originally intended to be the first of a series of scientific satellites, using further Redstone rockets that could be obtained cheaply from US defence agencies. But funds for the launcher purchase and satellite development were not forthcoming once WRESAT had achieved its prestige 'objective' of putting Australia in the 'space club', and so no further launches were made. Similarly, although the sophisticated command system developed for AUSTRALIS-OSCAR-5 was sold to other groups for use in later OSCARs, no viable follow-on work stemmed from this project in Australia.

Another lost opportunity for Australian industry was the lack of government interest in developing a geostationary launch facility near Darwin, proposed in the early 1970s. Had this development gone forward, it could have contributed enormously to the growth of Australian space capabilities and placed this country among the world's leading suppliers of launch services.

The Aero High, an Australian-designed and built sounding rocket, was a product of the WRE's Aerodynamics Division. It was used in upper atmosphere research at Woomera from 1968 to 1972 and is a good example of the space capabilities of Australian industry during the Woomera years.

after the transfer of the ELDO project away from Australia in the early 1970s, Australian space industry virtually disappeared, not to recommence until the 1980s. Along with the loss of Australian space industry ability, the cessation of ELDO's links with Australia led to the dismantling of their facilities at Woomera, which also meant the loss of Australia's ability to launch large rockets and thus participate in the commercial satellite launch market which has since become quite lucrative.

## WHEN IS AN INDUSTRY A SPACE INDUSTRY?

There is no generic technology which can be classified as exclusively space oriented. Spacecraft and other space products use a broad range of leading edge technologies such as communications, materials science, cryogenics, electronics and computer science. Space industry therefore has close links with several other sectors of the technology industry, particularly the aerospace and electronics industries, and many space firms are associated with major companies in these fields.

Space industry does not simply involve the manufacture of spacecraft and instrumentation and the provision of launch services: activities on the ground also form an integral part of the space sector. These activities include the construction and operation of ground stations and terminals for satellite command, control, data reception and retransmission, and the analysis of received data. Many ground sector activities related to the reception and analysis of satellite data also fall within the ambit of non-space activities such as communications equipment manufacture and software development. Consequently, a 'space' industry can be any industry that utilises or contributes to the manufacture, operation or processing of space products, services and received data.

Although the government drew back from supporting indigenous space science and technology projects during the 1970s, thus causing the established space industry to lapse, space applications such as meteorology, remote sensing and communications played an increasing role in Australian development at that time. As a result of this increasing use of space, Australia began to draw on its general industrial, scientific and technological skills to develop capabilities applicable to the ground sector of space activities. These capabilities and Australia's general skills in high technology would enable the redevelopment of a small local space industry in the 1980s, which is growing and expanding in the 1990s.

## THE 1980s—THE REVIVAL OF AUSTRALIAN SPACE INDUSTRY

The revival of Australian space industry began with the decision to develop the Aussat satellite communications system and the inception of the STARLAB project, which was outlined in chapter 6. The Australian Space Industry Symposium, which resulted from the developmental needs of STARLAB, was held in 1980 to gauge the level of space-related technical expertise in Australia and the interest of Australian industry in participating in space programs. It attracted more than 100 participants from fields as widely varied as battery manufacture and communications technology. As a result, the symposium identified areas of Australian

technological capability which could contribute to the development of a local space industry. Australian industrial firms attending this conference demonstrated that they were interested in participating in space activities as a means to enhance their own technological skills and capabilities.

Although the initial STARLAB program was cancelled in 1984, the intention that its ultraviolet detector should provide a space qualification payload for Australian industry lived on through the FUSE/LYMAN studies and eventually resulted in the ENDEAVOUR ultraviolet space telescope, the most sophisticated Australian instrument yet to fly in space. Although, as already mentioned, ENDEAVOUR's spaceflight proved to be controversial, the mission did space qualify the detector. However, due to the many delays the project encountered, by the time ENDEAVOUR actually flew, various Australian companies had already acquired space qualification status through other projects.

The STARLAB/ENDEAVOUR project also led to the creation of the first Australian company established specifically to undertake space-related industrial work, Auspace Ltd, which was formed by members of the original STARLAB team at the ANU. Established in 1983, Auspace Ltd is one of the leading companies in Australia's space industry today. It boasts world-class manufacturing facilities for the development and construction of high-

## THE CATCH-22 OF SPACE QUALIFICATION

The design and manufacture of spacecraft involves a high level of expertise in both engineering and project management. Consequently, space qualification is necessary to prove the spaceworthiness of components for major spacecraft when the manufacturers have not already proven their reliability in previous successful spaceflights. It is a catch-22 situation for many countries with emerging space programs: often an instrument cannot be flown until it is space qualified, yet it cannot be space qualified without a spaceflight!

At the start of the 1980s, Australian industry had experience in many areas of high technology that were relevant to space activities, such as electronics, high-reliability software, thermal sub-systems, and electro-optics. However, because Australia had been virtually absent from the space industry scene for so long, it had effectively lost its 'space qualification' and local industry needed to prove that it was equal to the demanding standards of space engineering through an initial qualification flight. Involvement with the STARLAB space telescope (and subsequent ENDEAVOUR GASCAN payload) was seen as a means by which Australia could space qualify an example of local technology and break the catch-22 cycle.

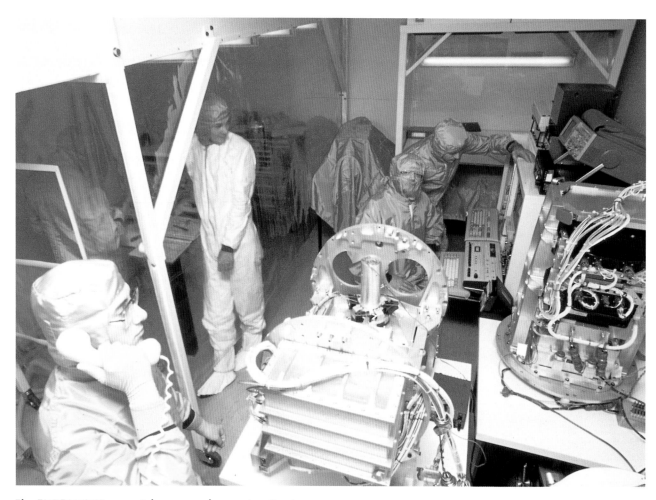

The **ENDEAVOUR** space telescope under construction in the state-of-the-art clean room facility established by Auspace Ltd for the **ENDEAVOUR** project.

technology equipment, including a 'space-qualified' dust-free clean room (used for the construction and storage of ENDEAVOUR) essential for the manufacture of space equipment.

The Australian government's decision to proceed with the Aussat communications satellite system provided another impetus to the development of local space industry, through the Civilian Offsets Program. Although Australia's lack of space-qualified industry at the time meant that, for the first generation of Aussat satellites, only cable harnesses and wiring systems could be contracted to local industry for the construction of the satellites themselves, Australia already had considerable experience and expertise in building communications satellite ground stations. Hence, local companies were contracted to provide advanced systems design and technology, high-accuracy microwave measuring techniques and sophisticated computer software for the ground segment of the system.

In addition, six Australian engineers (four from Aussat and two from the Government Aircraft Factories) were placed at the Hughes spacecraft construction facility in Los Angeles to participate in the Aussat satellite construction during 1985. These engineers took part in many areas of satellite construction to ensure that adequate technology transfer to Australia occurred.

## SPACE INDUSTRY AND THE NATIONAL SPACE PROGRAM

In the mid 1980s, Australian space industry received yet another boost from the establishment of the first government space agencies, the CSIRO Office of Space Science and Applications (COSSA) in 1984 and the Australian Space Board (ASB) and Space Office (ASO) in 1986-87. The CSIRO had long had a wide range of space science and applications interests and was developing some involvement in space industry through its participation in the ERS-1 remote sensing satellite. The ASB and its secretariat, the ASO, were created as a response to the Madigan Report, *A space policy for Australia*, which was released in 1985 (see chapter 8 for further details on this important report and its influence on Australian space policy).

The Madigan Report recommended that Australia's space activities should emphasise the ground sector areas in which Australia had, or was developing, expertise. It urged that

## THE OFFSETS PROGRAM

In order to encourage space technology transfer to Australia, the government included domestic satellite components as projects covered by its defence and civil offsets program. This program was originally set up to enable Australian industry to gain some benefit when huge capital expenditures were made overseas for high-cost items like military weapons systems and civil airliners.

The offsets program required overseas suppliers to place work orders, equivalent to some 30 per cent of the total value of the contract, with Australian industry for components, sub-systems and services that could be provided locally, as a way of 'offsetting' the loss to local companies of a major contract being placed overseas. This process was envisaged as a means of encouraging technology transfer, as well as providing business for local industry. At times, however, overseas contractors had difficulty meeting this requirement because Australian companies either did not have the necessary skills or could not match the prices of overseas suppliers.

Civil offsets for aerospace contracts were phased out in 1991, as the view was held that Australian industry had matured to a level at which offsets were no longer appropriate. They were replaced by Memoranda of Understanding to be established between the government and international aerospace companies.

**Australian engineers participated in the construction of the first Aussat satellites at the Hughes spacecraft construction facility in the US.**

government-funded research and development contracts be placed with Australian industry, with the goal of establishing local subcontractor or prime-contractor status for space hardware. Consequently, when the National Space Program was established in 1986, one of its major goals was to encourage greater Australian industry involvement in space research and development activities, and to promote the development of commercially viable industries based on space technologies.

As a result, the ASB, by virtue of its being an advisory body reporting directly to the Minister for Industry, Technology and Commerce, encouraged the growth of Australian space industry by funding and facilitating various projects which would enhance Australia's space capabilities. Despite low budgets, which at times prevented it from supporting various programs, the National Space Program, as administered by the ASB/ASO, has contributed to the growth of the Australian space industry to the extent that there were, in 1992, some 24 companies or organisations claiming various degrees of space qualification.

Today's industry faces global competitiveness and the ASO has accordingly implemented an Australian Space Industry Development Strategy, which seeks to encourage industrial activities that are internationally competitive, export oriented, based on comparative advantage, have high levels of local added value,

and do not rely on government assistance for commercial viability. This strategy concentrates on satellite communications, remote sensing and space launch services, with the infrastructure development of research and development, marketing, assistance schemes, education and information programs, all within an international context.

To encourage space industry development, the ASO has supported a variety of projects and programs which have provided space-qualification opportunities in both the space and ground sectors. The following is a brief survey of local projects that have enhanced Australia's skills and experience in the space industry.

### Aussat/Optus offsets

When the Aussat system went into operation in the mid 1980s, it was envisaged that a significant industry would develop around the future space and ground sector requirements of the system. There were even proposals that Australian industry would become a major subcontractor, or even a prime contractor, on the second generation Aussat satellite.

## TO BE, OR NOT TO BE... A PRIME CONTRACTOR

Although many Australian companies have skills and experience relevant to space work, they have not had significant experience in space project management, or as prime contractors on space projects. This lack of experience hampers local industry's ability to compete for space contracts overseas.

Around the time of the Madigan Report, the proposed MIRRABOOKA spacecraft offered Australian industry the possibility of achieving prime contractor status on a local satellite project. Unfortunately, this project did not proceed, nor did its successor, the AUSTRALIAN SCIENCE APPLICATIONS SPACECRAFT (ASAS). The ASAS project was initiated by Australian aerospace companies with the intention of developing a locally produced multipurpose satellite. In 1987 a feasibility study, partly funded by the ASB, was undertaken. Although it concluded that a spacecraft with a payload capacity of up to 250 kilo-

grams in low Earth orbit was technically feasible and commercially viable, funding for the project was not available, due to the ASO's low budgets.

Another low-cost Australian multi-role satellite called FLINDERS has been designed and proposed by Auspace Ltd as a means of achieving experience in space project management. FLINDERS is designed to be launched in piggyback mode on an ESA Ariane 4 launcher. It would weigh 400–800 kilograms, utilise a combination of off-the-shelf equipment and Australian industrial involvement (in order to minimise cost and yet provide beneficial work to local industry) and be adaptable to a number of missions including low and geostationary orbit science, surveillance, remote sensing, meteorology and communications. It, too, is currently unfunded and Australia still lacks prime contractor status for major space work.

### Space-qualified Australian companies and their capabilities, 1992

| Company or organisation | Manufacturing quality | Testing quality in support of manufacturing | Progressing towards qualification | Design and analysis |
|---|---|---|---|---|
| Aerospace Technologies of Australia | | Yes | | |
| AG Thomson & Co Pty Ltd | Yes | | | |
| Alcatel Australia Ltd | Yes | | | |
| ANU | | | | Yes |
| Auspace Ltd | Yes | | | Yes |
| Australian Defence Force Academy | | Yes | | |
| AWA Defence Industries Pty Ltd | Yes | | | |
| British Aerospace Australia Ltd | Yes | | | Yes |
| BTR Aerospace Australia Ltd | Yes | | | |
| Centre For Precision Technology | Yes | | | |
| CSIRO | | Yes | | Yes |
| DSTO | | Yes | | Yes |
| Hawker De Havilland Ltd | Yes | | | Yes |
| Integrated Spectronics Pty Ltd | | | Yes | Yes |
| James Optics Pty Ltd | Yes | | | |
| Jung Precision Optics Pty Ltd | | | Yes | |
| Longman Optical Pty Ltd | Yes | | | |
| Mitec Ltd | Yes | Yes | | Yes |
| NEC Australia Pty Ltd | Yes | Yes | | |
| Philips Defence Systems Pty Ltd | Yes | | | |
| Prime Optics Ltd | | | Yes | |
| SECV | | Yes | | |
| Tasmanian Diamond Tooling Pty Ltd | Yes | | | |
| VIPAC Engineers and Scientists Ltd | | | Yes | |

From *An integrated national space program* (report of the Expert Panel); source: Australian Space Office.

## SPACE INDUSTRY DEVELOPMENT CENTRES

In 1990 the ASB initiated a new means of encouraging commercially oriented research and development in space-related technologies, the Space Industry Development Centres (SIDCs). These centres are planned as jointly funded partnerships aimed at bringing together research institutions and commercial enterprises in the development and eventual marketing of commercially viable space products and services. With funding supplied by both the National Space Program and the private industry partners, SIDCs are intended to encourage space-related research and development in Australia, provide a visible focus for it, and promote industry and university collaboration in achieving it.

By 1992 four SIDCs had been approved: the Australian Centre for Signal Processing at the University of South Australia (already operational), the Australian Centre for Space Engineering at the University of Adelaide, the Space Industry Centre for Microwave Technology at Griffith University (Queensland) and the Space Centre for Satellite Navigation Technologies at the University of Queensland. In addition, the Expert Panel review in 1992 recommended the establishment of an SIDC devoted to remote sensing technologies.

**The CSIRO, in conjunction with Mitec and Codan Pty Ltd, plans to develop a range of portable antennas for mobile communications, like this vehicle-mounted prototype.**

Although this industry growth was not actually realised, by the second generation of Aussat/Optus satellites Australian space industry had developed to the point that it could supply high-technology equipment for the satellites. Mitec Ltd in Brisbane provided the satellite beacon transmitters used on the second generation satellites and has worked in conjunction with the CSIRO to develop mobile satellite ground terminals for use with Optus and INMARSAT mobile satellite communications systems. The CSIRO also designed an antenna for the Optus-B satellites which is designed to beam down a complex signal 'footprint' covering Western Australia, the North West Shelf and the Christmas and Cocos Islands.

Other Australian companies—notably Hawker de Havilland, British Aerospace Australia, Philips Australia and NEC Australia—also provided components for the Aussat/Optus satellites and gained considerable experience in the design, manufacture, integration and testing of internationally competitive ground and space sector hardware. Many companies invested heavily in new facilities to undertake this work and the follow-on contracts that were anticipated as part of the Aussat offsets agreement. Unfortunately, follow-on work has not been forthcoming, allegedly because of the lack of cost competitiveness of the Australian products, and many companies have had to close down the facilities that they established.

Notable exceptions to this situation have been Mitec, which continues to supply satellite beacon transmitters to Hughes; Philips Australia, which has won contracts to supply locally manufactured microwave switches to many of the Hughes HS601 satellites; and the CSIRO, which won a contract to analyse and redesign the onboard antenna system of the Hughes GALAXY HS601C satellite series. Australian-designed antennas are now transmitting specially shaped 'footprint' beams across the US.

### The telecommunications ground sector

The need for satellite ground stations to meet Australia's particular telecommunications requirements led OTC to develop its own ground station technology and a local production capability during the 1980s. In conjunction with the CSIRO, OTC produced a wholly Australian 18-metre antenna, which is now used throughout its ground station network. To achieve this, OTC drew on its own expertise in system engineering, project management and ground station operations, on the CSIRO's considerable expertise in antenna design (stemming from its involvement in radio astronomy), and on Australia's general engineering and electronics industry skills. The CSIRO has also contributed its antenna design skills to the development of antennas at the Australian Defence Satellite Communications Station at Kojarena in Western Australia.

In addition, OTC won the contract to supply new Telemetry, Tracking, Command and Monitoring (TTC&M) services to INTELSAT at the end of the 1980s, by developing a series of antennas utilising Australian antenna designs integrated with the most suitable components from a range of manufacturers. The

Australian antennas were ranked first technically and operationally by INTELSAT and their installation at the OTC Gnangara facility, in conjunction with new Australian antennas for INMARSAT and the ESA facilities, means that the Perth ground station has become recognised as one of the major centres for TTC&M and satellite operational expertise in the world.

The expertise of OTC and the CSIRO in antenna design, ground station systems engineering, project management and operations has enabled OTC/Telstra to win contracts to supply ground stations in the Asia-Pacific region and elsewhere. Australian-designed and constructed ground stations can now be found in Laos, Cambodia, Vietnam, Malta, Kazakhstan, Antarctica and various Pacific islands. OTC/Telstra has developed Very Small Aperture Terminal (VSAT) data networks in Thailand and the Philippines. The Pacific Area Cooperative Telecommunications (PACT) network, which has helped to assist in maintaining costly telephone circuits between various island nations with low telephone usage, has been designed and managed by OTC/Telstra, further enhancing its satellite expertise.

Mitec Ltd specialises in the design and manufacture of terrestrial and satellite microwave communications equipment using advanced microwave circuit technology. It has produced a range of satellite ground station equipment, under the brand name of Skylink, which has achieved sales not only in Australia but also in Asia and North America. Both Mitec and OTC have been involved with the design of VSAT satellite communications antennas for the development of commercial data networks.

Other recent Australian space industry developments in the ground station field have included the Orbtrack antenna control unit (developed by OTC and the University of Newcastle), which enables small antennas to track satellites in inclined orbits, and a solar powered ground station for use in remote locations (developed by OTC and Codan Pty Ltd), which is low cost, low maintenance and can operate in areas with little or no mains electricity available. Both of these developments would appear to have export potential.

Australian Space Office studies have also indicated that, in the future, Australian industry stands to be at the forefront in the

**Australian-designed satellite antennas at the OTC ground station at Gnangara, near Perth. From this station OTC receives and transmits signals via INTELSAT and INMARSAT satellites and provides TTC&M services for the ESA and the two international satellite communication agencies.**

**A ground station designed by OTC and built by Australian industry installed in Kazakhstan. OTC was contracted to establish ground stations in a number of countries in the late 1980s and early 1990s.**

ground sector of mobile satellite communications, as Australia becomes one of the first countries in the world to introduce L-band mobile satellite communications via the Optus satellites. The opportunities provided by mobile satellite systems will be further outlined in chapter 9.

### Remote sensing

Australia has developed considerable expertise in the development of image analysis systems for remote sensing data (see box on page 100). This position at the forefront of remote sensing applications has become the basis of a small but significant industry in data analysis software and hardware, which is generating export earnings for Australia.

In addition, the CSIRO and Australian industry have been directly involved in the development and fabrication of remote sensing instruments for spaceflight and ground reception hardware. British Aerospace Australia (BAeA) worked in conjunction with the CSIRO to produce Australia's first remote sensing flight equipment, the Digital Electronics Unit for the Along Track Scanning Radiometer (ATSR) instrument on board the European ERS-1, which was launched in July 1991. The ATSR was itself co-designed by an Australian scientist. The Digital Electronics Unit, which was designed to process data from the ATSR and add it to data from other instruments aboard the satellite, was one of the first projects to be funded under the National Space Program. The CSIRO was also involved in calibrating and developing software for the ATSR.

Australia's contribution to ERS-1 was considered so successful that Auspace Ltd was contracted to undertake the partial design and fabrication of the focal plane assembly for the ATSR-2, a component of the ERS-2 satellite, due for launch in mid 1994. Related to this work, an additional contract was given to BAeA for the development of electrical ground support equipment for the testing and calibration of the ATSR-2 prior to launch.

ERS-1 data is being received in Australia at the Tasmanian Earth Resources Satellite Station (a new remote sensing ground

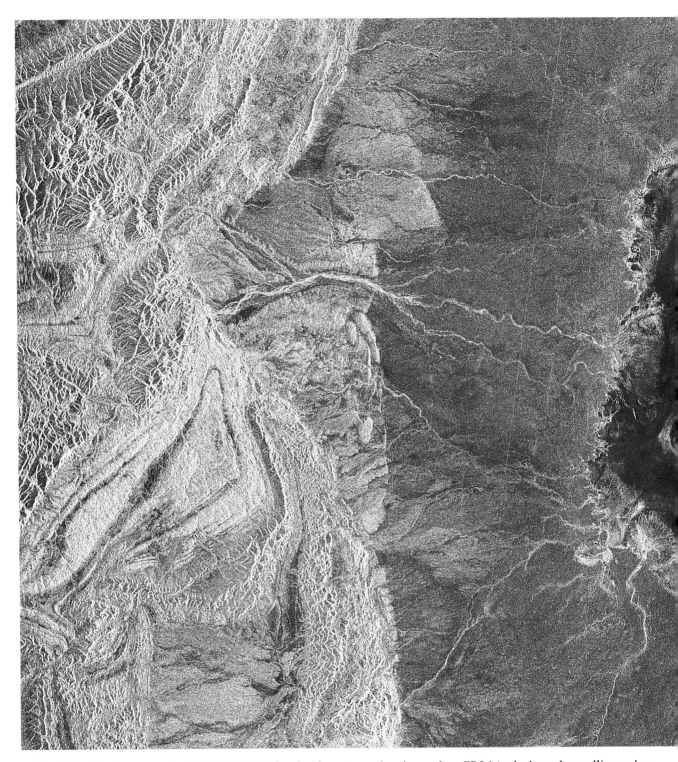

station designed and constructed by the CSIRO, the University of Tasmania and local industry), and at the ACRES facility at Alice Springs. The upgrade of the ACRES facility to receive the complex radar data from ERS-1 and future remote sensing satellites has enabled Australian industry to develop a leading-edge data processing system, AETHERS (Advanced Equipment to Handle ERS), which is extremely compact and relatively cheap.

The heart of the AETHERS system is an Australian-designed supercomputer called the Fast Delivery Processor (FDP), developed by BAeA. Ten of these processors work together in an array to produce images from ERS-1 (and other radar satellites such as JERS-1) at one-tenth of real time. This means that satellite data can be made available as an image in just two minutes, instead of the more usual four hours! In addition, the quality of the FDP processed image is higher than that specified by the ESA. The AETHERS system is now being marketed internationally and FDP technology offers other opportunities for Australian industry as the technology is adaptable to other high-speed data processing applications such as high-resolution medical imagery and military surveillance.

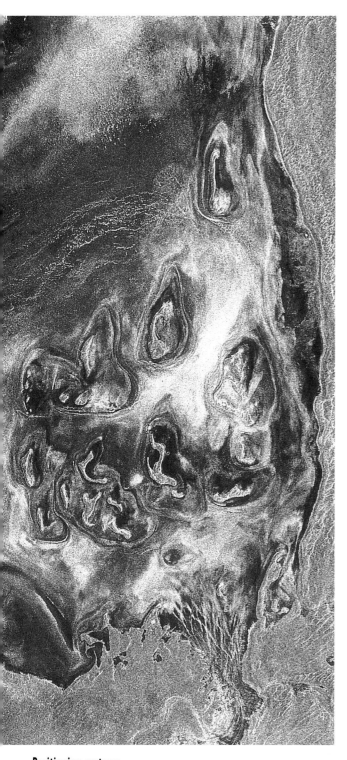

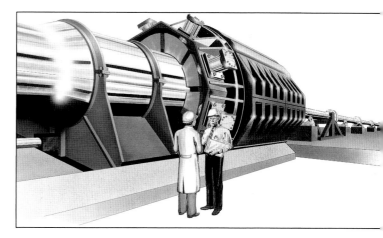

Australian image processing technology was used to produce this image of the Lake Frome district in South Australia. The image was taken by the ERS-1 satellite, which carries an Australian remote sensing instrument.

An artist's conception of the Rocketdyne Hypersonic Flow Laboratory, the world's largest shock tunnel, designed in Australia.

### Positioning systems

In recent years Australian companies have recognised the benefits to Australia of the use of positioning systems for commercial and emergency use and have begun to develop receivers, suited to local requirements and conditions, to enable this country to utilise these systems more fully.

A Sydney company, GME Electrophone, has designed and manufactured a completely Australian EPIRB (Emergency Position-Indicating Radio Beacon) which is now finding an international market, while Auspace Ltd has developed a world-leading compact Global Positioning System (GPS) receiver which is perceived to have major market potential in Australia and overseas. This device is produced in three versions: Miltrak, designed for military uses; Fleetrak, developed to enable fleet controllers to keep track of their vehicles; and Multinav, a light-weight, easily portable receiver for use by anyone needing positional information as part of their occupation or hobby.

### Hypersonic shock tunnels

Australian expertise in the development of shock tunnels for hypersonic research has already been outlined in chapter 6. An Australian company, WBM-Stalker Pty Ltd is taking this expertise to the world and winning contracts to design significantly larger new shock tunnels for aerospace companies and research institutions in the US. WBM-Stalker has already designed the world's largest free-piston shock tunnel for the Rocketdyne

## LEADING THE WORLD IN IMAGE PROCESSING

Many data users have their own computer processing facilities to allow data enhancement and manipulation that produce images with specially desired characteristics. A range of image processing software and hardware has been developed in Australia, reflecting the fact that we have become a world leader in the application of remote sensing technology, particularly in the meteorology, mining and agricultural disciplines. System brands including MicroBRIAN, CSIDA, DISIMP, SLIP and IMAGED are now sold in Australia and around the world. Some of these systems are the result of collaboration between the CSIRO, universities and private companies. Various CSIRO divisions have made significant contributions to the development of advanced image processing systems and analysis techniques, as well as sensing instruments. CSIRO remote sensing programs are coordinated by COSSA, its Office of Space Science and Applications, based in Canberra.

**The MicroBRIAN image analysis software package was originally developed for use with computer workstations by CSIRO scientists studying the Great Barrier Reef (BRIAN stands for Barrier Reef Image Analysis). Today the software is marketed for many applications in the remote sensing field.**

company in Los Angeles. At 120 metres in length, this shock tube will be able to test full-size engine hardware for the US National Aero Space Plane (NASP). Other shock tunnels have been commissioned by Germany and France, who are planning their own spaceplanes, while Japan is also seeking funds for the construction of a large shock tunnel of Australian design for its National Aerospace Laboratory.

Australia's space industry capability has developed tremendously since 1980. Stimulated by government cooperation and support, new skills and technologies have raised Australian space industry capability to a high level. Some 100 organisations now cover such areas as systems engineering, consulting, project management, computer software design and the space sciences. In 1993 the Australian Space Industry Chamber of Commerce was formed to further promote the entry of Australia's space industry into world markets.

Although still small and narrowly based by world standards, Australia's space industry is continuing to grow, focusing on those areas of local expertise (such as the ground sectors in satellite communications, and remote sensing) in which it is possible for Australia to develop niche market positions in the global space industry.

PROFESSOR DON MATHEWSON *is a former Director of the Mt Stromlo and Siding Spring Observatories of the Australian National University. He was instrumental in initiating the STARLAB project, which in turn inspired the redevelopment of Australian space industry. He comments on STARLAB and its role in encouraging Australian space industry.*

After I became Director of Mt Stromlo Observatory in '78, I started lobbying the ANU to give more money for space science. They funded us to initiate collaborative projects with other countries, particularly in the use of the International Ultra-violet Explorer satellite. Our collaborative projects were very successful and gave us a lot of good background experience in space astronomy.

One day I read that STARLAB, a NASA space telescope, was going to be discontinued because they had to cut their budget. STARLAB was going to be the 'seeing-eye dog' for the space telescope because it was a large field imager. They signpost the really interesting regions for the bigger telescopes like HUBBLE. So I phoned NASA and said that Australia was interested in participating in the project. I was invited over to the US and met with American and Canadian industrialists, scientists and a lot of NASA people.

I knew nothing about space really, and certainly not about constructing things for space, but we had a good detector system, useful for optical or ultraviolet work, which had been developed at the Observatory. It was called a Large Format Photon Counting Detector. It wasn't an absolutely unique principle, but it was very efficient and much more advanced than other detectors. We also had good experience in building ground-based astronomy instrumentation. When I presented our detector, I put a lot of emphasis on it. NASA, and also the Canadians, started to become interested and it developed into a tripartite collaborative project.

Then the cold light of realisation dawned—that one really needed money—and so came the new experience of starting to lobby government. You had to try to fire them: the initial reaction was 'space is something for NASA, for the big boys'.

We had to know what Australian industry could do, and at that point we didn't really know, so I called an Australian industrial symposium in 1980. Organising it meant identifying Australian companies that might be interested. So we put a big block advertisement in the newspaper: 'Anybody interested in space and space industry please contact me at Mount Stromlo.' We had a great flood of inquiries and the lecture theatre was filled to overflowing.

It was obvious that the industrialists, no matter whether they were from firms making batteries, or whatever, were fired. As a matter of fact, the thing that suddenly struck me was that everybody seems to like a challenge. This is exactly what turns people on and they become fired, they just want to get involved. At the end of this symposium fifteen of the companies pledged support for the project for a year. Some provided as many as three people in their firm who would do all this work for nothing. They all honoured that pledge and it must have been well over a million dollars that Australian companies put in off their own backs. This was the turning point because the government could see that this really had caught the imagination of Australian industry and they became interested themselves. Initially, though, we had government encouragement but no funding.

In 1981 Matra, the big French space company, wanted to join us. That was a great association that lasted for many years. They sent out expert space engineers who provided our base of expertise. In 1982 Matra and Australian industry were really rapt in STARLAB and, searching for funding, I invited the Minister for Industry and Commerce to Stromlo to look at our detector, as I thought there might be some advantages for us in the offset program. He came one evening and we observed with the detector. We showed him the planets and he became absolutely fascinated. This meeting was the break-point for the whole thing. We were told formally, in August 1982, that we had received $3.337 million

**The Auspace STARLAB team at the Mt Stromlo Observatory.**

for the ANU to become the prime contractor for the studies of the interim package for STARLAB [the preliminary design stage].

That was the beginning. Our little prefabbed hut at Stromlo became a meeting place of industry, government, universities, the CSIRO, and we all learnt something from each other. The government commissioned a study on just what would be the advantages to Australia in space. It took about a year and when this study was completed it found the benefits to Australia would be quite significant. I guess they were really magic times because we were moving around continually, lobbying, working hard at the design studies of how the instrument would be built. You always had to work with the big buck in mind and Australian industry was learning all the time.

We used to have lots of reviews, with teams from NASA and Canada putting us under the microscope, because the interim package was probably the most sophisticated instrument package that had ever been designed for space. In all these reviews they said we were of the very highest standard and better than what they could have done themselves. When we are given the opportunity, Australia can not only do the work, we can do it better. Therefore the most impressive thing I learnt in the whole time that we lived with STARLAB was that Australians can do anything they turn their minds to.

The government was supportive. Altogether we got $8.3 million up to end of 1984. Then came the tragedy: the Canadian Science Minister was sold on the Space Station rather than STARLAB, and they dropped it. I said that Australia wasn't going to let the project fall apart and so there came an enormous flurry of activity. NASA was still hanging in—if we could get another partner, they would continue. Then I learnt about a project called COLUMBUS, a European Space Agency ultraviolet satellite. We saw the ESA and signed a letter of intent that Australia would build an instrument for COLUMBUS, which was later renamed FUSE/LYMAN. Once again we had a tripartite agreement with NASA, the ESA and Australia.

In 1983 there had been a meeting in my room with the representative of Matra in Australia. In my office very late at night, over a bottle of whisky, we created the idea of the Australian space company called Auspace. This was started first with some of the Stromlo STARLAB team and with Matra—50/50 per cent. In 1986 they decided they should branch out on their own, so the complete STARLAB group left the university and started off as an independent space company, Auspace Ltd. The government gave Auspace $3 million to continue the studies for the instrument package for FUSE/LYMAN.

Because we needed to space qualify our detector, we came up with the concept of putting it in a Get Away Special canister in the payload bay of a Shuttle. This would verify that it could take a launch, the environment in space, the temperature gradients, all that sort of thing. I suggested the name 'Endeavour' and wanted to have ENDEAVOUR launched on Australia Day in 1988. It was more or less set for that date, to be accompanied also by an Australian astronaut. This Australian astronaut idea soon got carried away: the RAAF wanted it; I said it should be a scientist. People from Mt Stromlo, even the students, started going on special athletic training programs and wrote me letters saying could they please go. I got letters from lots and lots of people who wanted to be the astronaut that accompanied the instrument!

But there were times when I got very disappointed. In 1988 the ASO decided that they couldn't fund any more scientific activities in space and FUSE/LYMAN got wiped. So that was the death of STARLAB and FUSE/LYMAN, plus $11 million of Australian government money and eight years of back-breaking hard work.

But we did leave behind a legacy, including the ENDEAVOUR. We had learnt a lot; we had stimulated a whole body of Australian industry; we had earned the respect of NASA and the European Space Agency. The Australians were always the best: they presented the best papers, the best ideas, they did the best work in that entire period of eight years.

I was involved in one last desperate bid to build on that legacy and that was to get us to build our second generation Aussat in Australia. Not only did we have Matra and Hawker de Havilland as partners in Auspace, but as a result of ENDEAVOUR we had developed, for the very first time in Australian industry, the capability to become a prime contractor for such a high-tech project. We could have done it and this would have been, to me, the thing that made all our space projects worthwhile.

It was a pity that the great opportunities of STARLAB, FUSE/LYMAN and Aussat didn't eventuate, and I don't think you can blame anybody. I think the government was magnificent, I think the industrialists were great and the scientists were great. What it underwrites to me is that space is one big roulette wheel: it's got the biggest spin-offs but it's also the biggest gamble.

NASA tracking stations were just one facet of the close political ties between Australia and the US during the 1960s. The relationship was considered important enough for Prime Minister Menzies to officiate at the opening of the Tidbinbilla tracking station in 1965.

# CHAPTER 8

# GROUND CONTROL: Australian space policy

The various Australian space activities discussed in earlier chapters have been dependent upon government policies for much of their support and funding. The fortunes of local space science and industry, in particular, have been influenced by government attitudes and policy towards space activity. It has already been seen that Australia's space history is one of surprising achievements and disappointing lost opportunities, both situations stemming directly from government space policy.

Australia's early space activities resulted not from a national commitment to an Australian space program, but from a combination of other national requirements that such activities could satisfy: defence needs, the desire to encourage the immigration of skilled scientific and technical personnel, economic development (it was estimated that every £1 Australia spent on Woomera brought in another £1 from overseas), the availability of international collaborations and Cold War prestige considerations. Until relatively recently, local civilian space activities stemmed, with a few exceptions, from initiatives within industry and the scientific community, rather than from government. In fact Australia did not develop a comprehensive national space policy, or support an active national space effort, until the 1980s. Prior to this various government departments exercised control over different programs and budgets for space activities.

## THE 1950S AND 1960S—SPACE PROGRAMS SUPPORT DEFENCE REQUIREMENTS

Military programs rather than civilian applications led to the nation's first space programs through the Anglo-Australian Joint Project at Woomera. The Woomera rocket range, the Black Knight and other rocket and missile programs, and much of the upper atmosphere research were the result of the perceived defence needs of Australia, guided by the wider Cold War defence policies of Britain and the Western alliance. Early space activities in Australia that were essentially civilian still had to have some apparent military justification, although the sounding rocket programs of the Universities of Adelaide and Tasmania succeeded in maintaining their civilian status by gaining acceptance into the UK scientific sounding rocket program at Woomera as 'British' universities.

During the 1960s and the early 1970s, Australian space activities were primarily overseen by the Department of Defence and the Department of Supply, which managed the activities of the WRE and the NASA space tracking stations in Australia. Early attempts to 'civilianise' Australian space activities did not meet with much success. When, in 1961, Britain transferred its Blue Streak missile to the ELDO program and Australia, as a result, was given the opportunity to become a full member in the fledgling civilian European Launcher Development Organisation (ELDO), the offer was declined because the government of the day did not recognise the value of civilian space activities and the benefits that could flow to the nation from them. Consequently, while Australia was a member of ELDO (with a significant level of involvement), its role was that of a supplier of services rather than an active and contributing participant. As a result, space activities at Woomera did not survive the transfer of ELDO launch operations to French Guiana, or the wind-down of the Joint Project when Britain ceased its Australian-based military rocket and aerospace technology testing programs.

Another important space science opportunity was also blocked within the government in 1961, for reasons that are not readily apparent. The CSIRO prepared a paper regarding an offer from the US to launch a satellite for Australia (as they were soon to do for Britain and Canada). Despite strong support from the Australian scientific community, the proposal was 'killed' before ever being considered by the Cabinet. Subsequently, several well-placed scientific researchers gained access to the sounding rocket programs at Woomera, which were funded by the Defence Department. But when Woomera's programs faltered, so did local space science: with only limited funding received from government, it could not survive without the 'free ride' provided by the military.

## SPACE FOR DEFENCE

Australia's largest space programs have stemmed from military space activity, which has been predominantly foreign inspired. The space-related programs at Woomera, the activities of the WRE/DSTO, the US military space tracking stations and the Defence Signals Directorate's satellite interception activities have all been the products of defence and foreign policies rather than space policy.

Today, Australia's defence forces remain closely involved with military space systems and have interests in other space applications technologies such as communications (including mobile communications), navigation and position-fixing, environmental monitoring, search and rescue, and surveillance systems for military purposes. However, current defence policies mean that the defence forces are now primarily purchasers of space products and services rather than developers of space technologies. Although the DSTO conducts some space research and development activities and assists the development of Australian space industry, defence-related space activities remain outside the purview of the civilian National Space Program, with a consequent loss of the benefits and efficiencies that could be derived from an integrated space program without overlapping projects in the civil and defence sectors.

Despite the lessening of international tensions with the cessation of the Cold War, defence-related space activities will continue to play a large part in Australian defence policy. Whether or not they will be integrated more fully into the national civilian space policy, a current weakness commented upon by the 1992 Expert Panel report, remains to be seen.

## NASA PROMOTES AUSTRALIAN SPACE ACTIVITIES

Because of its significant space tracking programs in Australia and the intergovernmental arrangements that administered its facilities in Australia, NASA, which maintained an office within the Department of Supply, tried to encourage local interest in space affairs.

From 1965 NASA operated the Spacemobile education van in Australia, to promote awareness of both NASA and Australian space activities. This program, which operated into the early 1970s, reached many hundreds of thousands of students from intermediate school to tertiary level in all states. The program was tremendously popular, to gauge by the number of requests for additional lectures from interested public groups, professional bodies and social clubs, and made a positive contribution to public awareness of space activities in Australia.

**The official hand-over to Australia of the NASA Spacemobile education van was made at Parliament House, Canberra, in October 1965.**

In the early 1970s, NASA Administrator James Fletcher visited Australia to gain support for the proposed Space Shuttle program and solicit Australian involvement. As a result of his visit four governmental committees on local space activities were established. However, the prevailing attitude was that space was something for 'the big boys'—the major world economic and political powers—not smaller nations like Australia. Consequently, without any significant government support or commitment to funding, these committees were disbanded after infrequent meetings.

## THE 1970S—AUSTRALIAN SPACE ACTIVITY DIES DOWN

The 1970s saw a marked drop in Australian space activities, particularly after the downturn in programs at Woomera. As Australia withdrew from the international space scene, the space expertise and capabilities built up during the previous decade were lost as scientists and engineers, unable to find space-related work in Australia, went overseas or turned their attention to non-space interests. During this period the US space activities con-

ducted in Australia—the NASA tracking stations and US military bases—represented the nation's primary involvement with space.

Although Australian space activities at the time were under the control of various government departments, as early as 1970 an opportunity to coordinate them under one agency arose when a number of business executives, scientific bodies and industrial organisations submitted a paper to the prime minister calling for the creation of an Australian Space Research Agency (ASRA). The ASRA proposal recommended the establishment of a central authority to coordinate and plan Australia's efforts in space research and technology, develop and commercialise the space sciences, seek overseas contracts, develop an Australian technology base, and disseminate information. However, the prime minister informed the group that, on the recommendation of his advisers, there was no merit in the ASRA proposal, that there was no case for Australia to form a space agency, and that the relationship between NASA and the Department of Supply was totally adequate. As a result of this attitude, the ASRA proposal proceeded no further.

In 1974, because of its previous involvement with ELDO, Australia was invited to become a full member of the ESA. It was the only non-European country to which such an invitation was extended. However, Australia declined to take up ESA membership as the government of the day was not interested in furthering Australian space activities at that time. The government did, however, reserve the right to take up ESA membership at some time in the future.

It was not until 1983 that Australia actually rescinded all of its rights to ESA membership, ironically declining to join the Agency just at the time when local space science and industry were undergoing a significant rejuvenation as a result of the STARLAB project and the establishment of Aussat. ESA membership could have been very beneficial to Australia in the 1980s, both because of the opportunities it would have presented to Australian space science through its own active science program, and because of the potential work that Australian space industry might have obtained as a result of the ESA's policy of providing project contracts to countries on the basis of their financial contribution to that project.

Although the government drew back from supporting indigenous space science and technology projects and was unwilling to make a major financial commitment to international space programs, space applications such as meteorology, remote sensing and communications played an increasing role in Australian development in the 1970s. This use of space was funded by various government departments to meet specific national needs which could be assisted by space applications. Despite low budgets, Australian scientists and engineers were able to participate in space science and applications programs by utilising the satellites and joint-research opportunities provided by other nations (which were discussed in chapters 5 and 6).

Many ground sector applications programs, such as the reception and analysis of Landsat imagery, found support through general science funding and the CSIRO, while the construction of satellite telecommunications ground stations was supported due to the national requirement for international telecommunications. Because of this, Australia was able to develop strengths in

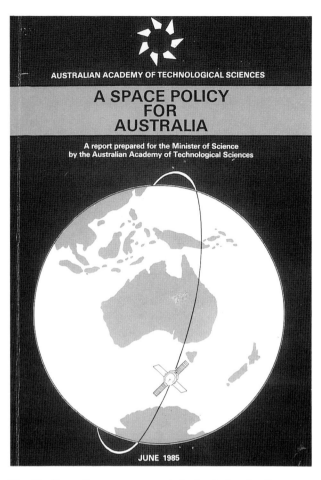

**The Madigan Report presented the basis for the first comprehensive national space policy.**

certain space disciplines which came to the fore in the 1980s when funding for space activities became more readily available.

## THE 1980S—THE REVIVAL OF AUSTRALIAN INTEREST IN SPACE

The 1980s saw a dramatic revival of Australian interest in space, stemming from the development of the STARLAB project and the decision to establish the Aussat satellite communications system. The opportunities that these projects afforded Australia paved the way for a rejuvenation of local space science and industry and led to the eventual development of Australia's first formalised national space policy and the creation of its first space agencies. In the light of government industry and technology policy at the time, STARLAB was seen as a way for Australia to regain its lost space qualification and to encourage the development of high-technology industries. It was seen as a way of utilising the offset provisions for Aussat in order to develop local space industry.

The year 1984 was an eventful one, probably the most important in the rebirth of Australian space activities. Although, ironically, it saw the cancellation of the STARLAB project, it also saw the fruits of the impetus it provided. The First National Space Symposium, in which more than 200 local and overseas representatives took part, was held. This conference was instrumental in providing the momentum that eventually led to the development of two governmental space agencies—the CSIRO Office of Space Science and Applications (COSSA) and the Australian Space Office (ASO). Also at this time, the Institution of Engineers, Australia, established its national panel (and later, committee) on space engineering, to consider and promote professional interest in the discipline.

In late 1984, following the Symposium, the CSIRO, which had long had a wide range of space science and applications interests and was developing some involvement in space industry, moved to consolidate its many areas of space activity. It established COSSA to link all of its space-related activities. COSSA's annual budget of around $6 million provided for remote sensing systems, communications research, radio astronomy and other related fields, with links to many international space programs. Since its inception COSSA has been active in many space applications projects, particularly those related to environmental monitoring, and has been involved in the development of sensors and instruments for spacecraft, such as components of the ERS-1 and 2 Along Track Scanning Radiometers. Many of COSSA's programs are undertaken in conjunction with the ASO.

## A SPACE POLICY FOR AUSTRALIA

Following the First National Space Symposium there were calls for Australia to develop a comprehensive national space policy to replace the ad hoc decision-making that had previously affected Australian space activities. The Australian Academy of Technological Science was commissioned by the Minister for Science and Technology to prepare a report on the potential of space science and technology in Australia.

In 1985 the Academy released the resulting report, *A space policy for Australia* (the Madigan Report), which considered a variety of issues relating to space programs in the nation. These included whether Australia had the potential financial, technological and industrial capacities to service a positive space policy. The report found that the country did indeed have these capabilities, but speculated as to whether Australia had sufficient commitment to support a national space program. It noted that no formal space policy existed, nor any agency capable of focusing national efforts on space affairs (even though the establishment of COSSA had at least focused CSIRO efforts).

In its extensive review of national space activities, the report concluded that Australia should establish a national space policy under government leadership, emphasising the space-related ground infrastructure sector, particularly involving remote sensing. The study also supported international collaboration, especially with neighbours in South-East Asia. The report further urged that government-funded research and development con-

tracts be placed with industry in order to establish local subcontractor or prime-contractor status for space hardware. It suggested an initial government commitment to spending $100 million over five years towards suitable programs, which would be coordinated under an independent national statutory space authority.

## THE AUSTRALIAN SPACE BOARD AND OFFICE

As a result of the Madigan Report, the government established, in 1986, the Australian Space Board (ASB) to oversee a National Space Program (NSP) within the Department of Industry, Technology and Commerce (DITAC). The major goal of the National Space Program was to encourage greater involvement by Australian industry in space research and development activities and to promote the development of commercially viable industries based on space technologies. The ASB's role was to act as an advisory and supervisory body in the formulation of a national space policy. Its main functions were to facilitate the development of Australian space science and technology, identify industry opportunities, and establish international programs of collaboration. Although the Madigan Report had recommended that a statutory authority be established to manage the National Space Program, the ASB was constituted as a non-statutory advisory body only.

The Australian Space Office (ASO) was established by the government in 1987 to act as the secretariat of the ASB and conduct the daily activities necessary for the coordination and management of the National Space Program. The ASO was situated

within DITAC, with the role of coordinating the development of commercially viable industries based on space technologies which were export-oriented and internationally competitive.

The ASO would eventually develop five sections: the Space Projects Section, which oversaw the contracts and specifications for NSP-funded space projects; the Launch Services Section, responsible for monitoring the progress of private sector launch facility proposals; the Space Policy Section, responsible for the development of Australian space policy and the programs necessary to achieve policy objectives; the NASA Administration Section, which handled the administrative, contractual and financial arrangements associated with NASA's activities in Australia; and the Canberra Deep Space Communications Complex (the formal

## WHO CONTROLS AUSTRALIA'S SPACE ACTIVITIES?

The National Space Program as managed by the ASB actually represented only a small part of Australia's overall space-related activities. Although the ASB worked closely with COSSA, Aussat/Optus, Telstra, the Bureau of Meteorology and other government departments (all of which participated as observers at ASB meetings), defence space activity, meteorology, communications and many other space applications activities operated outside the purview of the NSP and did not come under its jurisdiction.

This fragmentation of responsibility and the lack of coordination in the management of Australia's space activities has been criticised for creating duplication and overlapping of activities and responsibilities. It has also been criticised by international collaborators, who have difficulty determining who does what and who is responsible for funding particular types of projects (as funding for many Australian space activities lies outside the funding organised by the ASO).

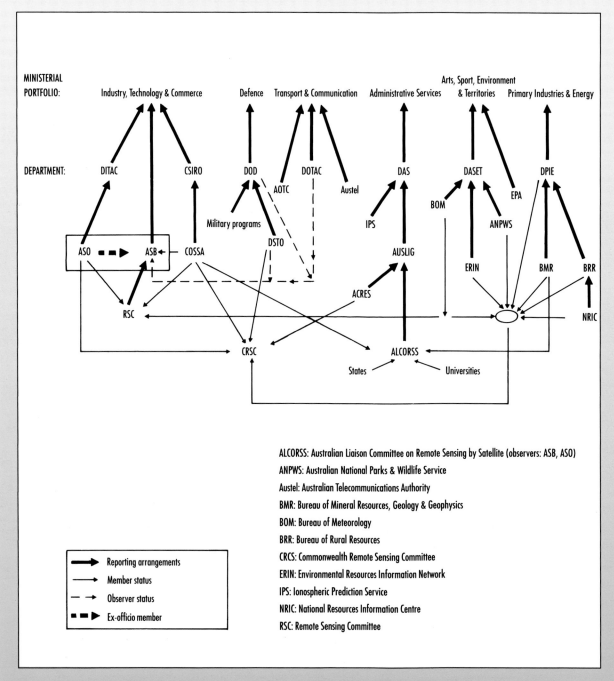

ALCORSS: Australian Liaison Committee on Remote Sensing by Satellite (observers: ASB, ASO)

ANPWS: Australian National Parks & Wildlife Service

Austel: Australian Telecommunications Authority

BMR: Bureau of Mineral Resources, Geology & Geophysics

BOM: Bureau of Meteorology

BRR: Bureau of Rural Resources

CRCS: Commonwealth Remote Sensing Committee

ERIN: Environmental Resources Information Network

IPS: Ionospheric Prediction Service

NRIC: National Resources Information Centre

RSC: Remote Sensing Committee

→ Reporting arrangements

→ Member status

--→ Observer status

■■► Ex-officio member

**The complex organisational arrangements existing in 1992 between different government departments controlling space activities is outlined in this chart, derived from the Expert Panel report.**

title of the Tidbinbilla space tracking station), which was considered a separate ASO section in its own right.

The initial objectives of the ASO were focused very much on the development of Australian industry and the fulfilment of Australia's space responsibilities under international space agreements. The ASO's funding went towards industry development projects and a range of studies examining potential areas of opportunity for niche-market development of Australian products. It sought to promote industry through its Space Industry Development Strategy and the establishment of the Space Industry Development Centres. Science objectives and national interests in space products and services were considered to have a lower priority, which provoked criticism from the Australian space science community.

By 1991 the ASO sought to redress the perceived bias in the National Space Program by promulgating the Balanced National Space Program, which refocused policy directions to include opportunities for public goods and services and national benefits from the use of space, while at the same time continuing to address the requirements of industry.

## FUNDING FOR AUSTRALIAN SPACE ACTIVITIES

Although the Madigan Report recommended that the National Space Program receive funding of approximately $20 million per year over a five-year period in order to develop an effective level of space activity, the ASB only received successive budgets of around $3–$5 million per year. By international standards, the National Space Program managed by the ASB has had a very low budget, representing a much smaller proportion of the national expenditure than that allocated by other countries. The percentage of its Gross National Product (GNP) that is actually devoted to Australia's space program is significantly smaller than that allocated to space activities in other countries, even those nations considered far less developed than Australia.

Critics of government space policy cite this low level of funding as indicative of a lack of government commitment to space activities. However, although these budgets have been much criticised within the space community as only allowing coverage of ongoing commitments, they actually represent only a small proportion of the money spent annually on space in Australia. Indirect expenditure on space-related systems by various government agencies has amounted to around $100 million each year, mostly spent overseas on such things as the communications satellites for the Aussat/Optus system, meteorological and communications satellite ground receiving stations, and ongoing operation of remote sensing satellite ground stations and processing facilities not under ASB control.

## THE 1992 SPACE PROGRAM REVIEWS AND FUTURE SPACE POLICY

International Space Year, 1992, saw the release of three government reports on space activities and opportunities in Australia that were to have an important effect upon the country's space policy and the National Space Program. The first of these reports, the Senate Standing Committee on Transport, Communications and Infrastructure's *Developing satellite launching facilities in Australia and the role of government,* considered the feasibility of the Cape York Space Port and Woomera revival proposals (see chapter 9) and made positive recommendations for non-financial government support of both these projects.

More significantly, the five-year review of the National Space Program, as suggested in the Madigan Report, was undertaken by two independent groups, both assessing the performance of the National Space Program from very different perspectives. The first was an Expert Panel consisting of three recognised space or technological experts, one foreign and two Australians, having between them a wealth of experience in both government and private sector space activities. It was appointed by DITAC to review the performance of the National Space Program and to make recommendations for its future direction. Concurrent with the Panel's study was an economic evaluation undertaken by the Bureau of Industry Economics (BIE).

The Expert Panel conducted extensive interviews within the Australian space community and overseas in order to judge the effectiveness of the current National Space Program. It found that, despite criticisms in regard to coordination of activities among different agencies, lack of support for space science and small budgets, the NSP and the ASB/ASO had performed well, particularly in developing Australian space industry capability significantly within a relatively short period of time.

Noting the various criticisms that had been levelled at the NSP, the Panel recommended in its report (*An integrated National Space Program*) that a high-level Australian Space Council be established to formulate space policy and set priorities for the National Space Program. The Panel also advocated a threefold increase in the space budget over three years, emphasising commitment to remote sensing for environmental monitoring, mobile communications systems, aspects of launch services, space science, and the space industry.

The BIE report, however, evaluating the NSP from an economic perspective, found that there was no economic case for an independent National Space Program. Although the BIE report concurred with the Expert Panel on the importance of remote sensing and strong funding for a national remote sensing program, it recommended that future funding for space industry development be provided through general industry development

## THE SPACE SCIENCE CONTROVERSY

The place of space science in the National Space Program has been somewhat controversial, with criticisms that the ASO has not devoted sufficient resources to space science, despite the fact that space science has always had a greater proportion of the space budget than the 10 per cent minimum recommended by the Expert Panel in 1992.

Space science programs (notably the LYMAN/ENDEA-VOUR and ATSR projects) were initially part of the NSP. They were transferred to the ASB on its creation from the Department of Science, under which they had been commenced. Many of the projects that the ASO has supported have been science driven, but each has been carefully tailored to have relevance to the development of the Australian space industry. It could be said that science was playing its part in contributing to the industry development that government required.

In 1989 the *Space science in Australia* (Cole) report, funded by the ASO and prepared under the auspices of the Australian Academy of Science, recommended consistent government support of an active program of space science. It outlined a five-year plan, with special funding for programs in ultraviolet astronomy, airborne science, and remotely sensed data use. The report urged specific funding to establish a space and astronomy data storage capability, and the design, construction and launch of an Australian science and applications spacecraft, as well as support for space science and education programs.

There was little evident reaction generated by this study—if anything, it marked the start of a period of uncertainty in the relations between some scientists (particularly those in the field of astronomy), the ASO and COSSA. By 1992 some Australian astronomers were criticising the National Space Program for failing to promote the development of space astronomy and the creation of an associated database. They called for the creation of a completely independent and professional space agency that would directly employ engineers and scientists, oversee contracts and maintain a space database with international collaboration. The remote sensing community, on the other hand, has generally expressed itself as being satisfied with the support that it has received from government for research in this field.

support programs, while space science should become a possible priority for funding within general science programs. As such, this report's thrust was quite contrary to the philosophy expressed by the Expert Panel, and the government was required to make a decision as to which of the reports it would follow in establishing the direction of Australia's space policy.

The government ultimately accepted the recommendations of the Expert Panel's report for an ongoing National Space Program and decided to replace the Australian Space Board with a statutory body, the Australian Space Council (ASC), supported by an enhanced Space Office within DITAC (which in mid 1993 became the Department of Industry, Technology and Regional Development). The ASC mission statement is: to secure for Australia net benefits from the development and use of space-related science, technology and industry. In March 1993 the government announced the membership of the ASC, which reflects a wider range of interests than its predecessor. Chaired by Dr Don Watts, who has diverse expertise as an adviser to governments on science and technology matters and a distinguished academic background, the ASC membership includes executives from space industry companies, scientific advisers and government departments with a strong space interest. The Executive Director of the Australian Space Office is also a member of the Council.

In mid 1993 Australia appeared to be on the verge of another renaissance of government support for space activities. Recognis-ing the potential cost to this country of access to satellite data and space-based services, the Minister for Science and Small Business, Chris Schacht, outlined a program for Australian space activities in the 1990s that includes the development and manufacture of instrumentation to fly on international satellites, the construction of an all-Australian satellite, and the establishment of launching services using locally made or imported rockets. The minister indicated that he expected the ASC to take a more active role in space activities, managing the National Space Program as a private enterprise, and not merely providing advice to government. The ASC has been given the task of developing a five-year plan, to be updated annually, for the implementation of this revitalised National Space Program.

However, despite the establishment of the ASC, very little additional funding for space activities has been provided, due to prevailing economic conditions. Hence the ASC budget remains at $7 million plus $2.6 million for running costs.

The National Space Program is scheduled for review again in 1997-98 to evaluate its achievements and develop appropriate recommendations for the future shape of the program for consideration by the government at that time. Perhaps by then, Australian space science and industry will have developed further and be involved with many new and exciting projects, some of which will be described in the next chapter. The potential exists for significant and productive involvement in international collaborative efforts to benefit the future of Australia.

MR ROBERT SOMERVAILLE *was Chairman of the Australian Space Board from its inception. A lawyer with a professional interest in aerospace law, he has also served on the Boards of the ABC and OTC and is Chairman of the Board of one of Australia's leading space companies. He comments on Australia's space future in light of the 1992 reviews of the National Space Program.*

I believe that unless we have an effective national space program, which includes a need to review policy from time to time, Australia will lag behind most of the advanced or semi-advanced nations in the world. It would be a handicap from which we would never be able to recover and we would be a second-class nation in space research and industrial development.

The Australian government has accepted the broad thrust of the recommendations by the Expert Panel on the evaluation of the National Space Program. Basically, I think you can say that the Australian Space Office and the Australian Space Board got a tick for the work which had been done. There is no dramatic change in the thrust or direction recommended by the Expert Panel: they have said, 'You are on the right track but you have to have a coordinating body.' That is why they have recognised that the creation of an Australian Space Council, which may evolve to a Space Agency in due course, is necessary. The ASC is to involve, as a matter of statutory base, government departments which are relevant in the space field, plus industry, universities, research agencies and representatives of the science community and academia. In other words, the intention will be to put them all together.

In the past, the Australian Space Board has recommended to the government the national space policy and developed a national space program which, for funding purposes, needed the approval of the budget process each year. Most of the projects the ASB has been involved in have been long lead-time matters, requiring the commitment of government to a continuation of the funding to enable these programs to be satisfactorily achieved. You are much better off if you have a budget provision which is related solely to that particular agency or council, rather than what has happened in the past. As part of DITAC we relied on the funding for that department and each of the divisions was keen to get its cut of the overall pie. So there was always the matter of compromise and there are occasions, of course, when the compromise doesn't give you the result that you desire in formulating a program.

For that reason it has been quite impossible for the ASB and the ASO to embark on programs as ambitious, for instance, as the revitalisation of Woomera, because such a project cannot be financed from the recurrent expenditure of the National Space Program. It requires the additional allocation of resources: you've

got to satisfy the government that such expenditure is for the national benefit and that there is a national priority in making that expenditure.

The BIE Report, which was done concurrently with the Report of the Expert Panel, was not as positive as the report by the Expert Panel. But the BIE had no particular input with regard to the experience and knowledge of the space industry or space activities generally. It is very hard when you are looking at a project where you cannot measure its dollars and cents and tangible assured benefits. These people are economists: if Australia took the attitude that for every dollar you put in a program, you must have a measured reward out of each dollar, nothing would get done in Australia for the future. It is as simple as that.

I don't mean this to be a scathing criticism of the BIE—they have their work to do—but they do necessarily have to relate their findings to a close examination on clear economic grounds and the benefits must be tangible. The potential benefits are not something that they are involved in.

The Space Council replaces the Australian Space Board and will oversee the management of the Space Office which will continue, not necessarily in its present form, but in a significantly simpler format. In future the ASO will be the executive arm of the Australian Space Council. It will have its own budget, allocated direct to it as a unit. One of the things we found very difficult to do in the Australian Space Office and Board was to recruit the specialist personnel which you need if you are going to get involved in ambitious projects requiring special skills. A lot of money therefore has been spent on consultancies, because that has been the only way to get the body of expert opinion to focus on a particular aspect or a particular project.

The new ASO will be strengthened by the recruitment of specialists in different areas, which will be particularly important if a more ambitious program than we have been able to get so far comes into being. Because we have not had the funding or the assurance of funding which enables you with confidence to get into a major continuing project, it has been a stop and go process over the last five years. That situation is not conducive to the establishment of a national space program which, as a matter of policy, will project Australia into a new dimension.

The funding recommendations of the Expert Panel, so far, have not been accepted by the government. The government has been virtually saying, 'Well, let's wait and see how we get on with this new invention [the ASC].' I think what the government wants to do at the moment, because of tremendous calls on its finances, is to wait and see if the National Space Program develops along the predetermined lines in accordance with the plan. The ASC will be a tremendously comprehensive body and it will have commitment attached to it. So far, with the ASB, we have not had commitment. We have had observers at our meetings from the Department of Transport and Communications, from the CSIRO, who are obviously closely involved in space activities, from the Department of Defence and from ACRES, but they only represent departments without a commitment themselves. What we are looking for is commitment and a program which will require the active adherence and commitment of different government departments—that once decisions are made, they will have the commitment to go ahead and finish them off. That is of great importance.

The ASB had no sanctions whatsoever. It was an advisory body and without muscle, if one could call it that. So I think that the funding is much more assured than it was, but the level of funding is going to require the persuasive ability of the Space Office plus the ability of the Chairman of the Australian Space Council, to be able to persuade the government that future projects are worthy of support. In the past we have been unable to obtain special funding for major projects, because the government was not committed. Massive investment is required if you want to get into the space industry and that's why local industry has been slow in responding to the development of an Australian space industry. To do it properly means you have got to have programs which will enable you to amortise your investment over an acceptable period of years. None of the programs so far has been able to do this.

Now I hope that the Australian Space Council will ensure that the ad hoc aspects of space programs will disappear and be replaced by a progressive movement into project work, which

**Sounding rocket launch facilities at Woomera in the 1960s. Will Woomera be the site of a new Australian spaceport in the '90s?**

ensures that the national benefit is there. This requires international cooperation, access to world markets, access to technology we may not have in Australia and the tremendous ability of Australians to adapt technology. It is the marriage of all those ingredients which will produce a sound and viable space industry for Australia.

For the future, I think that we have to concentrate on the areas in which we have plenty of ability to hold our own at international level. I would like to see Woomera up and running, as it will be the catalyst for further development of the Australian space industry. I'd like to see the SCRAMJET technology proceed and more Australian participation internationally. Remote sensing offers unique opportunities for the world and Australia is in a unique position to benefit from further involvement in remote sensing projects. The benefits to Australia from Cape York would be a catalyst for major development for Australia's space industry and civil engineering. The development of mobile communications and the development, for that purpose, of small communications satellites are also providing Australia with a unique opportunity to have a position within the small satellite field which entitles it to international recognition. You have got to ensure that the national benefits are clearly observable and we are working on that aspect now.

# CHAPTER 9

# FINAL FRONTIER: Space futures and opportunities

The Queensland Mach 20, an Australian hypersonic aerospace plane proposal which would use locally developed SCRAMJET technology.

What is the future for Australian space activities? Over the last decade this country has developed considerable expertise in certain areas of space-related technology. With government support for the new National Space Program recommended in 1992, Australia has many opportunities to develop a vibrant space program that would utilise its strengths and capabilities and meet the needs of the nation in industrial development, communications, remote sensing, meteorology and space science.

## INDUSTRIAL DEVELOPMENT

Although no Australian company could currently compete as a prime contractor on international satellite programs, local firms, with their high production quality standards, could join international space consortia, to participate in space projects and further enhance their space qualification and capabilities. Opportunities for commercial enterprises are growing in a number of space-related fields, including communications, transportation, position location applications, financing and insurance, payload processing and spaceport safety (if Australia should proceed to develop the space launch capabilities currently proposed). Australia could participate in any of these areas, utilising its specific space industry skills and geographical advantages to further its involvement in world space activities.

Opportunities exist within the satellite communications field for adroit government use of the leverage it obtains when purchasing high-cost technology items overseas in order to secure contracts for space and other services to Australia. The government could also use the strength of its financial contributions to both INTELSAT and INMARSAT to lobby for greater Australian participation in the construction of their satellites.

Australian companies could also capitalise on their specific areas of expertise by developing products designed to fit specific international market niches, some of which are outlined below. The two current proposals to develop space launch facilities within Australia would also provide a significant boost to many sections of local industry, if they proceed.

## SATELLITE COMMUNICATIONS AND POSITIONAL SYSTEMS

Australia is already a significant customer for satellite communications and positional services, with its national satellite system, its participation in INTELSAT and INMARSAT, and its use of navigation satellites and the emergency search and rescue systems.

Australia's expertise in the development of satellite ground stations and reception antennas has considerable commercial

### COMMUNICATIONS FROM LEO—MOBILE SATELLITE SYSTEMS

Unlike satellites in geostationary orbit, which remain fixed above a particular spot on the Earth, satellites in Low Earth Orbit (approximately 200–5000 kilometres) quickly pass over and out of the line of sight of any single location. Because of this they require complex tracking and control systems and this rendered them unsuitable for communications use until relatively recently.

However, the development of powerful computing and signal processing technologies in the 1980s has made the use of LEO satellites for communications more feasible in the 1990s and an attractive idea for the development of global systems for mobile communications. Instead of using large, very expensive geostationary communications satellites, the new mobile satellite concepts propose to use small, relatively inexpensive light satellites, which can be launched reasonably cheaply. Constellations, or groups, of LEO satellites are planned to form networks in which a number of satellites would occupy different positions in each of a number of different orbits. This would mean that there would always be at least one satellite in the line of sight of any location on Earth, thus overcoming the main drawback of LEO.

LEO communications satellite systems, which would orbit at 420–3000 kilometres, have been proposed using constellations of 12–77 satellites for voice, data transmission, messaging services and emergency communications. At least ten different proposals were put forward for systems in the early 1990s, perhaps the best known of which is Motorola's Iridium system, which originally planned to use 77 satellites (with 11 satellites in each of 7 orbital planes) in 760-kilometre orbits. Using small, hand-held terminals, not unlike current cellular phones, Iridium users would be able to utilise this system to call anywhere on Earth, because the satellite would connect with the public telephone networks around the world.

In addition to providing communications services, LEO satellites could also provide positional services, by taking advantage of the Doppler effect inherent in a LEO system to calculate the location of the user's terminal in relation to the satellite. The proposed Globalstar network is just one LEO system intending to offer a positioning system as part of its communications services. This opens a lucrative market for terminals combining communication and location facilities, both areas of technology in which Australia has expertise.

The large numbers of small satellites required for LEO satellite systems also mean the opening of an important opportunity for light satellite launch services, both to put the initial satellite constellations into orbit and to place replacement satellites into the systems over time. Current geostationary launch vehicles are not well suited to the requirements of LEO systems, and the launch requirements of these satellites could present another opportunity for Australia to provide specialised lightsat launch services. Australia's expertise in the Telemetry, Tracking, Command and Monitoring (TTC&M) field could also be utilised to provide the tracking and control systems that will be needed for these satellite constellations.

potential. OTC began producing its own satellite ground stations in the 1980s and has already won many contracts to provide ground stations and telecommunications systems development in the South Pacific, South-East Asia and parts of the CIS. As the burgeoning economic powerhouse of the Asia–Pacific rim develops further, increased opportunities will exist for Australia to become a major supplier of satellite ground stations and other telecommunications equipment.

Australia has become one of the first countries in the world to introduce national L-band mobile satellite communications, via the second generation Optus satellite. L-band mobile satellite communications can supplement and complement the existing cellular mobile phone networks by providing mobile communications in those areas not serviced by terrestrial cellular systems. Australia is taking the initiative to become a world leader in this field by being the first country to develop and sell L-band mobile satellite communications terminals and antennas.

Two consortia of Australian industry and researchers, assisted by funding from the National Space Program, are already devel-

oping mobile satellite terminals and antennas with the objective of capitalising on the world satellite service market which is expected to develop through the increasing use of mobile satellite communications systems. Thus Australia's growing expertise in mobile communications technology has the potential to provide significant export income through the development of satellite-based mobile communications and GPS receivers.

The real growth of opportunity in this field will come with the development of global mobile satellite systems which provide the overseas markets for locally developed and manufactured mobile satellite equipment. INMARSAT has introduced the first global L-band mobile system and Telstra is working with an international consortium, which includes France and Canada, to develop an INMARSAT system which offers worldwide mobile communications to the aviation industry. As INMARSAT expands its range of mobile services, there are increased opportunities for Australian involvement in equipment development.

Another opportunity will be the use of small Low Earth Orbit (LEO) satellites in a constellation to provide global mobile

**The Iridium satellite system will use a constellation of small satellites to provide global mobile communications. It is one of many similar systems proposed in recent years for development in the latter half of the 1990s.**

communications coverage. There are a number of proposals for systems of this type, such as Iridium, Starsys and Odyssey, which would require large numbers of light satellites in LEO to provide continuous communications. Australian-designed antennas and mobile terminals could service these systems and Australia is also geographically well placed to benefit from the need for launch services which these systems will require. South Australia is particularly interested in the opportunities provided by the lightsat market and aims to have a National Space Industry and Research Complex operating by 1995. This facility would focus on the development of lightsat. It would be based around the Australian aerospace companies already in the state and its two SIDCs, the Centre for Space Engineering and the Centre for Signal Processing.

In addition to the satellite mobile capabilities of the Optus satellites, Australia could also develop its own lightsat, a 'store and forward' LEO communications satellite that would receive L-band signals from ground stations as it passes over and then transmit them directly to a ground station, or to another satellite (such as the Optus and INMARSAT spacecraft) for relay to the Earth. A system like this, using UHF (ultra high frequency) terminals, would have considerable applications for low-cost data gathering as well as search and rescue use. Applications include utility meter readings, meteorological and environmental data gathering, electronic funds transfer, store inventory management, general data retrieval, mailgrams, and voice data services such as the time and weather.

One proposal for an Australian 'store and forward' system already under development is the Remote Area Satellite Service (RASS). With an Australian-designed communications lightsat to be launched from a revitalised Woomera, the RASS system proposes using a small polar orbiting satellite at an altitude of 1000 kilometres for data communications with sensors located in remote areas. These sensors would be used to measure environmental data such as plant growth, water levels in dams and creeks, rainfall and wind speeds, and also to monitor bushfires and other events. As the RASS satellite passed over, the data would be relayed to it, for transmission to a ground station.

The construction of such a satellite would considerably enhance Australia's space industry capability in communications satellite construction. Australian industry could also look to utilising its expertise in microwave components, antenna design, and satellite navigation, not only on an Australian satellite, but also for the world market. The RASS system itself could be utilised beyond Australia, if the satellite constellation were suitably expanded. As the Earth rotates beneath a satellite in polar orbit, a RASS constellation could service Africa, South America, Siberia or northern Canada, providing additional market opportunities for the system and its Australian-designed hardware.

## SPACEPORT AUSTRALIA—WOOMERA LIVES!

Since Woomera first served Australia as a launch facility, it has been proposed that Australia should maintain and expand its role in this space service industry. Although Australia lost its space launch capability after the initial wind-down of the Woomera rocket range, the late 1980s saw two serious proposals to establish new facilities to satisfy part of the global demand for space launches: to build a launch facility at Cape York in far north Queensland and to renovate and revitalise Woomera. Both these proposals provide considerable opportunities for the development of Australian space activities in the 1990s.

Since 1985, the Woomera range has been used for an average of ten weeks a year for such tasks as tracking, Global Positioning System tests, explosive tests, vehicle and missile tests. Due to the high cost of maintaining the range, the Minister for Defence Support announced a proposal for the commercialisation of Woomera in early 1989. The new proposal sought to find a commercial developer to meet the cost of maintaining and developing the range to service new markets, both military and non-military. Initially it was thought that the range might be redeveloped as a major facility offering air combat manoeuvring, electronic warfare and advanced bombing test facilities, missile testing and rocket launching on a commercial basis to military forces in the Asia-Pacific region.

One of the plans put forward for the revitalisation of Woomera involved the reactivation of the rocket launching facilities to provide the basis of a light satellite launch service, using an Australian-designed launch vehicle, to take advantage of the market that was seen to be developing for this type of launch. One Australian group, Australian Launch Vehicles (ALV) of Adelaide, saw that Woomera offered considerable potential as a launch site for polar orbiting LEO satellites and proposed both the redevelopment of the facilities there and the development of an Australian rocket to provide the launch service.

In the ALV proposal, the successful revitalisation of Woomera was based on securing at least part of the launch contract for the Iridium series of satellites. Unfortunately, the Iridium opportunity did not eventuate as the Motorola company decided to delay its appointment of a launch service supplier and the ALV group decided not to pursue the project further.

Although the attempt to commercialise the Woomera facility seems to have failed, with the RAAF now in control of the range, the impetus towards the revitalisation of Woomera, at least as a space launch facility, has not been not lost. The Southern Launch Service (SLS) consortium was formed in 1991 to continue where the ALV proposal left off, planning for the development of lightsat launch facilities at Woomera. Composed of three Australian space companies, Auspace, British Aerospace Australia and

**ELDO launchpad 6A at Woomera, scrapped and partially demolished in the 1970s. The 6B launchpad may yet be rebuilt, if future plans to use Woomera as a satellite launching facility come to fruition.**

Hawker de Havilland, with the backing of the South Australian state government, the SLS group believes that Woomera has many advantages. It is an existing and internationally regarded launch range suited to polar orbits. A stable site and close to Adelaide, it has considerable existing infrastructure. It is also a good location, because of its favourable weather, for the recovery of re-entry capsules used in microgravity experiments. In addition, it is regarded as complementary to the Cape York project for equatorial orbiting satellites, should that proposal proceed. Using its proposed Southern Launch Vehicle (SLV), the consortium, which in 1993 changed its name to Space Australia, plans to offer launch services tailored to four market areas: LEO communications satellites, small remote-sensing satellites, microgravity work and space research.

One of the three major space reports of 1992 was a Senate Standing Committee report on developing satellite launching facilities in Australia and the role of government (see chapter 8). The committee recommended increased government support in terms of assistance to the SLV project, reviewing the future of Woomera, and revitalised organisation of space policy in Australia. The report of the Expert Panel also indicated that the government should give further consideration to the revitalisation of Woomera.

Another proposal to reutilise the Woomera range involves designating parts of the range area as potential landing sites for emergency landings from the international space station FREE-DOM, or a combined MIR/FREEDOM complex. Although FREEDOM would be regularly serviced by the US Space Shuttle, an Assured Crew Return Vehicle (ACRV) would be permanently attached to it to ensure that there is a capability for the crew to return to Earth in an emergency, and the CIS SOYUZ-TM ('union') spacecraft has been chosen to fulfil this role initially. Currently, a SOYUZ-TM spacecraft is permanently attached to the MIR space station for this purpose.

However, unlike the reusable Shuttle, the SOYUZ-TM does not touch down on a runway but 'hard lands' on the ground, with the landing shock cushioned by parachutes and retro-rockets. Because this method of re-entry is imprecise, the Soyuz craft requires a clear landing area of at least 30 square kilometres, to avoid the possibility of it coming down slightly off course and crash-landing into a populated site.

Due to the orbital path of the space station, suitable landing sites are limited and none at all are available in the US. Consequently, the Woomera range is a prime location to act as a re-entry landing area in the case of an emergency onboard the space

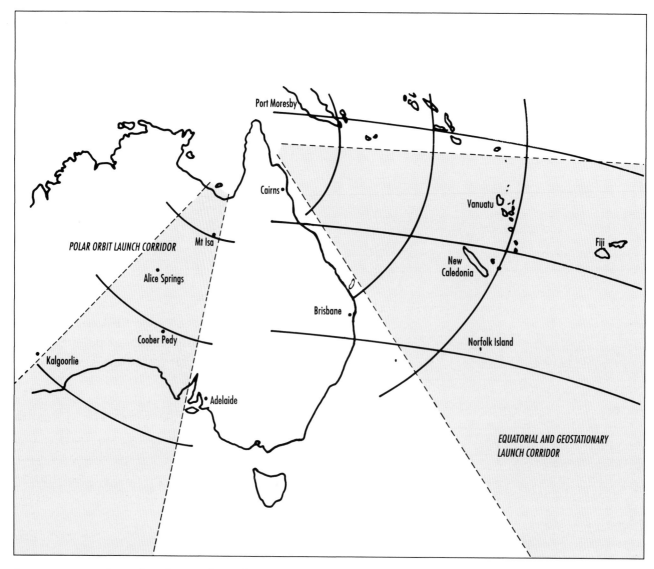

**From a spaceport located on Cape York satellites can be launched into both geostationary and polar orbits. Geostationary satellites would be launched out over the sea, while polar satellites would reverse the old satellite trajectories from Woomera and fly over the old rocket range in a southerly direction.**

station. Its selection as the designated landing site would provide further impetus for the rejuvenation of the range and its facilities. It would allow Australia to play an important service role in world space activities again.

The proposed German–Japanese Express program for recoverable microgravity research vehicles also envisages using the Woomera range as a landing area. This venture would use a small self-contained Japanese rocket to launch the Express carrier with its cargo of experiments. After up to five days in space, the carrier would re-enter the Earth's atmosphere, landing in Australia, so that the experimental equipment could be recovered.

Given the international interest in using Woomera for space-related activities, a refurbishment of facilities would have the potential to serve both national defence interests and commercial uses. The novel and exciting project to revitalise Woomera as a launch site would facilitate Australia's move back into the mainstream of world space activities and provide developmental opportunities for local space industry and high technology industry generally.

It is, however, disappointing to note that none of the preceding proposals has given consideration to the land rights claims of the Kokatha people. The revitalisation of the range is likely to continue to restrict the Kokatha's access to their traditional lands, unless provisions are made to recognise their tribal land rights. It is to be hoped that the supporters and proponents of Woomera's revival will work cooperatively with the Kokatha to establish an equitable recognition of their claims, while allowing Australia's space development to continue. The 1992 Mabo land rights decision of the High Court of Australia, which recognised for the first time the prior claims of indigenous people to their land, may have significant ramifications for the Kokatha people's land rights claims and Woomera's redevelopment, but the outcome could not be anticipated at the time of writing.

## SPACEPORT AUSTRALIA—THE CAPE YORK COMMERCIAL SPACEPORT

Preceding the proposals for the revival of Woomera, an international commercial spaceport was proposed for the Cape York area of far north Queensland in 1986, to take advantage of the area's geographical advantages for launching geostationary satellites. In the 1980s geostationary satellites provided the majority of commercial launch service business and the proposed spaceport's location in proximity to the equator was therefore an important factor: the closer a launch site is to the equator, the easier it is to place a geostationary satellite into orbit, because of the added 'push' given to the launch vehicle by the Earth's rotation. Because of this it is possible for a rocket to launch larger payloads, or make considerable fuel savings, when using a launch site that is near the equator.

In the mid 1980s, when the spaceport was first proposed by Hawker de Havilland Technical Services Director Mr Stanley Schaetzel, there was a shortage of commercial satellite launch services (due partly to the Shuttle CHALLENGER accident and the failure of both US Titan and Delta rockets in the same period). Consequently several proposals were put forward for commercial spaceports in various parts of the world. The Cape York location had an advantage over most of the other proposed sites in that it was not troubled by either geological or economic instability, unlike Indonesia, Brazil or Hawaii.

In 1987, with the support of the National Committee on Space Engineering of the Institution of Engineers, Australia, an in-depth feasibility study of the proposal to establish an international commercial spaceport at Cape York began. Sponsored by the Queensland government, the study assessed possible orbits, launch vehicles and payloads, site locations, and environmental, economic, legal and commercial matters. It suggested that a commercial operation could be established for a cost of $1 billion. This meant that the Cape York Spaceport would have to capture at least a quarter of the world commercial launch market in order to become profitable. Although a key aspect of the proposal was to serve overseas private launch vehicle companies by offering a cheap, deregulated launch facility, open to all comers, federal government commitment was also required, as certain international space legal agreements require Commonwealth support.

Two companies formed in 1987 to undertake more detailed feasibility research into the venture. The Cape York Space Agency (CYSA), which became totally owned by Essington Developments Ltd, representing a consortium of more than 30 engineering, financial and supporting companies, completed a two-year study focusing on the establishment of a major spaceport, defence and tourist facility located on the eastern side of Cape York. The CYSA study concluded that the venture was commercially viable without government support or reliance on any military payloads or tourist complex, considering Western satellite launch requirements alone. But it would only be viable with a marketable rocket launcher to offer to potential clients, rather than user-supplied vehicles.

The second company considering the Cape York proposal was the Australian Spaceport Group (ASG), comprising BHP, Bond Corporation, Comalco, Aussat and Martin Marietta (a major supplier of US launch vehicles). Unlike the CYSA study, which envisaged a long-term development with the spaceport commencing operations in the mid 1990s, the ASG followed a shorter timeframe, examining the near-term prospect of constructing a launch site on the Cape's west side near Weipa. Unlike the CYSA group, they concluded that a spaceport was not viable and terminated their interest in the project.

Despite ASG's negative assessment, the CYSA remained convinced of the feasibility of the project if a suitable launch vehicle could be identified and provided. In 1988 the CYSA signed an agreement with the Soviet space agency Glavkosmos for the purchase of Soviet Zenit rockets in a deal which included the training of Australian operators in launch procedures. This was the first time that a Western nation had completed such a deal with Glavkosmos. The Zenit rocket is a commercial version of the highly reliable Soviet/Ukrainian Tsyklon ('cyclone') launch vehicle, a three-stage rocket fuelled with liquid oxygen and kerosene, capable of placing a payload of up to 2200 kilograms into geostationary orbit. The Zenit rockets would be purchased from the CIS and assembled, integrated and launched from the spaceport by an Australian launch crew.

In late 1989 the federal and Queensland state governments announced full non-financial support for the project, provided that environmental and other impact studies presented satisfac-

### CAPE YORK SPACEPORT—THE PERCEIVED BENEFITS

The proponents of the spaceport considered that there would be many benefits to the nation in the construction of the facility, which would provide offset contracts to local industry. Such work would include ground transport infrastructure, safety and computer systems, propellant supply and ground tracking stations. According to the 1987 feasibility study, a spaceport operating on Australian soil would generate a new pro-technology attitude that would stimulate national industries.

The spaceport was generally conceived not just as a launchpad and control centre, but as a combination of major elements including an Air Force base, seaport and tourist complex. It was felt that only with these combined elements could the project be viable, and they were perceived as valuable assets in opening up the largely undeveloped areas of far northern Queensland.

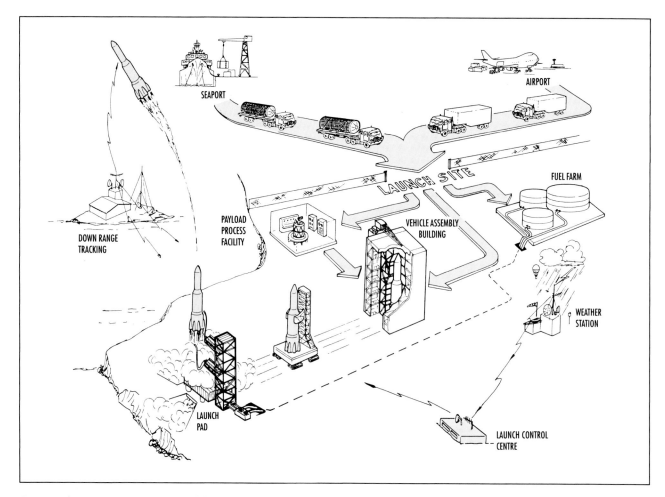

**Cape York Spaceport as envisaged by the CYSA, showing the assembly, launch and control facilities.**

tory results. The CYSA also reached agreement with the US aerospace company United Technologies Corporation, contracting it as program manager for deployment of the Zenit rockets combined with payloads developed in Western nations. In mid 1990 the US State Department legislated to permit such an operation (which may have been considered to contravene US regulations governing technology transfer if American-built satellites were to be launched on Soviet rockets), to the concern of US rocket manufacturers, who opposed the use of lower-cost Soviet rockets by Western satellite agencies.

### Cape York Spaceport—into the 1990s

By 1990, purchase of 60 000 hectares of land was proceeding at the chosen site at Temple Bay, and an environmental impact study had begun for the project. The CYSA expected to use only 200 hectares for the launch site, and had shelved proposals for a tourist complex, aside from a small town for the expected 700 site staff and their families. Although the proposed RAAF base had been relocated further to the west, the CYSA proposed a long aircraft runway to handle cargoes and personnel, with a sea barge ramp for bringing in spacecraft and equipment by water.

The CYSA expected a rocket launch rate of five per annum, commencing with two in 1995. This, it was claimed, would bring significant benefits to Australia through export income and import replacement, plus high-technology opportunities. According to the CYSA, the capital cost of the project would be $323 million in ground equipment leases to Glavkosmos, plus $277 million infrastructure investment: a total of $600 million. Annual operating costs would be $297 million. The total cost was not far short of the $1 billion estimate that had been made in 1987.

During 1990-91 the CYSA's parent company, Essington, experienced financial difficulties due to the recessionary economic climate, and work on the Cape York project slowed to a halt. Progress on the environmental impact study ceased, as did discussions with Aboriginal communities. The CYSA withdrew from further negotiations with Glavkosmos at the end of 1990 and a liquidator was finally appointed to it in October 1991. As a result of the CYSA's difficulties, the federal government, wishing to maintain the viability of the project, invited parties interested in participating in the spaceport project to come forward in October 1990. Some two dozen groups expressed their interest to government.

In February 1991 the Australian Space Office commissioned the Australian Industry Development Corporation (AIDC) to undertake an independent pre-feasibility study of the Cape York project, which would provide information that could be placed before potential alternative investors. The AIDC's report was released in November 1991 and confirmed that the project could be profitable on reasonable business and investment assumptions, although at a much higher investment cost than that claimed by the CYSA.

After the failure of the CYSA, one of the companies that had expressed interest in the Cape York Space Port, Space Transportation Systems Ltd (STS), was granted an exclusive mandate by the Queensland government as the preferred developer for the Cape York project. The federal government agreed to recognise this status on condition that STS achieved a series of developmental milestones, in terms of securing finance and suitable contractual support, for its $800 million project. Unfortunately, due to the prevailing economic climate, STS was unable to meet the condi-

tions imposed by government and in the end faltered, losing its preferred developer status in late 1992.

The Australian government then invited other consortia to take on the project, and currently it is in the hands of Cape York International Spacelaunch Ltd (CYISL), a group representing six companies with interests in infrastructure and launch site development, plus facilities and logistics management. In March 1993 CYISL was reported to have secured investment capital, although no formal announcements were made to indicate the level of investment funding that had been achieved. The consortium was also reported to be assessing the world launch market and its potential growth in order to confirm that the project was financially viable. Due to the many issues surrounding the Temple Bay site, CYISL has investigated other possible sites in the Cape York region and had not, as of June 1993, indicated the final location of its proposed spaceport. It was also reported to be considering other launch vehicles as alternatives to the Zenit, should the political situation in the CIS make it unavailable.

**The Ukrainian Zenit rocket, seen here on its launch cradle before being raised into position for firing, was originally chosen as the launch vehicle to be used at the Cape York Spaceport.**

Although the Expert Panel report recognised the potential for the nation of the Cape York Spaceport, it did not recommend that it be made a priority under the new National Space Program, since the project is viewed as a commercial, not a government, undertaking. However, if the spaceport proceeds it could place Australia at the forefront of commercial satellite launch services and, in 1993, this opportunity attracted other consortia into the space launch market. Apart from the CYISL project, a separate Cape York facility has been proposed, as well as a launch site near Eucla in Western Australia (ironically, one of the early locations suggested for Woomera). In addition, Space Transportation Systems re-entered the picture in April 1993 with a proposal to establish a commercial spaceport on an island off the coast of Papua New Guinea. As of June 1993, no further information was available on these new proposals, but all offer the potential of the Cape York project, should they come to fruition.

Despite the setbacks, the spaceport's potential is still exciting, as no other country has yet established a fully commercial space launch facility. The ASO has estimated that the spaceport would offer the following benefits to Australia: 2700 jobs in the design, construction and operation of the spaceport; export earnings of $130 million per year; $400 million in economic growth; opportunities for the provision of flight hardware integration, testing and supply of sub-systems.

## THE AUSTRALIAN AND SOUTHERN LAUNCH VEHICLES

Many of the major spacefaring countries have a launcher program as an integral part of their space activities. With the demise of the ELDO program in this country and the close-down of our sounding rocket production, Australia lost its early launch capability, but the exciting possibilities of the Cape York Spaceport and the revival of Woomera open up new opportunities for the development of Australian launch vehicles.

Launch services and launch vehicles around the world have been designed to service the launch of large satellites into geostationary orbit. Launch vehicles like the ESA's Ariane, the CIS's Proton and the American Atlas and Delta launchers require large payloads to make their launches cost effective: they are not intended to serve the needs of the small satellite launch market. Consequently, in the late 1980s (particularly as potential LEO satellite systems began to be proposed), commercial groups in many countries, including Australia, recognised the opportunity that was present and began to develop lightsat launch vehicles to service the small satellite market.

In 1988 the Australian Launch Vehicle (ALV), a three-stage rocket combining local expertise with overseas components, was proposed to take advantage of the foreseen lightsat launch market.

## WILDCAPE NOT SPACECAPE

The Temple Bay site has been the cause of much controversy, with environmental groups expressing concern over damage to rainforest areas and the Great Barrier Reef, due to the exhaust products of spacecraft launch and possible launch accidents. Similarly, Aboriginal groups are also concerned about the effect of the spaceport development on tribal lands and sacred sites in the area.

The CYSA dismissed many of the environmentalists' concerns, claiming that much of the site had already been damaged by cattle farming and had lost any environmental or wilderness significance. They also cited the successful operation of Kennedy Space Centre in the US, which is surrounded by national park and has an excellent environmental record, as evidence that spaceports and wilderness areas can coexist in harmony.

However, the Environmental Impact Study, which would have assessed these conflicting claims and considered the concerns of the local Aboriginal community, remains unfinished at the time of preparation of this book, due to the slow progress of the project in recent years. Consequently the issues surrounding the environmental soundness of the Cape York project are still unresolved.

**Wildlife and spacecraft coexist at NASA's Kennedy Space Centre in Florida. Could the same coexistence occur at Cape York if the spaceport is developed?**

## CAPE YORK—A MISSED OPPORTUNITY?

Although the opportunities for Australian industry and the Australian economy offered by the Cape York Spaceport concept are considerable, there are many who now believe that the 'window of opportunity' is past and that Australia has lost the chance to develop a commercial geostationary launch service.

With the entry into the commercial launch market of China and the CIS, and the drop in demand for geostationary launch services now occurring due to the longer service life of satellites and the trend towards LEO satellite systems, some question whether the Cape York Spaceport could now establish itself as a commercially viable operation. The report of the Expert Panel actually recommended that, unless solid financial backing could be found for the project, the ASO cease to accord it any further priority assistance.

An Australian company, Australian Launch Vehicles Pty Ltd, was founded in May of that year, with major backing from the Transfield engineering group, to develop a satellite launch service using the ALV launcher. The ALV rocket was designed using proven foreign technologies and hardware, which allowed the development of a low-cost launcher that could carry one or two light satellites, weighing up to 1000 kilograms in total. The ALV company proposed to launch their rocket from a reactivated Woomera site, providing access to polar orbits.

Originally planning for project development to start in 1991, the ALV team sought to provide launch services for the proposed Motorola Iridium LEO communications system, which envisages the launch of many small communications satellites to provide services all over the globe. As Motorola did not choose the ALV proposal, Transfield and ALV decided by 1991 not to pursue the project further.

However, building on the ALV work, the Southern Launch Vehicle (SLV) has been proposed by a group of three space industry companies—Auspace, Hawker de Havilland and British Aerospace Australia—that have banded together to form the Space Australia consortium. The SLV has been designed to provide a lightsat launch service based on an affordable small rocket. It would serve the emerging international launch market for LEO spacecraft up to 1000 kilograms, which includes communications, positioning, remote sensing, space research and microgravity experimental satellites.

The 21 metre tall SLV is intended to be a low-cost, reliable launch vehicle which would require minimal infrastructure and support equipment. The design is for a three-stage rocket, with an additional post-boost propulsion stage which would actually

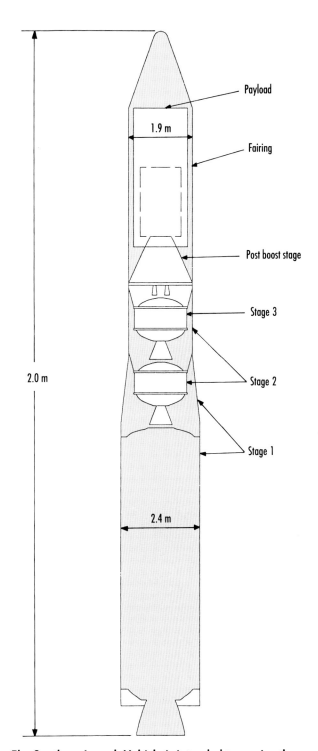

**The Southern Launch Vehicle is intended to service the lightsat launch market which is expected to eventuate over the next few years. It is planned to use existing hardware with a proven record of reliability.**

place the satellites in their required orbits. Proposals for the SLV include utilising cheap rocket hardware from the CIS, or combining purchased US rocket engines with an Australian fabricated body to create a vehicle adaptable for a range of launch services.

An important aspect of the SLV proposal is its intention to revitalise the Woomera range to place its satellites into orbit. One option proposes using the former ELDO pad 6B, which was never used for ELDO launches, as the SLV launchpad. The Space Australia group also intends to utilise other structures and facilities at Woomera to provide an integrated satellite processing and launch service.

In 1992 the total investment required by the project was estimated to be around $50 million. This figure included a project definition study, the development of a demonstration launch vehicle by 1994 and a protoflight launch vehicle in 1995, with commercial operations commencing in 1996. Since there is currently no purpose-built launcher like the SLV available to serve the lightsat market, some international interest has been received from major US aerospace companies.

The first two test launches of the SLV have been planned with the intention of providing a launch opportunity for Australian satellites, to aid local space industry development. The RASS satellite is proposed for the first test launch, which will qualify the key system elements of the launch vehicle and its ground control segment. The second test launch, which would qualify the system for operational applications, could potentially carry an Australian remote sensing payload, like GAMS (Global Atmospheric Methane Sensor) or the Imaging Spectrometer, or a second RASS satellite. Government support for the two demonstration launches has been sought and the Expert Panel recommended that funding for the proposal be considered favourably under the National Space Program when it is further developed.

## SCRAMJET TECHNOLOGY AND FUTURE LAUNCH SYSTEMS

Further in the future, however, standard rocket launch vehicles like the SLV may be replaced by spaceplanes, which will use special combination rocket-jet engines known as Supersonic Combustion Ramjets (SCRAMJETs) to take off and land like normal aircraft. Several designs are now under development and Australia is at the forefront of this technology due to the hypersonic research being undertaken at the University of Queensland.

Designs for SCRAMJET-powered aerospace planes like Britain's HOTOL, the US National Aero Space Plane (now under design development by NASA and the US Air Force), and the German-proposed SANGER two-stage reusable system, have been tested in Australia at the University of Queensland hypervelocity shock tunnel, which is the only facility in the world able to simulate real gas effects at hypersonic speeds. As it is also the only test facility in the world large enough to accommodate full-scale SCRAMJET engine models, the shock tunnel has made key contributions to SCRAMJET design theories.

In 1991 a proposal was put forward for an Australian SCRAMJET-powered expendable launch vehicle, the Queensland Mach 20, which would utilise Australian SCRAMJET exper-

### WHAT IS A SCRAMJET?

SCRAMJETs are air-breathing engines that draw their oxygen from the atmosphere, instead of carrying it with them, and operate at speeds between Mach 5 and Mach 20 (5–20 times the speed of sound). Because they do not need to carry supplies of oxygen in order to burn their fuel, SCRAMJETs provide considerable savings in launch weight, which is of crucial importance in determining the amount of payload that a launch vehicle can carry—the less fuel it has to carry, the more payload it can launch. SCRAMJETs are also environmentally clean, producing only water vapour.

Although other forms of propulsion are needed to raise a launch vehicle to supersonic velocity and to boost it at near orbital velocities (when the atmospheric oxygen has become too thin to enable a SCRAMJET to function), SCRAMJETs are very useful for the middle stages of a launch vehicle's flight and can help to reduce the size of the first- and third-stage engines required for those portions of flight when a SCRAMJET cannot itself be used.

tise and aviation skills to build a lightweight SCRAMJET vehicle. This would be a forerunner of future spaceplanes. Another innovative Australian proposal calls for the development of a hybrid vehicle which uses both SCRAMJET and rocket technology. It would replace the second stage of the conventional SLV launch vehicle with a SCRAMJET booster creating a more cost-effective rocket with a higher Australian industrial content.

The University of Queensland, WBM-Stalker Ltd and Australian Defence Industries are currently developing a SCRAMJET engine made of light, strong composite materials (like carbon fibre) that would be cheap enough to be considered expendable. An engine of this type would avoid the tremendous structural and material problems that are inherent in designing a reusable engine hardy enough to withstand the rigours of multiple flights. A prototype of this engine has already achieved the world's first 'flight' of a SCRAMJET. In May 1993 a scale version of the complete SCRAMJET engine was tested in the University of Queensland shock tunnel, achieving a velocity of over seven times the speed of sound. The test demonstrated that the engine could develop the forward thrust that would produce acceleration in flight and proved the validity of the design. This success paves the way for future developments, giving Australia a two-year lead on the rest of the world in this field.

With strong continued funding support from government, Australian SCRAMJET research could enable this country to claim about 25 per cent of the world space launch market by the turn of the century. Locally designed SCRAMJET engines may yet provide the power for an Australian light launch vehicle, or for overseas spaceplanes that would considerably reduce the travel time between Australia and the Northern Hemisphere.

## INSURANCE

Australia is already a small but active player in the space reinsurance business, offering launch insurance for rockets and satellites. Satellite owners and launch providers or operators must cover not only the loss or damage of their property, but also any damage caused by a launch accident or by a falling satellite, as UN agreements specify that the owners of spacecraft and rockets are responsible for making restitution for any damage caused by their craft or rockets.

Although the failure of a spaceflight can incur large insurance payouts, in the order of several hundred million dollars for each mission failure, space reinsurance ventures are not without profit. Currently, Australian insurers provide insurance against physical loss or damage to satellites, whether they are Australian or foreign-owned.

Should Australia revive its space launch capacity, there is a potential for large third-party liability claims to result, although such claims have been relatively rare to date. The re-entry of the SKYLAB space station over Western Australia in July 1979 could have resulted in considerable claims for damages had the station crashed into a heavily populated area. Fortunately, no apparent damage to life or property occurred, and no third-party claim

resulted. However, the possibility for damage and injury from a launch or re-entry mishap is always present, and Australia will undoubtedly expand its space insurance activities if the Cape York Spaceport or Woomera revival proceeds.

## SPACE SCIENCE

The recommendations of the Expert Panel that space science should form part of the Integrated National Space Program (with a recommended funding level of not less than 10 per cent of the space budget) have paved the way for an increase in Australian space science activities for the rest of this decade.

Currently, Australian scientists are guest investigators on a number of long-term space astronomy projects, many of which will continue to operate beyond the end of this decade. Australian astronomers have been highly successful in gaining access to observing time on the HUBBLE SPACE TELESCOPE. It is a tribute to Australian space astronomy that, in fact, Australian guest investigators have received the highest priority for observers outside NASA and the ESA, and have been allocated more observing time than either France or the UK. Australian observers are also working with the IUE (International Ultraviolet Explorer) satellite, the EXTREME ULTRA-VIOLET EXPLORER and the ROSAT X-ray and extreme ultraviolet telescope. In the future they will have access to the LYMAN ultraviolet space telescope when it is launched in 1999.

The support for space science given in the 1992 review of the National Space Program will hopefully encourage the establish

---

### SKYLAB WAS HERE

Contrary to a popular complaint at the time, NASA did not deliberately guide SKYLAB to crash down on Australia. NASA controllers had actually intended for the re-entering space station to come down in the Indian Ocean. However, when the station did not break up as expected on re-entry, this altered its descent path. Although much of it did fall into the ocean, some debris fell on Australia. Fortunately, there were no injuries or property damage—it is claimed that the only casualty of SKYLAB was a rabbit, which was killed by a piece of debris! When NASA scientists came to collect any pieces of SKYLAB that they could find, local authorities in Western Australia presented them with a fine for littering, as a joke.

**Fragments of the SKYLAB space station displayed in the Esperance Museum in Western Australia. Had these pieces landed in a built-up area, they could have caused tremendous damage and resulting claims for compensation.**

**A model of the RADIOASTRON satellite to which Australia is contributing an instrument. RADIOASTRON will form part of a gigantic VLBI radio telescope capable of very high resolution of remote radio sources in space.**

ment of a proposed guest investigator support program. This would enable Australian space scientists to take advantage of future opportunities, such as those presented by the AXAF (Advanced X-ray Astrophysics Facility) and SIRTF (Space Infrared Telescope Facility) space telescopes proposed for launch shortly after the year 2000.

Australia has already participated in space VLBI (Very Long Baseline Interferometry) studies and experiments and will, over the rest of this decade, be participating in two major space-based VLBI programs: the CIS's RADIOASTRON and Japan's VLBI Space Observatory Program. RADIOASTRON, due for launch in 1994, has wide international participation and Australian radio telescopes will work in conjunction with those of Canada, China, Germany, Britain, Italy, India, Hungary, Japan, the Netherlands, Poland, South Africa and the US in simulating a gigantic radio telescope with an effective diameter many times that of the Earth.

With its onboard 10-metre radio telescope linked to facilities on Earth, the RADIOASTRON satellite will be used to study remote space radio sources with very high temperatures. Australia's contribution to the satellite itself is a 1.7 GHz L-band radio receiver, one of four receivers that will operate at different wavelengths to detect radio signals from space. Designed and built by British Aerospace Australia and Mitec Ltd in conjunction with the CSIRO, the Australian RADIOASTRON receiver was one of the earliest projects funded by the Australian Space Office.

Like the RADIOASTRON mission, Japan's VSOP (VLBI Space Observatory Program) satellite (also called MUSES-B) will carry a 10-metre radio telescope into orbit which will then link with radio telescopes around the world, including the Parkes radio telescope and the Australia Telescope. Australian astronomers have participated in the detailed planning of the mission, which is to be launched in 1995. VSOP will also complement the

research being undertaken in the RADIOASTRON program. With the new emphasis on space science encouraged by the Expert Panel report, it is expected that Australian scientists will participate in the science programs to be conducted with both RADIOASTRON and VSOP.

Australia will also participate in these VLBI programs through a new tracking network which NASA is constructing to provide data acquisition facilities and linkages between the two spacecraft. A new 10-metre tracking dish will be built at the Tidbinbilla tracking station for these VLBI programs.

In addition to space astronomy, Australia has had a long involvement with solar-terrestrial physics (the study of the interrelationship between the Earth and the Sun) and has been participating since 1990 in the Solar-Terrestrial Energy Program (STEP), which is scheduled to continue until 1995. Australian scientists may also become involved with investigations of the atmosphere that will be conducted in the latter part of the 1990s from the Japanese Equatorial Radar, a high-powered radar, designed specifically for atmospheric research, to be located on the equator in Indonesia.

The Waves in Space Plasma (WISP) experiment, scheduled to fly on the Space Shuttle in January 1995, is among the many ground and space-based programs in this field in which Australia is participating. A joint US/Canada project, with a significant Australian contribution, WISP will carry out active experiments by transmitting controlled radio transmissions from the Shuttle, which will be monitored from the ground (in Australia and other locations around the world) to determine resulting plasma instabilities and ionospheric irregularities in the regions the signals pass through.

## REMOTE SENSING

Australia is a major user of satellite remote sensing data and currently accesses much of that information through its own local reception stations. However, the economic value of remotely sensed data is now widely recognised and there are strong indications that within the next ten years it will not be so freely available as at present. In future satellites may beam their data, via data relay satellites, back to their country of origin, from which possibly only processed, not raw, data will be available. This would greatly increase the cost of data products and would exclude Australian companies and institutions from the remote sensing value-added market for processing raw data images, a field in which Australia has considerable expertise.

Because it is vital for Australia to have direct access to remotely sensed data, the National Space Program proposed by the Expert Panel report stressed that Earth observation should be a clear priority in Australia's future space activities. In order to ensure its continuing access to data, Australia must consider ways in which

## AN AUSTRALIAN SPACE ASTRONOMY DATA CENTRE

Because of the number of large space telescopes already in orbit or due to be launched within the next ten years, there have been proposals for an Australian Space Astronomy Data Centre that would provide a national archival centre for the analysis and dissemination of space science data from NASA and ESA space missions. Such data are currently available without cost to internationally recognised archiving centres and the establishment of such a centre in Australia (while the data is freely available) would serve the needs of both basic scientific research and industry in this country.

The ready availability of scientific data would stimulate research and create opportunities in areas of space astronomy not currently developed in Australia. Local access to space data would also encourage local expertise in the manipulation and analysis of such data, which could generate new hardware and software for data handling, with potential commercial applications.

it can participate in remote sensing and meteorology satellites. Australia has already undertaken collaborative remote sensing projects with its participation in the ERS-1 and 2 satellites. These contributions give Australia ready access to ERS data and have established a strong credibility for Australian space industry with the ESA and the UK. In-principle commitment has now also been made to the Advanced Along Track Scanning Radiometer, a further development of the instrument already flown on the ERS satellites, which is due to fly on the ESA ENVISAT environmental satellite in 1998. Australia will be a joint owner of this instrument. It is the first time that Australia has invested at such a level in a major space instrument.

The development of remote sensing instruments, to be flown on either Australian-designed lightsats or the remote sensing satellites of other countries, is one way for Australia to maintain its access to necessary data. At present there are a number of instruments under development for use as airborne scanners on aircraft that could eventually be adapted for satellite remote sensing. The CSIRO-developed Atmospheric Pressure Sensor (APS) and the Global Atmospheric Methane Sensor (GAMS) are both potential remote sensing satellite payloads. The Airborne Volcanic Ash Detection System, developed by the CSIRO Division of Atmospheric Research as a prototype, would also be suitable for spacecraft deployment. Another CSIRO development, the Ocean Colour Scanner (OCS), could assist in the monitoring of the world's oceans, as could the DSTO-developed Laser Depth Sounder (LADS). Multi-spectral sensors already developed for airborne mineral exploration and the Imaging Spectrometer currently under development by the ASO, CSIRO and BHP also have the potential for space deployment.

Australia will hopefully continue to lead the world in the development of remote sensing data analysis systems, and there are opportunities for the nation to become more heavily involved with remote sensing training and education in the Asia-Pacific region. Australia has already participated in UN-sponsored remote sensing training programs in South-East Asia (which relies heavily on remote sensing technology for environmental monitoring due to the inaccessible nature of the terrain in many areas). Australia already serves the general education market in South-East Asia, with students coming here to study in many professions, ranging from architecture to medicine. There is considerable potential for Australia to market its excellent education courses in remote sensing, space engineering and related disciplines throughout the Asia-Pacific area, and to conduct training programs in other countries and in Australia.

## AUSTRALIA'S FUTURE IN SPACE

What is the future for Australian space activities? The foregoing brief survey of the potential available to Australia over the next decade indicates that the future is bright. With funding and support from a reinvigorated National Space Program, Australia could take advantage of many opportunities to develop and implement a vibrant space program that would utilise its special strengths and capabilities, meet the needs of the nation in the areas of industrial development, communications, remote sensing and space science, and propel the country back into the forefront of international space activities through the provision of launch services and niche-market space products.

## REMOTE SENSING AND GLOBAL CHANGE

Global change, the changes in the structure and functioning of the Earth's ecosystem over time scales ranging from decades to centuries, is a major focus of scientific research in the 1990s. Major international projects like the International Geosphere–Biosphere Project, the International Land Cover Project and NASA's Mission to Planet Earth are all concentrating upon studies of the Earth's environment and the changes that are taking place in it as a result of human activities.

It is primarily space-based remote sensing systems that have revealed the global changes occurring now, caused by the effects of overpopulation, energy resource depletion and climate change. Space-based environmental surveillance of the Earth will continue to increase in importance as the most appropriate way of monitoring

global change. Already there are indications that military intelligence and economic assessment agencies are transferring their interests to the complex study of environmental effects: it may be that the age of the military superpower is ending, to be replaced by the more challenging role of environmental superpower.

Australian scientists are already involved in all the important global change space missions currently underway or planned, thus assuring this country's access to their data and design information. With its experience in the development of software systems for analysing environmental data, and its growing expertise in designing environmental monitoring instruments, Australia can look forward to taking an active role in the global monitoring of environmental change.

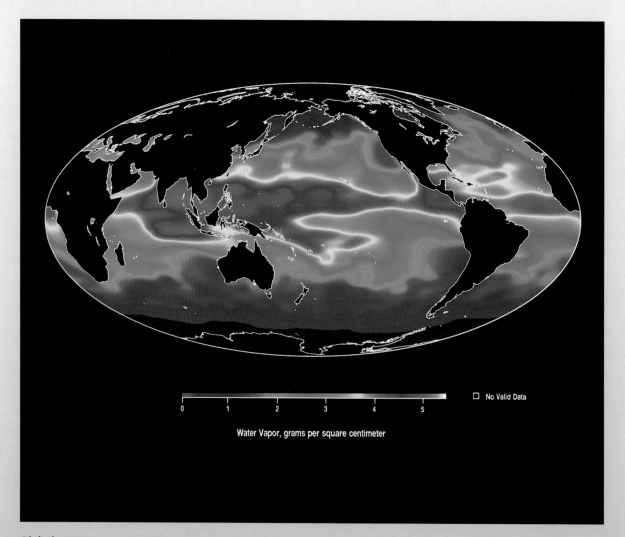

Water Vapor, grams per square centimeter

☐ No Valid Data

**Global water vapour content, important for understanding the role of the oceans in weather and climate change, as seen by the NASA/ESA TOPEX/POSEIDON satellite, one of the many environmental research satellites currently in orbit. Satellites have been monitoring the environmental health of our planet for more than 20 years, providing a database of information which is now being used to study global change as a result of human activity.**

## C O M M E N T A R Y

PROFESSOR RAY STALKER *is Australia's first Professor of Space Engineering based at the Department of Mechanical Engineering, University of Queensland. The pioneer of hypersonic shock tunnel technology and a world leader in SCRAMJET research, he comments on the value of hypersonic technologies to the future development of an Australian space program.*

Australia is a natural market for satellite operations, but domestic development of this market has not been feasible in the past because of the large scale of the space technology needed for its exploitation. However, it has lately become obvious that hypersonic technology, by contributing to the development of aerospace planes, can make it possible for us to satisfy our need for satellite services with an independent, affordable space program tailored to our own needs.

In terms of the values assigned by countries similar to our own, general civilian space operations are worth about $100 million a year to Australia, and at such a cost current space technology would afford us perhaps one launch a year, with reasonable launch economics. A space program based on one launch a year of a large satellite would be very difficult to manage, and is unlikely to satisfy the range of our needs. We need a program based on small satellites.

Until recently, it appeared that launch vehicle technology discriminated against the small satellite, and there was no solution to the Australian problem. However, no technology stands still, and in space technology new developments include the concept of 'micro-spacecraft' together with basic changes in launch technology.

This basic change in launch technology is centred around hypersonic technology, which is presently in the research laboratories, particularly in the US and Australia. The major development is a very simple engine, with no moving parts, described technically as a supersonic combustion ramjet, or more simply a 'SCRAMJET'. Like a conventional aircraft jet engine, it burns onboard fuel with air drawn from the atmosphere. However, it holds the promise of being able to operate at speeds approaching orbital velocity—six to eight times faster than any air-breathing engine has operated before.

By eliminating the need to carry onboard oxygen, this engine also allows a great reduction in the total amount of fuel which must be carried. Consequently the vehicle design is no longer dominated by the need to carry large stocks of onboard propellants. Because of that, small launch vehicles can be designed to be almost as efficient as large ones. Research on these engines has now reached the stage where enough is known to start planning development of SCRAMJETs for use in flight.

SCRAMJETs could be used to power the second stage of an Australian three-stage, expendable, light launch vehicle. The other two stages would use conventional rockets. Such a launch vehicle could be designed to place into orbit satellites which are only one-quarter of the mass of present satellites, without suffering a penalty in launch cost efficiency. It would break the present nexus between launch vehicle size and launch cost efficiency, making it possible to realise the smaller capital costs associated with smaller payloads and launch vehicles, without paying a penalty in launch cost per kilogram.

It becomes possible for Australian users to have, at a reasonable cost, dedicated satellites in orbits which are efficiently matched to their purpose. With satellites weighing a few hundred kilograms each, it is feasible for Australia to do its own research into the space environment near our own part of the world, to have its own mineral exploration satellites, to perform its own marine resource monitoring by satellite, to maintain its own search and rescue satellite, and so on. In short, it is possible to satisfy our growing need for satellite services with an independent, affordable space program.

## APPENDIX 1
### SPACE ADVOCACY SOCIETIES

A BRIEF HISTORY OF SPACE ADVOCACY SOCIETIES IN AUSTRALIA

Like people all around the world, Australians have been fascinated by the excitement and challenge of space exploration. Apart from two early rocketry societies in the 1930s, it is not known whether there were any space advocacy groups in Australia prior to the 1960s, when a small body was operating in Adelaide as the South Australian Group of the British Interplanetary Society. Around the same time, astronautical societies were formed at Melbourne and Monash Universities in Victoria, the University of Melbourne group eventually going on to produce the AUSTRALIS-OSCAR-5 amateur radio satellite.

The real growth of pro-space societies occurred in the early 1970s. At this time the wind-down of the activities at Woomera and the cancellation of the Apollo program initiated a groundswell of public response, leading to the formation of space advocacy societies whose aim was to promote space exploration and encourage a reinvigoration of the Australian (and American) space programs.

Early in 1972 members of the Melbourne University Astronautical Society formed a national body, the Astronautical Society of Australia (ASA), with branches in other states. In May 1973, the ASA held an aerospace congress in Melbourne and later became an Australian representative in the International Astronautical Federation (IAF), the international professional body in the field of space technology.

In 1975 the Western Australian branch broke away to become the Astronautical Society of Western Australia (ASWA). ASWA conducted the 1975 and 1977 Australian Astronautics Conventions in Perth, attracting international and Australian papers. Among its projects, the Society helped with the construction of the Mount Gungin Radio Observatory, and carried out a feasibility study for a planetarium in Perth. The ASWA joined the International Astronautical Federation in 1976, becoming the National Voting Member for Australia in 1978.

The university societies at Monash and the University of Melbourne continued until 1985. By 1976 the Monash University society had established a tracking station receiving weather satellite images, and produced a national magazine. In 1981 the inaugural meeting of the public Space Association was held in Melbourne. It later became the Space Association of Australia Inc (SAAI) and replaced the Monash and Melbourne University societies in 1985. The SAAI later joined the IAF and continues today as a small but active society promoting space through education programs, a radio show and other activities.

Small groups representing the US-based L-5 Society, which promoted space exploration and colonisation, were formed in Adelaide and Sydney in the late 1970s. With the amalgamation, in America, of the L-5 Society and the National Space Institute (NSI), another leading US pro-space group, to become the National Space Society (NSS), the Australian L-5 groups amalgamated with small local NSI chapters to become Australian chapters of the NSS.

Since the mid 1980s, the NSS has expanded rapidly and now has chapters in Sydney, Newcastle, Brisbane, Adelaide, Canberra, Perth and Melbourne. In 1990 the individual NSS chapters banded together to form the National Space Society of Australia (NSSA), the most active public space advocacy body in Australia today, catering to both professional and public space interests. The NSSA works actively to promote Australian space industry and business development, and public space education.

A number of independent space groups also arose in the 1980s. The Australian Space Education Association in Brisbane organised the Space Shuttle Science Contest for secondary school students in 1985, in which entrants designed experiments for Getaway Special canisters. The Sydney Space Association, which grew from the Sydney chapter of the L-5 Society in the early 1980s, has mounted a number of space education displays and activities. In 1986 it was responsible for bringing a Soviet cosmonaut to Australia as part of its Sydney Space Festival, to celebrate the 25th anniversary of the first person in space. It also operated a small Space Camp in 1988 and has held many other small symposia. In the mid 1980s, the Endeavour Astronautical Society flourished in Sydney, providing the STARTEL astronomy and astronautics computer bulletin board.

In the 1990s the groups listed below are active, to varying degrees, in promoting space in Australia. In addition to the Australian societies, two international space advocacy groups, The Planetary Society and the British Interplanetary Society, have considerable memberships in Australia, although they do not have an organised structure of local chapters.

## SPACE ADVOCACY SOCIETIES

Many space advocacy societies are active in Australia today. These groups provide opportunities for interested people to become members of bodies which seek to promote space science, technology, applications, and space education in Australian and overseas. Some of the more active groups act as political lobby groups for Australian space activities and also encourage the development of local space industry. In the following list both Australian groups and some international societies active in Australia are listed. Local groups can be contacted for further details, but please include a stamped, self-addressed envelope.

*National Space Society of Australia Inc (NSSA)*
 GPO Box 7048, Sydney NSW 2001
 The NSSA, an affiliate of the US National Space Society, is the most active space advocacy group in Australia in the 1990s. Operating at international, national and local levels, the society's initiatives include space business roundtables, the Australian Space Industry Chamber of Commerce and the Australian Space Development Conferences, as well as a wide range of space education activities.

### The state chapters are:
*Adelaide Space Frontier Society*
 18 Charmaine Avenue, Para Vista SA 5093
*Canberra Space Frontier Society*
 GPO Box 227, Canberra ACT 2601
*Melbourne Space Frontier Society*
 GPO Box 2476V, Melbourne VIC 3001
*Newcastle Space Frontier Society*
 PO Box 1150, Newcastle NSW 2300
*Perth Space Frontier Society*
 37 Lowth Road, Beckenham WA 6107
*Queensland Space Frontier Society*
 GPO Box 1908, Brisbane QLD 2001

*Sydney Space Frontier Society*
 5/10 Templeman Crescent, Hillsdale NSW 2036
*Western Sydney Space Frontier Society*
 PO Box 1183, Auburn NSW 2144

### Independent space societies
The following societies undertake space advocacy activities in their various states, but accept members from around Australia and overseas:

*AMSAT Australia*
 GPO Box 2141, Adelaide SA 5001
*Astronautical Society of Western Australia*
 PO Box 278, South Perth WA 6151
 The ASWA is the oldest Australian space advocacy society still operating.
*Ausroc Projects*
 42 Broadmeadows Road, Elizabeth North SA 5113
*Australian Space Education Association*
 11 Butler Street, Bellbird Park QLD 4300
*Australian Space Engineering and Research Association*
 PO Box 184, Ryde NSW 2112
*Space Association of Australia*
 PO Box 351, Mulgrave North VIC 3170
*Sydney Space Association*
 PO Box R45, Royal Exchange, Sydney NSW 2000
 The Sydney Space Association is an affiliated society of the Powerhouse Museum.

### International space societies in Australia
*The British Interplanetary Society*
 27/29 South Lambeth Road, London SW8 1SZ England
 The British Interplanetary Society is the oldest space advocacy group in the world.
*New Zealand Spaceflight Association*
 PO Box 5829, Wellesley Street, Auckland NZ
*The Planetary Society (US)*
 65 North Catalina Avenue, Pasadena CA 91106 USA
 The Planetary Society is the world's largest space advocacy group.

### APPENDIX 2
### GOVERNMENT AGENCIES AND PROFESSIONAL BODIES
Most Australian states have established space development and/or remote sensing offices. For information on these agencies contact the state government information service in each state.

*Association of Australian Aerospace Industries*
 GPO Box 817, Canberra ACT 2601
 Space companies mentioned in this book may be contacted through the Australian Association of Aerospace Industries at this address.

*Australia Telescope National Facility*
PO Box 76, Epping NSW 2121

*Australian Centre for Remote Sensing (ACRES)*
PO Box 28, Belconnen ACT 2616

*Australian Space Office*
PO Box 269, Civic Square ACT 2609

*Bureau of Meteorology*
Head Office, GPO Box 1289K Melbourne VIC 3001
The Bureau can also be contacted through its regional offices in each state capital.

*Centre for Remote Sensing*
University of New South Wales, PO Box 1, Kensington NSW 2033

*CSIRO Division of Radiophysics*
PO Box 76, Epping NSW 2121

*CSIRO Office of Space Science and Applications (COSSA)*
GPO Box 3023, Canberra ACT 2601

*Defence Science and Technology Organisation*
GPO Box 2151, Adelaide SA 5001

*Department of Transport and Communications*
GPO Box 594, Canberra ACT 2601

*NASA Senior Representative in Australia*
Australian Space Office, PO Box 269, Civic Square ACT 2609

*National Committee on Space Engineering*
Institution of Engineers Australia, 11 National Circuit, Barton ACT 2600

*Optus Communications (formerly Aussat)*
GPO Box 1512, Sydney NSW 2001

*Telstra Corporation Ltd (formerly OTC/AOTC)*
GPO Box 7000, Sydney NSW 2001

*Tidbinbilla Space Tracking Station*
PO Box 4350, Kingston ACT 2604

## APPENDIX 3
### SPACE EXHIBITIONS AND EDUCATIONAL RESOURCES

Note that the following list does not include planetaria or astronomy displays unless they have some space technology component.

*Astronomy and Space Communicators of Australia*
c/o Manager, Visitors' Centre, Parkes Observatory,
PO Box 276, Parkes NSW 2870
Astronomy and Space Communicators of Australia (originally the Astronomy and Space Exploration Liaison Group) is a space education organisation founded in 1980 by leading educators and scientists to promote astronomy and space education and awareness. It promotes an annual Astronomy and Space Week.

*CSIRO Visitors' Centre*
Parkes Observatory, PO Box 276, Parkes NSW 2870

This CSIRO Visitors' Centre at the Parkes radio telescope provides an excellent exhibition on radio astronomy and CSIRO activities in the field.

*NASA Teacher Resource Centre*
Curriculum Development Centre, University of Canberra, PO Box 1, Belconnen ACT 2616
The centre provides a wide range of NASA educational materials for teacher use in subjects ranging from astronomy and geography to social science.

*National Science and Technology Centre*
PO Box E28, Queen Victoria Terrace ACT 2600
The NSTC's hands-on exhibitions demonstrate much of the basic physics applicable to spaceflight.

*Perth Scitech and Planetarium*
PO Box 1155, West Perth WA 6005
This science centre includes an exhibition on space travel and astronomy, as well as a planetarium.

*Powerhouse Museum*
PO Box K346, Haymarket NSW 2000
The Powerhouse is the home of Australia's first major space exhibition, 'Space—beyond this world', which provides an overview of Australian and international space history and activities.

*Scienceworks*
Museum of Victoria, Booker Street, Spotswood VIC 3015
A hands-on science centre which includes exhibitions on space-related technologies.

*Sir Thomas Brisbane Planetarium*
Mt Coot-tha Road, Toowong QLD 4066
A small space history exhibition forms part of the displays at this excellent planetarium.

*Sky and Space Magazine*
PO Box 976, Bondi Junction NSW 2022
The only Australian-produced space and astronomy magazine.

*Tidbinbilla Space Tracking Station Visitor Centre*
PO Box 4350, Kingston ACT 2604
Tidbinbilla's Visitor Centre presents displays about the work done at the tracking station and also provides an overview of NASA space tracking activities in Australia.

*Woomera Heritage Centre*
Woomera Village, Woomera 5720
This local history museum at Woomera provides a broad overview of the history of the Woomera township, the rocket range and the region. Its outdoor display shows examples of many rockets and missiles launched at Woomera, including the WRESAT first stage that was recovered from the Simpson Desert.

# GLOSSARY

**Aperture synthesis:** use of one or more pairs of instruments of relatively small aperture (opening for electromagnetic waves) to act as an interferometer capable of resolving objects as if they were a much larger device.

**Applications satellite:** orbiting spacecraft which provide functional services that apply space technology to earthly requirements.

**Beacon satellite:** orbiting spacecraft emitting signals for timekeeping or navigation purposes.

**Cosmic radiation:** electromagnetic waves or atomic particles emanating from the depths of space.

**Doppler shift:** change in signal frequency due to the relative motion of the observer of the signal.

**Dropsonde:** atmospheric sensor dropped from an aircraft or satellite.

**Early warning satellite:** orbiting spacecraft for detecting missile launches.

**Electromagnetic radiation spectrum:** the entire range of energy waves characteristic of the physical universe, including, in increasing frequency, radio, microwaves, infra-red, visible light, ultraviolet, X-rays, gamma rays.

**Fairing:** the nose-cone or top part of a rocket which surrounds and protects a satellite during launch.

**Focal plane array:** set of sensors arranged at the prime focus of a telescope, where the light or other electromagnetic radiation concentrates, for greatest sensitivity.

**Frequency:** the rate of repetition of a signal, or complete cycles per unit time.

**Hypersonic technology:** technology for flight at speeds greater than five times the speed of sound.

**Infra-red:** a portion of the electromagnetic radiation spectrum of energy waves, below that of visible light.

**Interferometry:** technique which uses a number of smaller sensors spaced apart from each other to effectively represent one very large antenna. This enables weaker signals to be received without requiring a single large unit for good resolution.

**Ionosphere:** portion of the Earth's atmosphere above 50 km. It contains charged particles created by the impact of ultraviolet radiation and other emissions from the Sun on air molecules in the upper atmosphere.

**Ionospheric soundings:** measurements of the characteristics of the upper atmosphere of Earth.

**Kinetheodolites:** tracking instruments that measure the distance and direction of moving objects.

**Laser ranging:** technique using laser light to measure distance, such as to the Moon.

**Microgravity:** the almost zero gravity condition that is experienced in an Earth-orbiting spacecraft. Less correctly called 'weightlessness'.

**Multi-spectral sensors:** remote sensing instruments capable of detecting a range of electromagnetic wavelengths.

**Nose-cone:** top of a rocket or missile, often enclosing satellites, experiments or weapons.

**Numerical weather prediction:** the use of computer analysis of meteorological data to estimate future conditions.

**Orbit:** the closed path followed by a natural or artificial body around a centre of gravity.

**Passive magnetic attitude stabilisation system:** system used to maintain spacecraft orientation in orbit by reference to the Earth's magnetic fields.

**Payload:** the cargo that a rocket carries into space. A payload can be people, satellites or experimental equipment.

**Photon:** atomic wave/particle that is the fundamental unit of visible light energy.

**Quasar:** quasi-stellar or star-like object at the edge of the known universe which seems to emit enormous quantities of energy.

**Radar:** radio direction and ranging system that locates distant objects using reflected radiowaves.

**Radio:** portion of the electromagnetic radiation spectrum of energy waves, below infra-red radiation.

**Rays:** an alternative term for electromagnetic radiation, eg, cosmic rays.

**Real-time imagery:** remotely sensed images which are immediately processed when received from a spacecraft, rather than processed later on.

**Resolving power/resolution:** degree to which distant objects can be discerned clearly by an instrument such as a telescope.

**Rocket:** vehicle that emits gas at high speed in one direction, in order to move in the other direction.

**Scientific satellite:** orbiting spacecraft that contains science experiments or sensors for scientific research.

**Sensor:** scientific instrument which detects particular characteristics of remote objects.

**Shortwave:** portion of the radio spectrum of energy waves, used for long-distance communications.

**Sounding rocket:** small rocket generally used for sub-orbital flights of scientific or experimental payloads.

**Space qualify:** to test fly in space a new technology or instrument under development.

**Spectrometer:** an electronic detector instrument used for spectroscopy.

**Spectroscopy:** analysis of the electromagnetic radiation spectrum to determine the chemical nature of an object emitting or reflecting energy waves.

**Telemetry:** information transmitted from a spacecraft that tells its ground controllers about its performance.

**Transponder:** electronic device which receives or transmits signals when a predetermined signal is received. It is usually found on a satellite.

**Transponder capacity:** ability of a satellite's transmitter to handle many different signals.

**Ultraviolet:** portion of the electromagnetic radiation spectrum of energy waves, above that of visible light.

# ACRONYMS

| | |
|---|---|
| ACRES | Australian Centre for Remote Sensing |
| ACRV | Assured Crew Return Vehicle |
| ACT | Australian Capital Territory |
| ADEOS | Advanced Earth Observation Satellite |
| ADF | Australian Defence Force |
| ADFA | Australian Defence Force Academy |
| ADS | Australian Department of Supply |
| ADT | Australian Department of Trade |
| AETHERS | Advanced Equipment to Handle ERS |
| AIDC | Australian Industry Development Corporation |
| ALV | Australian Launch Vehicle |
| AMSAT | Amateur Radio Satellite Corporation |
| ANU | Australian National University |
| ANZUS | Australia-New Zealand-United States |
| AOTC | Australian and Overseas Telecommunications Corporation, formed by the merger of the Overseas Telecommunications Corporation (OTC) and Telecom Australia in 1992; renamed Telstra Corporation Ltd in April 1993 |
| APS | Atmospheric Pressure Sensor |
| ARC | Aggregation of Red Cells |
| ARDU | Aircraft Research and Development Unit |
| ASA | Astronautical Society of Australia |
| ASAS | Australian Science and Applications Spacecraft |
| ASB | Australian Space Board (replaced in 1993 by the ASC) |
| ASC | Australian Space Council |
| ASERA | Australian Space Engineering Research Association |
| ASG | Australian Spaceport Group |
| ASO | Australian Space Office |
| ASRA | Australian Space Research Agency |
| ASRI | Australian Space Research Institute Ltd |
| ASWA | Astronautical Society of Western Australia |
| ATS | Applications Technology Satellite |
| ATSR | Along Track Scanning Radiometer |
| AUSLIG | Australian Surveying and Land Information Group |
| AXAF | Advanced X-ray Astrophysics Facility |
| BAeA | British Aerospace Australia |
| BHP | Broken Hill Proprietary Company Limited |
| BIE | Bureau of Industry Economics |
| BIOSAT | Biological Satellite |
| CIA | Central Intelligence Agency |
| CIS | Commonwealth of Independent States, formerly the Union of Soviet Socialist Republics (USSR) |

| | |
|---|---|
| CNES | Centre National d'Etudes Spatiales (French National Centre for Space Studies) |
| COMSAT | Communications Satellite |
| COSPAR | Committee on Space Research |
| COSPAS | Acronym derived from the Russian Cosmicheski Spasetel (Space Rescuer) |
| COSSA | CSIRO Office of Space Science and Applications |
| CSIRO | Commonwealth Scientific and Industrial Research Organization |
| CYISL | Cape York International Spacelaunch Ltd |
| CYSA | Cape York Space Agency |
| DITAC | Department of Industry, Technology and Commerce; renamed Department of Industry, Technology and Regional Development in 1993 |
| DRC | Defence Research Centre, formerly the Weapons Research Establishment (WRE), later the Defence Science and Technology Organisation (DSTO) |
| DSCS | Defence Satellite Communications System |
| DSN | Deep Space Network |
| DSTO | Defence Science and Technology Organisation, formerly Defence Research Centre (DRC) and Weapons Research Establishment (WRE) |
| EAST | Eastern Australian Standard Time |
| ELDO | European Launcher Development Organization |
| ELINT | Electronic Intelligence |
| ENVISAT | Environmental Satellite |
| EPIRB | Emergency Position-Indicating Radio Beacon |
| ERS | European Remote Sensing Satellite |
| ERTS | Earth Resources Technology Satellite |
| ESA | European Space Agency |
| ESRO | European Space Research Organization |
| ET | Extraterrestrial |
| FDP | Fast Delivery Processor |
| FUSE | Far Ultraviolet Spectroscopy Explorer |
| GAMS | Global Atmospheric Methane Sensor |
| GASCAN | 'Get Away Special' Canister |
| GCF | Ground Communications Facility |
| GEOS | Geostationary Earth Observation Satellite |
| GMS | Geostationary Meteorological Satellite |
| GNP | Gross National Product |
| GPS | Global Positioning System (see also, NAVSTAR-GPS) |
| HAD | High Altitude Density |

| | |
|---|---|
| HARP | High Altitude Research Project |
| HASP | High Altitude Sounding Projectile |
| HAT | High Altitude Temperature |
| HCMM | Heat Capacity Mapping Mission |
| HEAO | High Energy Astronomical Observatory |
| HOTOL | Horizontal Take-Off and Landing |
| HRMS | High Resolution Microwave Survey |
| HRV | Hypersonic Research Vehicle |
| IAF | International Astronautical Federation |
| IBM | International Business Machines |
| ICBM | Intercontinental Ballistic Missile |
| INMARSAT | International Maritime Satellite Organisation |
| INTELSAT | International Telecommunications Satellite Organisation |
| ISEE | International Sun-Earth Explorer |
| ISO | Infrared Space Observatory |
| ITOS | Improved TIROS Operational Satellite |
| IUE | International Ultraviolet Explorer |
| JEM | Japanese Experiment Module |
| JERS | Japanese Earth Resources Satellite |
| JPL | Jet Propulsion Laboratory |
| LADS | Laser Depth Sounder |
| LAGEOS | Laser Geodynamics Satellite |
| LASER | Light Amplification by Stimulated Emission of Radiation |
| LDEF | Long Duration Exposure Facility |
| LEO | Low Earth Orbit |
| LIGHTSAT | Lightweight Satellite |
| LRWE | Long-Range Weapons Establishment |
| LUT | Local User Terminal |
| MASER | Microwave Amplification by Stimulated Emission of Radiation |
| METSAT | Meteorological Satellite |
| MINISAT | Miniature Satellite |
| MINITRACK | Minimum Weight Tracking |
| MIT | Massachusetts Institute of Technology |
| MSFN | Manned Space Flight Network |
| MUAS | Melbourne University Astronautical Society |
| NASA | National Aeronautics and Space Administration |
| NASCOM | NASA Communications |
| NASP | National Aero Space Plane |
| NAVSAT | Navigation Satellite |
| NAVSTAR-GPS | Navigation System using Timing and Ranging-Global Positioning System |
| NOAA | National Oceanographic and Atmospheric Administration |
| NSI | National Space Institute |
| NSP | National Space Program |
| NSSA | National Space Society of Australia Inc |
| NSW | New South Wales |
| OCS | Ocean Colour Scanner |
| OSCAR | Orbiting Satellite Carrying Amateur Radio |
| OTC | Originally the Overseas Telecommunications Commission (1946), later Corporation (1989). Merged with Telecom in 1992 to form the Australian and Overseas Telecommunications Corporation (AOTC), now Telstra. |
| PACT | Pacific Area Cooperative Telecommunications (network) |
| PAGEOS | Passive Geodetic Earth Orbiting Satellite |
| PMG | Post Master General's Department (split into Telecom Australia and Australia Post in 1975) |
| QUASAT | Quasar Satellite |
| RAAF | Royal Australian Air Force |
| RAE | Royal Aircraft Establishment (now Royal Aeronautical Establishment) |
| RASS | Remote Area Satellite Service |
| READS | Re-entry Air Data System |
| ROCKOON | Rocket Balloon |
| SA | South Australia |
| SAREX | Shuttle Amateur Radio Experiment |
| SARSAT | Search and Rescue Satellite |
| SAS | Small Astronomy Satellite |
| SCRAMJET | Supersonic Combustion Ramjet |
| SETI | Search for Extraterrestrial Intelligence |
| SIDC | Space Industry Development Centre |
| SIGINT | Signals Intelligence |
| SIR | Shuttle Imaging Radar |
| SIRTF | Space Infrared Telescope Facility |
| SLS | Southern Launch Service |
| SLV | Southern Launch Vehicle |
| SMM | Solar Maximum Mission |
| SPAN | Solar Particle Alert Network |
| SPOT | Satellite Probatoire d'Observation de la Terre (Satellite Probe for the Observation of the Earth) |
| STADAN | Satellite Tracking and Data Acquisition Network |
| STC | Standard Telephones and Cables Pty Ltd |
| STEP | Solar-Terrestrial Energy Program |
| STS | Space Transportation System (the Space Shuttle); also Space Transportation Systems Ltd |
| STV | Satellite Test Vehicle |
| TDRS | Tracking and Data Relay Satellite |
| TDRSS | Tracking and Data Relay Satellite System |
| TERSS | Tasmanian Earth Resources Satellite Station |
| TIROS | Television and Infra Red Observation Satellite |
| TOMS | Total Ozone Monitoring System |
| TTC&M | Telemetry, Tracking, Command and Monitoring |
| UFO | Unidentified Flying Object |
| UHF | Ultra High Frequency |
| UK | United Kingdom |
| UN | United Nations |
| UNCOPUOS | United Nations Committee on the Peaceful Uses of Outer Space |
| US | United States |
| USNCOS | United States National Commission On Space |
| USSR | Union of Soviet Socialist Republics, now the Commonwealth of Independent States (CIS) |
| V-2 | Vergeltungswaffe-2 (Vengeance Weapon-2) |
| VEGA | Venera/Galley (Venus/Halley) |
| VfR | Verein für Raumschiffahrt (Society for Space Ship Travel) |
| VLBI | Very Long Baseline Interferometry |
| VLF | Very Low Frequency |
| VSAT | Very Small Aperture Terminal |
| VSOP | VLBI Space Observatory Program |
| WA | Western Australia |
| WISP | Waves in Space Plasma |
| WMO | World Meteorological Organization |
| WRE | Weapons Research Establishment, later Defence Research Centre (DRC) and Defence Science and Technology Organisation (DSTO) |
| WRESAT | Weapons Research Establishment Satellite |

# BIBLIOGRAPHY

The following bibliographic lists are annotated to assist readers in selecting books applicable to their interests and level of knowledge. None of these lists is exhaustive, but they reflect the range of references called upon by the authors of this book and provide a good foundation for further reading.

## GENERAL BOOKS ON AUSTRALIAN SPACE PROGRAMS

These books are basic references covering Australia's past and current space activities.

Australian Senate, *Developing satellite launching facilities in Australia and the role of government*, Senate Standing Committee on Transport, Communications and Infrastructure, Parliament of Australia, April 1992
Report of a parliamentary inquiry into the Cape York and Woomera reactivation proposals, as well as a commentary on general space policy. It reflects the submissions made by the Australian space community.

Ball, D J, *A suitable piece of real estate: American installations in Australia*, Hale and Iremonger, Sydney, 1980
—— *A base for debate*, Allen & Unwin, Sydney, 1987
—— *Pine Gap*, Allen & Unwin, Sydney, 1987
—— *Australia's secret space programs*, Canberra Papers on Strategy and Defence No 43, Australian National University, 1988
—— *Australia and the global strategic balance*, Canberra Papers on Strategy and Defence No 49, Australian National University, 1989
—— *Code 777: Australia and the US Defense Satellite Communications System*, Canberra Papers on Strategy and Defence No 56, Australian National University, 1989
A series of reports and books by this noted academic that document the role of American military space bases operating in Australia and consider Australia's own military space activities.

Ball, D J and Wilson H, *Australia and space*, Canberra Papers on Strategy and Defence No 94, Australian National University, 1992
The proceedings of a conference held to cover matters of global space policy and defence programs relating to Australia. Many of the papers were presented by local and international space policy experts.

Banister, M and Harris, G (eds), *Australian space activities to the year 2000*, Commonwealth Scientific and Industrial Research Organization, Office of Space Science and Applications, 1992
A series of invited papers by space technologists covering developments in various space applications without too much technical content. Published to record a series of seminars given by the authors.

Bureau of Industry Economics, *An economic evaluation of the National Space Program*, BIE Research Report 43, Australian Government Publishing Service, Canberra, 1992
An economic analysis of the effectiveness of previous space activities, with recommendations for the future that suggest abolition of a national space program. Its recommendations were not subsequently adopted by the government.

Cole, K, *Ready for launch: space science in Australia*, Australian Academy of Science, Canberra, March 1989
A space policy report prepared by space scientists, describing existing programs and future proposals.

Dare, T and Scully-Power, P, *Voyage on the Challenger*, Weldon, Sydney, 1986
This commentary of a flight on the Space Shuttle was prepared by the first Australian-born person to travel in space. It includes many pictures, presented in a magazine format.

Department of Industry, Technology and Commerce, *An integrated National Space Program*, Report by the Expert Panel, DITAC, Commonwealth of Australia, July 1992
A complete review of the national space policy by a learned panel, which made recommendations adopted in principle by the government.

Gooden, B, *Spaceport Australia*, Kangaroo Press, Sydney, 1990
Provides a brief history of modern rocket development and the events leading to Woomera's establishment, then discusses the Cape York proposal.

Leslie, R A, 'Space tracking stations', *Canberra's engineering heritage*, 2nd edition, The Institution of Engineers Australia, Canberra Division, 1990, pp 187-199

A concise historical account of the development of the various space tracking facilities used in Australia, prepared by a person involved with their management.

Madigan, R, *A space policy for Australia*, Australian Academy of Technological Sciences, Canberra, 1985

This important report was prepared by a committee of space professionals. It was the first report to describe Australian space involvements in a policy setting and indicate possible means of formalising those activities. Many of its recommendations were adopted by the government.

McCracken, K and Astley-Boden, C (eds), *Satellite images of Australia*, Harcourt Brace Jovanovich, Sydney, 1982

An introduction to remote sensing and the various uses to which it has been put in Australia. Heavily illustrated with images of Australia taken from the Landsat remote sensing satellites.

Morton, P, *Fire across the desert*, Australian Government Publishing Service, Canberra, 1989

An official government history of the Anglo-Australian Joint Defence Project. The book is encyclopaedic in scope and somewhat anecdotal and chronological in style. There are chapters covering space and space-related activities at Woomera.

Southall, I, *Woomera*, Angus and Robertson, Melbourne, 1962
—— *Rockets in the desert*, Angus and Robertson, Sydney, 1964

These two books by a well-known children's author describe the activities of the rocket range, its people and their lives during Woomera's busy heyday. The first and longer book is intended for adult readers, and the second is for older children.

### FURTHER READING ON AUSTRALIAN SPACE ACTIVITIES

This list covers books and articles which are more technical, or which provide further detailed coverage of particular aspects of Australian space activities.

## OVERVIEWS OF AUSTRALIAN SPACE ACTIVITIES

Australian Space Board, *Annual report*, Australian Government Publishing Service, Canberra (various years)

Official government report of the activities and annual summary of government expenditure administered by the Space Board since 1987.

Harris, G, 'Overview of space developments in Australia 1988-89', *Space Industry News (SpIN)* 32, Commonwealth Scientific and Industrial Research Organization, Office of Space Science and Applications, Canberra, February 1990, pp 2-3

This editorial analysing government space policy appears within a bimonthly newsletter produced by the CSIRO. *SpIN* provides good overview information on new Australian space involvements and programs.

James, M L, 'Into space from Down Under: the early days', *Australia and space: a bicentennial perspective*, special issue of the *Journal of the British Interplanetary Society*, 41, 12, December 1988, pp 539-554

This paper provides a historical summary of Australian space

programs, and serves to introduce ten other papers which examine current programs in more technical detail, as part of a special issue prepared by the Institution of Engineers, Australia.

Tuohy, I R, 'Space activities', *The Australian encyclopedia*, Australian Geographic Society, Sydney, 1988, pp 2679-2685

A concise summary of local space programs, with some pictures, which was prepared by a space scientist.

## ACTIVITIES AT WOOMERA

Goodfield, J, Hannaford, C and Gunn, J, *Weapons at Woomera*, Anti Bases Campaign (SA), Adelaide, 1991

A booklet produced to highlight the many controversial military and weapons-related activities that have been carried out in South Australia, and the effects of these activities on the local Aboriginal people and the environment.

Woomera High School, *A sense of urgency: a social history of Woomera*, Woomera High School, Woomera, 1978

A social history booklet compiled by students from Woomera High School. It includes an anecdotal history of the Woomera township from 1948-1965 and a history of education at Woomera from 1950-1978.

## SPACE TRACKING

'Carnarvon Tracking Station', Canberra, 1964

'Tidbinbilla Deep Space Tracking Station 42', Canberra, 1965

'STADAN Facility, Orroral Valley, ACT', Canberra, 1966

'ATS Station Cooby Creek, Darling Downs, Queensland', Canberra, 1967

'Honeysuckle Creek Tracking Station', Canberra, 1967

'Island Lagoon Tracking Station', Canberra, 1967

'Weapons Research Establishment', Canberra, 1967

'Weapons Research Establishment Satellite', Canberra, 1967

'Recent space activities of the Department of Supply', Canberra, 1968

This series of booklets was prepared by the Australian Department of Supply as guides to each of Australia's then active space tracking and ground facilities. Written for the general public, with diagrams and photographs, they provide non-technical background information, and some program summaries.

## SATELLITE COMMUNICATIONS

Australian Department of Communications, *AUSSAT: a chronology*, Australian Government Publishing Service, Canberra, 1986

Historical summary of Aussat's establishment expressed as a concise list of key events without comment.

Barrett, W E, 'OTC's involvement in space', *Proceedings: International Aerospace Congress, Sixth National Space Engineering Symposium*, 3, Melbourne, 1991, pp 1-11

A paper providing an overview of OTC activities without too many technical explanations. It was presented at a regular international aerospace conference.

Brown, A, 'Golden bird or white elephant?: Australia's AUSSAT satellite system', *Telecommunications policy*, June 1991, pp 248-262

A rigorous, independent historical assessment of Aussat's economic performance is presented in this academic paper.

Heyman, J, *Communications satellites*, Astronautical Society of Western Australia, Perth, 1980

This is a concise listing of communications satellite types and missions. It has recently been developed into a computer database covering all types of launches and satellites.

Innes, U E, 'Critical choice and public interests', *Proceedings: Domsat 79*, Canberra, February 1979, pp 406-414

An academic paper assessing the possible sociological impact of Aussat, presented at one of the conferences held to consider the scheme before its establishment.

Lamberton, D McL, 'Satellite communications: social consequences', *Proceedings: Domsat 79*, Canberra, February 1979, pp 130-145

An academic paper assessing the possible sociological impact of Aussat, presented at one of the conferences held to consider the scheme before its establishment.

Masterton, R and Frances, M, *Invisible bridges*, Overseas Telecommunications Corporation, Sydney, 1986

A book sponsored by OTC to mark its achievements, it provides a historical account of Australian telecommunications development and its links to space.

Nowland, W, 'AUSSAT's second generation system', *Ascent*, 14, Australian Department of Science, Canberra, December 1987, pp 16-17

A specialist government magazine article describing the satellite system, written by an Aussat representative.

Pike, G H S, 'Commercial launch systems: the foreseeable future for AUSSAT', *Proceedings: Second National Space Engineering Symposium*, The Institution of Engineers Australia, Sydney, March 1986, pp 1-11

An academic paper assessing alternative rocket launch vehicles for the second generation Aussat satellites.

Tonkin, R and Mace, O, 'AUSTRALIS Oscar V: an Australian amateur radio satellite', *Proceedings: Third National Space Engineering Symposium*, The Institution of Engineers Australia, Canberra, July 1987, pp 192-195

A general paper, written by two of the leading figures involved, providing a historical account of this amateur satellite project.

## REMOTE SENSING AND METEOROLOGY

Astley-Boden, C, 'Seeing Downunder from up there', *Geo*, 7, 1, 1985, pp 28-45

General overview of remote sensing in Australia, highlighting some of the main remote sensing projects being undertaken at the time. Well illustrated.

Aubrey, M C, 'Remote sensing in Australia: current activities and future trends', *Proceedings: 4th Australian Remote Sensing Conference*, Adelaide, September 1987

Written by an active industry participant to outline policy options for the future, the paper assesses the various remote sensing programs involving Australia.

Fairall, J (ed), *Australian remote sensing industry capability*, South Pacific Science Press, Sydney, 1992

A commercially produced guide to Australia's remote sensing industry, its capabilities and the many companies involved. Provides a useful list of remote sensing contacts.

Greatz, D, Fisher, R and Wilson, M, *Looking back: the changing face of the Australian continent, 1972-1992*, CSIRO Division of Wildlife and Ecology, Canberra, 1993

An excellent coffee-table book which examines the changes in the Australian landscape and environment as revealed by 20 years of satellite imagery.

Griersmith, D C, A brief history of meteorological satellite utilisation in the Australian Bureau of Meteorology, Australian Bureau of Meteorology, Melbourne, unpublished, 1988

A summary paper providing a chronology of weather satellite usage.

Griersmith, D C and Kingwell, J, *Planet under scrutiny: an Australian remote sensing glossary*, Australian Government Publishing Service, Canberra, 1988

Glossary of terms covering all aspects of remote sensing and meteorology in Australia. Contains many useful explanations and diagrams and an excellent reference list for further technical reading in remote sensing and meteorology.

Walker, R D, Aubrey, M C, Fraser, S J, Milne, A K and Jeremy, R, *Remote sensing in Australia*, Australian Government Publishing Service, Canberra, 1986

A promotional colour booklet which provides an overview of Australia's remote sensing industries and their activities. It includes a list of contact addresses, and an overview of significant remote sensing projects.

## SPACE SCIENCE

Australian Science and Technology Council, *The future of Australian astronomy*, Australian Government Publishing Service, Canberra, 1989

A government policy report which reviews astronomical programs and facilities, in a non-technical manner, assessing support and management arrangements for their continued operation.

Carver, J H, 'Space science: future directions for Australia', *Proceedings: National Space Symposium*, Sydney, March 1984, pp 39-53

A policy paper listing space science achievements and topics for possible future involvement, prepared by a senior Australian scientist who has represented Australia on a United Nations' committee.

Tuohy, I R (ed), *Australian space research 1990-1992: report to COSPAR*, Australian National Committee for Solar Terrestrial and Space Physics, Australian Academy of Science, Canberra, 1992

This concise summary of local space science activities was prepared by a space scientist for the Academy.

## AUSTRALIAN SPACE INDUSTRY

Australian Department of Trade, *Australian aerospace*, Australian Government Publishing Service, Canberra, 1985
A promotional colour booklet which provides an overview of Australian aerospace industries and their activities. It includes a list of contact addresses and an overview of significant aerospace projects.

Australian Space Office, Department of Industry, Technology and Commerce, *Remote sensing opportunities for Australia*, Australian Government Publishing Service, Canberra, 1989
A government report examining remote sensing industries in Australia with a view to developing a remote sensing industry strategy and action plan.

Australian Space Office, Department of Industry, Technology and Commerce, *Australian space industry development strategy*, Australian Government Publishing Service, Canberra, 1990
A government policy report which examines options for the local development of space industry. It examines various sub-industry categories, and assesses support and structural arrangements for their development. It led to the formation of Space Industry Development Centres.

COSSA, 'Getting into the space business', *Proceedings: Australian Space Board, CSIRO Office of Space Science and Applications Industry Opportunities Seminar*, Canberra, 1987
A collection of seminar papers prepared by various speakers involved with the Australian space industry. They cover local space activities and commerce in a not too technical manner.

Department of Industry, Technology and Commerce, *Australian aerospace capability directory 1991*, Marsland, Sydney, 1991
A reference directory covering Australian companies with space-qualified capabilities. Useful list of contacts with company profiles.

Furniss, T, 'Competing for the space stakes', *Space*, May-June 1990
A specialist magazine article assessing the economics of space activities and applications.

Shirley, W A, 'Status of the Cape York project', *Proceedings: Fifth National Space Engineering Symposium*, The Institution of Engineers Australia, Canberra, 29-30 November 1989, pp 229-232
An overview paper prepared by a member of the Cape York consortium advising on progress with the spaceport.

Tambosi, P, 'Financing in space', *Proceedings: France-Australia Space Opportunities Forum*, Canberra, March 1987
A financial paper examining commercial aspects of space activities, presented at a special forum.

## SPACE POLICY

Australian Space Office, Department of Industry, Technology and Commerce, *Observing Australia: the role of remote sensing in a balanced national space program*, Australian Government Publishing Service, Canberra, 1992
A government policy report examining the role of remote sensing in Australia and its place in the National Space Program. This report provided seminal input into the report of the Expert Panel and its recommendations for the future directions of the program.

James, M L, 'Australian space and scitech policy, and society', *Proceedings: 38th International Astronautical Federation Congress*, Brighton, UK, October 1987
A brief paper providing an overview of space activities from a social viewpoint.

Kennedy, D, *An overview of Australia's space program*, Legislative Research Service Current Issues Paper No 9, Canberra, December 1987
A general policy paper prepared for parliament which notes the influence of Australian space programs on the national direction and government policy.

Schaetzel, S S, 'A space policy for Australia', *Proceedings: Fourth National Space Engineering Symposium*, The Institution of Engineers Australia, Adelaide, July 1988, pp 74-77
—— 'The space age and Australia', *Working Paper No 200*, Strategic and Defence Studies Centre, Australian National University, Canberra, 1989
These papers, by a representative of the Australian space industry, critically analyse government space policy in relation to the development of an Australian space industry.

## SELECTED GENERAL BOOKS ON WORLD SPACE PROGRAMS

Burgess, C, *Space: the new frontier*, Ashton Scholastic, Sydney, 1987
A general introduction to space activities and history for young people, written specifically for an Australian audience.

Clark, P, *The Soviet manned space programme*, Salamander, London, 1987
A comprehensive account of the personalities, equipment and programs that characterised the Soviet side of the space race. Many diagrams and photographs accompany the text, which was written by a noted commentator on Soviet/CIS space activities.

Dougherty, K, *Space: beyond this world*, exhibition brochure series, Powerhouse Museum, Sydney, 1989
This illustrated brochure briefly outlines the history and nature of spaceflight. It is linked to the exhibition at the Powerhouse Museum.

Forestier, A M, *Into the fourth dimension: an ADF guide to space*, Air Power Studies Centre Fellowship Paper No 2, RAAF, Canberra, 1992
A comprehensive guide to the space technologies relevant to military applications. Prepared for use in the ADFA, this book includes useful information on specific Australian military use of space.

Gatland, K, *The illustrated encyclopaedia of space technology*, 2nd edn, Salamander, London, 1990

A comprehensive treatise, by space professionals, on many aspects of space programs around the world, including the technology involved and the discoveries made. Many diagrams and photographs accompany the text.

Hart, D, *The encyclopedia of Soviet spacecraft*, Bison, London, 1987

A concise guide to the equipment and missions achieved under the former Soviet Union.

Hartman, W K, Miller, R and Lee, P, *Out of the cradle: exploring the frontiers beyond Earth*, Workman, New York, 1984

Jointly produced by space philosophers and artists, this unique book focuses on the reasons for space exploration, outlining discoveries, and hypothesising about the future.

Kelly, K W, *The home planet*, Macdonald & Co Ltd, London, 1988

A glorious picture book showing how the planet Earth looks from space. The images are accompanied by text from the astronauts who have seen the view in person.

King-Hele, D, *Observing earth satellites*, Macmillan, London, 1983

A practical guide for the interested amateur to understand satellite types and orbits and then observe them in the sky, written by an authority in the field.

Lewis, R S, *The illustrated encyclopaedia of space exploration*, Salamander, London, 1983

A comprehensive treatise about interplanetary exploration, the spacecraft involved, the missions, planetary characteristics, and the discoveries made. Somewhat out of date for recent missions, but excellent for the period 1957-1982.

McConnel, M, *Challenger: a major malfunction*, Simon and Schuster, London, 1987

An investigative journalist's account of the politics and problems in NASA that led to the CHALLENGER tragedy. A fascinating look at the behind-the-scenes politics of the US space program.

McDougall, W M, *The heavens and the earth: a political history of the space age*, Bantam, New York, 1985

Awarded a Pulitzer Prize, this highly praised account of the space race and the politics behind it provides a thorough introduction to the early years in space.

Pahl, D, *Space warfare*, Bison, London, 1987

This non-technical book attempts to document the basis and direction of the Strategic Defence Initiative program. Using many diagrams and pictures, it is designed to show the general reader the often neglected sphere of military space activity.

Plant, M, *Dictionary of space*, Longman, Harlow, UK, 1986

This useful book outlines the meaning of space jargon and acronyms to the general reader, but is not illustrated.

Rycroft, M (ed), *The Cambridge encyclopaedia of space*, Cambridge University Press, Cambridge, 1990

A comprehensive treatise about space exploration and technology prepared by many of those involved with space projects. It is categorised by projects and has many illustrations and photographs.

Sheffield, C, *Earthwatch: a survey of the world from space*, Octopus, London, 1981

This collection of remotely sensed images of Earth provides a unique introduction to geography and Earth resource studies for the general reader.

Sherman, M W, *TRW space log*, TRW, annual until 1991

Produced by a leading aerospace corporation, each edition of this small book lists annual space activity highlights and provides brief details and statistics of all spaceflights to date.

Smolders, P, *Living in space*, Princeton, Melbourne, 1987

An account of the problems and requirements for human habitation in space. Written at high school level, it covers life on board the US Space Shuttle and space stations.

Trento, J J and Trento, S B, *Prescription for disaster: from the glory of Apollo to the betrayal of the Shuttle*, Harrap, London, 1987

An alternative source to government statements, this controversial account of the development of the Space Shuttle program and the CHALLENGER tragedy provides a useful introduction to contemporary space politics.

United States National Commission on Space, *Pioneering the space frontier*, Bantam Books, New York, 1986

Prepared by space industry experts appointed by the president, this report attempts to set out a future for American space activities and exploration. Its recommendations helped form the basis for the US Space Exploration Initiative.

Von Braun, W, Ordway, F and Dooling, D, *Space travel: a history*, Harper and Row, New York, 1985

A comprehensive history of rocketry and spaceflight, written by experts in the history of astronautics. Copiously illustrated and thoroughly researched.

White, F, *The overview effect*, Houghton Mifflin, Boston, 1987

This philosophical book attempts to describe the effects on humanity that have occurred as a result of the universal perspective provided by spaceflight.

Wilson, A (ed), *Interavia space directory 1992-1993*, Jane's Information Group, Coulsdon, UK, 1992

An encyclopedic reference to world space activities, listed by both country of origin and subject. Covers both military and civilian space activities and is considered a standard work within the space community.

Yenne, B, *The encyclopedia of US spacecraft*, Bison, London, 1985

—— *Space Shuttle*, Bison, London, 1986

—— *The pictorial history of world spacecraft*, Bison, London, 1988

—— (ed), *To the edge of the universe*, Bison, London, 1986

—— (ed), *Interplanetary spacecraft*, Bison, London, 1988

—— *The astronauts*, Bison, London, 1988

A series of popular books covering various aspects of spaceflight and space exploration. Well-written and illustrated, each provides a good introduction to its subject for the general reader.

# INDEX

## PHOTO CREDITS

The permission of the following individuals and organisations to reproduce pictorial material is gratefully acknowledged. Numbers refer to page numbers.

AUSLIG 38; Auspace Ltd 63a, 75, 92, 101a; The Australian 83, 84, 103; Australian Academy of Technological Sciences and Engineering 106; Australian Anti-Bases Campaign Coalition 39; Australian Maritime Safety Authority 64; Australian National University, photo by Bob Cooper 87; Australian Space Office 107, 108, 121; Mark Blair 82; British Aerospace Australia 89; Bureau of Meteorology 14, 59, 60, 66; CSIRO 95; CSIRO Australia Telescope National Facility 46a, 126; CSIRO Marine Laboratories and the CSIRO Office of Space Science and Applications 58; CSIRO Office of Space Science and Applications 77; Defence Science and Technology Organisation 17 + cover, 20, 21a, 21b, 22, 23, 24, 25, 68, 69, 71, 72, 90, 112; Department of Defence 40; Esperance Museum, WA 125; John Fairfax Group 10 + back cover; GME Electrophone 63b; Dr Brett A Gooden 18; Hawker de Havilland 123; Institution of Engineers, Australia 120; Iridium Inc 115; Mrs Julie Kroschel 105; Owen Mace 51, 52, 53; Ken McCracken 65; Ken McCracken & Powerhouse Museum, photo by Penelope Clay 74; Macquarie Publications, Dubbo 57; Mount Stromlo and Siding Spring Observatories 67 + cover, 75, 101b; MPA Communications Pty Ltd and CSIRO Office of Space Science and Applications 100; NASA 5, 9, 11, 12, 16, 29, 31, 32, 34, 35, 42, 62, 79, 85, 86, 122, 128; Optus Communications 43 + cover, 46b, 47, 48, 49; Optus Communications and Hughes Aircraft Company 93; Oxford University Press, from Science and life by Nielsen, Ford & Doherty, 1991 56; Tony Pelling 37, 41; Powerhouse Museum, photo by Penelope Clay 50, by K Dougherty 117; RAAF Museum 78; Mark Rigby 82; Robert Somervaille 111; Telstra 8, 45, 96, 97; Richard Tonkin and The Age 54; University of Queensland 81, 113, 129; United Nations, UN photo 179384 / M Tzovaras 88; The West Australian 33; WBM Stalker Pty Ltd 99b; Mary Whitehead 27a, 27b, 28;

Images courtesy Australian Centre for Remote Sensing (ACRES), Australian Surveying and Land Information Group (AUSLIG): Earth image courtesy Bureau of Meteorology, contrast enhanced by ACRES cover + 3; satellite data acquired and processed by ACRES 1; Landsat TM imagery acquired by ACRES 55 + back cover; ERS-1 SAR imagery (c) ESA 1991, acquired by ACRES 98.